Irish Eccentrics

Peter Somerville-Large was born in 1928 and educated in
Dublin. After leaving Trinity College, he spent a decade
working abroad before returning to Ireland and taking up a
writing career. He lives in Dublin with his wife and daughter.

He has written four thrillers as well as works on travel
and social history. These include *The Coast of West Cork*
(1972); *From Bantry Bay to Leitrim: a journey in search of
O'Sullivan Beare* (1974); *Dublin* (1979); *The Grand Irish Tour*
(1982); *Cappaghglass* (1985), a record of changing rural life
in Ireland; *To the Navel of the World* (1987), which describes
a journey to western Tibet; and *Skying* (1989), an account of
flying in a microlight over England and Ireland.

Irish Eccentrics was first published in 1975.

Some reviews of the 1975 edition

'Mr Somerville-Large writes with *élan* and erudition' —
Tim Heald in *The Times*

'If, as sociologists suggest, eccentricity is a luxury, Ireland is
portrayed in this book as one of the most luxurious countries anywhere' — Malcolm Macpherson in *Newsweek*

'Mr Somerville-Large has probed the annals of dim Anglo-
Irish families to produce a rare gallery of human curiosities.
. . . All human life is here with a vengeance, and in these
affectionately presented pages its vagaries know no bounds'
— William Trevor in the *Guardian*

'Peter Somerville-Large has parcelled up as colourful a batch
of nature's sports as could be found a whisker this side of
lunacy, and has written about them in a witty, detached
prose style which admirably sets off their extraordinary
behaviour . . . delightful reading' — Frank Muir in *The
Spectator*

'Mr Somerville's book might be taken as a Modern Irish
Aubrey, though he is rather more factually accurate than
the Master' — John Jordan in *Hibernia*

PETER SOMERVILLE–LARGE

Irish Eccentrics

A SELECTION

THE LILLIPUT PRESS
DUBLIN

First published by Hamish Hamilton Ltd, London, 1975.
First paperback edition published in 1990 by
THE LILLIPUT PRESS LTD
4 Rosemount Terrace, Arbour Hill, Dublin 7, Ireland.

British Library Cataloguing in Publication Data
Somerville-Large, Peter
Irish eccentrics.–2nd ed.
1. Ireland. Eccentrics – Biographies – Collections
I. Title
920.0415

ISBN 0 946640 67 X

Reprinted in 1997

Cover design by Jole Bortoli (The Graphiconies)
Printed by Betaprint of Dublin

Contents

List of Illustrations

The illustrations have been reproduced by kind permission of the National Library of Ireland, 1a, 1b, 2a, 2b, 3, 4, 5, 6a, 6b, 7a, 11a, 11b, 12, 13a, 13b, 14a, 14b, 16b; of the National Gallery of Ireland, 7b, 8, 10; of the Library of the Northern Ireland Tourist Board, 9a, 9b; and of Jack Loudan, 15.

Acknowledgements

I would like to thank Francis Bonham and John Somerville-Large for directing my attention to Adolphus Cooke; also Mrs. Bayly-Vandeleur of Killucan, Co. Westmeath who kindly lent me a copy of Dr. William's sworn opinion that he was sane in spite of believing that he was turning into a screech owl. The Royal Academy of Ireland has allowed me to use its marvellous library to search for other eccentrics. I am also grateful for the assistance I received at the National Library of Ireland, the library at Trinity College and the library of the Religious Society of Friends in Dublin. Finally I must thank Giles Gordon who gave me the idea for the book.

Preface to the Lilliput Edition

ECCENTRICITY is a slippery word to define. The dictionary puts it down to 'being off centre' and cites several synonyms: peculiarity, freakishness, queerness, aberration. *Roget's Thesaurus* is more unkind, filing eccentrics under misfits and cranks: crackpot, nut, screwball, oddity, fogey, laughing-stock, freak; and only on reflection including in its stockpot of comparisons rhapsodist, enthusiast, knight-errant, Don Quixote.

In Ireland eccentricity still has a conditional charm, and much of it lies in not being a public nuisance. Rereading my book I find that, apart from men of violence like George Robert Fitzgerald, most of my eccentrics were, if not adornments to society, people who commanded affection. Even Fitzgerald is still remembered with nostalgia around Castlebar because 'he hunted by moonlight and won all his duels' and, no doubt, because he was hanged.

In Ireland the word 'touched', which *Thesaurus* does not include but which can be applied to so many eccentrics, was always less of a matter for opprobrium and more a mark of respect. A tolerance of diversity and strangeness in people's character was one of the more attractive features of Irish life. It spread through many aspects of day-to-day routine. Some of us will remember that before driving-tests became mandatory, there were only two qualifications for potential drivers: one was not to be blind, the other was to declare simply that no one in the family suffered from mental disease. Unfortunately, with Euroconformity it may well be that Irish eccentricity will become unacceptable.

Times change rapidly. For a number of reasons, social, pecuniary, environmental, the Anglo-Irish have produced numerous eccentrics, particularly in the environs of the big house. When I wrote my book in the early seventies there was still a whiff of sulphur about the big house. Today, however, its inmates have become high fashion, and the decaying world of the Anglo-Irish is revived in numerous novels and coffee-table books. An endangered species, the Anglo-Irish are no longer a threat. The landlord has ceased to be an ogre and has become picturesque, while the eccentric landlord is now presented as an ornament, a contrast to the grey conformity of modern life.

When Lilliput Press told me that they wished to bring out a new edition of *Irish Eccentrics*, my gratification was tinged with regret for all those gifted and golden people whom I had not written about. Some of them I came across since in my travels around Ireland; others were encountered through reading. Some I knew personally, like Pope O'Mahony, universally beloved as much for his generosity as his dottiness. Another acquaintance, a well-mannered lady, took up residence at the bottom of my garden and hung her clothes on a tree. She would go round at night opening farmers' gates to release the animals.

'It is most cruel shutting them in like that.' She had plans for storming the zoo and returning suitable animals to Africa.

I encountered for the first time a number of unusual personalities through reading for a book called *The Grand Irish Tour.* Among the travellers whose route I traced was the saintly Asenath Nicholson, American by birth and only Irish by association or by Conor Cruise O'Brien's convenient methods of defining Irishness. In 1840, wearing a coat covered in polka dots, a capacious bonnet and a huge bearskin muff, and carrying a carpet-bag full of Bibles, she set off around Ireland to distribute the Bibles to anyone she met. Mrs Nicholson embodied courage, toughness and an engaging personality that could only be described as eccentric.

Another discovery was a native of Moate, Co. Westmeath, who called himself A. Atkinson, Gent. In 1812 Atkinson published a philosophical treatise entitled *The Roll of a Tennis-ball through the Moral World*, and then, abandoning his wife and six children, toured Ireland in search of subscribers who would enable his second travel book, *The Irish Tourist*, to be published. He listed his subscribers in four categories denoting their generosity or meanness; Lord Meath and Daniel O'Connell were entered under class one, while numerous impoverished or avaricious clergymen, tradesmen and gentlemen were listed under class four. Anyone familiar with *Tourist*'s reflective, garrulous, sermonizing and gossipy style ('[At] Ballyconnell . . . I obtained a few subscribers and some marks of civility from Mr Whitelaw the curate, who is married to a daughter of the late valuable Mrs Angel Anna Slack of the county of Leitrim whose character and the remarkable termination of whose life have often been the subject of conversation in select parties . . .') would not hesitate to include A. Atkinson, Gent., in any compilation of Irish eccentrics.

I would like to end this introduction — and I hope Fernie will forgive me — with a memory of one of the most charming of living eccentrics whom I encountered on the Antrim coast.

When I met Fernie in Glenarm he was wearing a waterproof suit and polythene wrappings taken from bread loaves over his hands to keep them dry as he prepared to take his 400-c.c. Honda south to Drogheda in the Republic. His motor-bike was burdened down with over two hundred pounds of equipment, not to mention Fernie himself on top. The equipment included a set of Swiss bells, a ventriloquist's doll, a Punch and Judy show and a fez. There was scarcely a town in Ireland which he had not visited in thirty years. He ignored political and religious divisions, and had not yet found a Republican or Loyalist stronghold where he was not welcomed. He had encountered only one spot of trouble, a stray shot through the Honda's front wheel. He specialized in giving shows for children and charity performances, presented with a blend of enthusiasm and innocence.

I still have a poster advertising his performance: MAD CON-JUROR, MAGIC AND SCAPO VENTRILOQUISM, YOU BELL BAND AND DUET CONCERTINA, CHAPEAUGRAPHY TROUBLE WIT, BA–LOONATIC AND THE ROLLO, LAOUGHS, SCREAMS AND YELLS.

Fernie told me he was English — another only to be included among Irish eccentrics by association. Long settled here, married to an Irish girl, a quiet, well-spoken family man, he did not consider himself or his work in any way unusual. No doubt this unselfconsciousness is an essential ingredient in an eccentric's make-up.

I will leave the last word on the subject with Mary Manning, who wrote in her review of this book when it first appeared:

> It would seem to me that the true eccentric is not only a nonconformist; he is usually a gifted person who transforms the dance of life from a pavane into a merry polka; one who wilfully embroiders harsh reality so that it becomes a tapestry of golden nonsense, but at the same time he maintains the balance between eccentricity and insanity; he is never an enemy of mankind, but is often a delight.

Peter Somerville-Large
Glenageary, Co. Dublin,
Spring 1990

Introduction

ALTHOUGH Irish people as a whole are considered unconventional, it is the Anglo-Irish who generally make the records for eccentricity. Comparatively few Celtic Irish are remembered solely as eccentrics. For hundreds of years the majority of the nation was poor, and the behaviour of the poor is seldom recorded or tolerated. 'I wonder if you've noticed', wrote Margaret Powell recently, 'but when rich men are peculiar it's called eccentricity. But when poor men act a bit strange they're promptly classed as loony.' But is it only for reasons of wealth that the Anglo-Irish have produced so many eccentrics during the past two hundred and fifty years? There is scarcely a family that cannot number two or three, past and present. Why should so many flourish in the eighteenth century? It may have been a matter of timing. Transferred to Ireland, moulded by their new environment and contact with those whom they had subjected, the English settlers suddenly found they had lost touch with their immediate origins. This was the moment when the country house was transferred into a forcing house for eccentricity. The eighteenth century, which until its close was a period of peace and comparative prosperity, was the first time that the newcomers could take advantage of the circumstances which had given them an undisciplined licence to behave just as they chose. The choice was conditioned not only by wealth, but by isolation, prejudice, deficiencies in education and boredom. Bishop Berkeley may have noticed what was happening when, in June 1736, he wrote to a Mr. Urban that 'we also in this island are growing an odd and mad people. We were odd before, but I was not sure of our having the genius necessary to become mad.' But we should not search too closely for a reason. Maurice Craig has

I

confessed that when he was asked whether he thought living in country houses made people eccentric, or was it merely that eccentric people tended to live in country houses, he did not attempt an answer.

It may also be that among Celts the trait is transformed into fanaticism. Pure eccentricity is a luxury that native Irishmen have been unable to afford. Wherever it exists in Ireland it tends to be sombre. There is far less of the gaiety that characterizes the English eccentric, who according to Edith Sitwell has 'that peculiar and satisfactory knowledge of infallibility that is the hallmark and birthright of the British nation'. A proud definition of an English village is that it is a collection of eccentrics. This hallmark can be seen in the behaviour of Lord Bristol or Archbishop Whately, who tripped across the sea to join the odd and whimsical among the Irish. How lighthearted they were in comparison with their Irish counterparts! Irish eccentrics are a desolate crowd; one is reminded that the profligacy, violence, and even the extremes of austerity that form a basis for much of their behaviour have been linked by Dante in the seventh circle of Hell. Few make good family men; most have a preoccupation with death. The country houses are homes for tyrants. No buck oppressed with debt, drinking himself senseless, shooting his friends or throwing away his money under the chandeliers at Daly's appeared to be experiencing any enjoyment. Ascetics earnestly flogged themselves. Garish figures have roamed Ireland's cities, imposing a harsh familiarity, typified by Zozimus' grating voice chanting recitations.

The line between eccentricity and madness is blurred as Swift knew when he left his money to found a madhouse because 'no nation needed it so much'. Wars, poverty and loneliness have contributed to the erection of the asylums that rise like cathedrals outside Irish towns. The weather exerts its pressures as grey moody skies shot with cloud help to govern Irish behaviour. 'You feel ... an exhaustion rising into the air to meet you,' V. S. Pritchett found, visiting Ireland. 'You reach for the whiskey glass. Those wan sick clouds only a few hundred feet above the earth, might be damp souls of little value leaving gods that cannot cure. Yet a day or two, even an hour or two later, you could be flying into theatrical anarchy, swaying from one bizarre piece of break-up vapour to another . . . you have arrived at the beginning and end of creation.'

The true insane flicker through history. Here is just one, described by James Hamilton, Lord Abercorn's agent, in the terrible year of 1798:

> I lament to tell you that poor Harry Hood, your Lordship's surveyor is mad, and not likely to recover . . . (He) fancies that he will be murdered by United Irishmen and that his own family are trying to poison him . . . His first essay was in the middle of a most stormy and inclement night to leap out of a 2nd storey window with his breeches, a loose coat and nightcap on; the pockets of his coat he filled with stones, got a long pitchfork in his hand, and in this trim marched in the dead of night as far as Raphoe 8 miles: day appearing, he concealed himself in a waste house and took the first opportunity of the Bishop of Raphoe's gate opening to run in and call for protection . . .

Harry Hood had to be restrained, but although I have written about a number of people who were acknowledged as lunatics, others as mad as he were tolerated and flourished at liberty.

The eighteenth century in Ireland was so rich with distortions of human behaviour that we turn with reluctance to the more distant past where a scale of standards is difficult to determine. We can only use our own estimate in describing the edifying routines of anchorites and ascetics. Along with these formidable holy men are assembled other people with preoccupations that were pursued with unnatural singlemindedness. To quacks, healers, almanack makers, witches and wizards, have been added giants and centenarians who could not help stepping outside the normal pattern of our existence. The list is not nearly comprehensive. I have left out most modern people altogether and all that goes on in pubs and behind lace curtains in country towns. There is too much material. 'To a certain extent all of us are a bit odd, all of us are eccentric,' Chekov has said.

Irish Eccentrics

I have followed the example of recent anthologists in accepting Conor Cruise O'Brien's useful comments on being Irish:

Irishness is not primarily a condition of birth or blood or language; it is the condition of being involved in the Irish situation and usually of being mauled by it.

This is a definition that allows the compiler to take enormous liberties. I have included people who travelled abroad, one or two who never set foot in Ireland, and Englishmen like Lord Bristol and Translated Asgill who spent time there and suffered for it.

Familiars

THE people who have shuffled out of line emphasize by their appearance that their world is apart from ours. Generally they have singular clothes which are either parrot-bright or cobweb-dirty; usually they are solitary, sometimes they are deformed. They have haunted us over the centuries. For a few years a figure is as much an adornment of a city as any landmark of brick or stone; then he vanishes and is replaced by someone equally strange and equally well known. Sometimes one or two brief appearances may make a character remembered for a generation. Captain Debrisay, Crazy Crow, Zozimus, Stoney Pockets—they are some of the figures who have wandered up and down or lingered on corners, or, like Paginini, the Window Pest, glared out for a couple of decades from the window seat of the Kildare Street Club to reveal his head twisted in a hunting accident so that it was on the same level as his neck.

An early Dublin familiar was Joseph Damer, the usurer and miser, who came over from England with Cromwell to make a fortune out of moneylending. From the Swan and London Tavern, 'a timber house slated' where he lived,

> He walked the streets and wore a threadbare cloak;
> He dined and supped at charge of other folk.

Around 1740 the dramatist, John O'Keefe, took notes on some of the city's best-known characters. He lovingly described the elderly veteran, Captain Debrisay, who insisted on wearing clothes that had been fashionable in the reign of Charles II. They consisted of 'a large cocked hat, all on one side of his face, nearly covering his left eye; a great powdered wig hanging at the side in curls, and

5

in the centre of the back a large cockade with a small drop curl from it; his embroidered waistcoat down to his knees; the top of the coat not within three inches of his neck; the large buttons about a foot from it; buttons all the way down the coat, but only one at the waist buttoned; the hilt of the sword through the opening of the skirt; a long cravat, fringed, the eye pulled down through the third buttonhole, small buckles . . .'

Another Dubliner observed by O'Keefe was a conjuror. 'He was unalterable in regard to dress, and would have died rather than change his old fashion, although it were to prevent either a plague or famine. On his head was a broad slouchy hat and white cap. About his neck was tied a broad band with tassels hanging down.

'He wore a long dangling coat of good broad cloth, close-breasted and buttoned from top to bottom. No skirts, no sleeves, no waistcoat. A pair of trouser breeches down to the ankles, broad-toed, low-heel shoes which were a novelty in his time and the latchets tied with two pack threads, a long black stick, no gloves; and thus bending near double, he trudged slowly along the streets with downcast eyes, minding nobody, but still muttering something to himself.'

In the eighteenth century Dublin beggars were notorious; they were perpetually threatened with the lash, the stocks and imprisonment. They crowded the coaches wherever they stopped, and were the first sight for new arrivals coming in to Dublin by jaunting car from the Pigeon House after crossing the Irish Sea. Their general appearance was such that one traveller wondered what English beggars did with their cast-off rags 'til he went over to Ireland and then he perceived that they were sent on to the Irish beggars'.

The most notable was a cripple named Corrigan, known as His Lowship, Prince Hackball, or The King of the Beggars. Every morning a little cart drawn by a mule or two dogs brought him down to his spot on the Old Bridge which spanned the Liffey opposite Church Street. Here he begged for fifty years, in spite of the disapproval of city functionaries who sought to tidy him away. In 1744 the parish beadle of St. Werburgh's Church had him seized; 'but on his way to the House of Industry he was rescued by a riotous mob'. This was the beginning of a tug or war between the parish and Hackball's own people who sought to protect him. A public advertisement warned 'the friends of Hackball . . . the noted beggar . . . that if they do not prevent him from begging in the streets, [the authorities] will apprehend him tho' it should be with a military force, which they are determined to use against the multitudes who assemble to rescue those who are in the custody of parish offices'. When he was an old man the parish was able to arrest him and confine him for good.

Billy the Bowl was another beggar hard to shut away. He had been born without legs and moved about by the use of his arms with the stump of his body encased in a wooden bowl shod with iron. He was handsome with 'fine dark eyes, aquiline nose, well-formed mouth, dark curling locks, with a body and arms of Herculean power'. But his temper was unsteady, and when he was put in an institution the Board resolved 'that the man in the bowl-dish is not a proper person to be discharged from the House'. He managed to escape and somehow wandered around Dublin un-detected for two years in spite of his unmistakable appearance, until he attacked two women in a lane near the Royal Barracks. He was taken in a wheelbarrow to Green Gaol and sentenced to hard labour for life, a legal action that made him for a time a hero of the Dublin mob.

Crazy Crow flourished some decades later towards the end of the eighteenth century. He was not a beggar, but made a living as porter to musical bands and as a body snatcher. Bully Acre near the Royal Hospital and the Poor Man's Burial Ground were said to provide work for at least fifty resurrection men like Collins and Daly, who thought nothing of strewing the public highway with bodies they were forced to abandon. William Rae, a Scots naval surgeon on half pay, did better and conducted an export trade. The goods sent over the Irish Sea in barrels marked 'pickled pork' or cases labelled 'pianos' sometimes became so offensive that travellers were forced to transfer ship.

Crazy Crow was more of an amateur sack-em-up and had mixed success, with a period of imprisonment for stealing corpses from St. Andrew's graveyard. He was better known as a boozy personality carousing around the city, loaded with cymbals and trumpets looking like a one-man band. He was caricatured in an engraving which showed him weighed down with musical instruments and was accompanied by a verse:

> With looks ferocious and with beer replete
> See Crazy Crow beneath his minstrel weight;
> His voice as frightful as great Etna's roar
> Which spreads its horrors to the distant shore,
> Equally hideous with his well known face
> Murders each ear—till whiskey makes it cease.

The Female Oddity lived on the outskirts of Dublin, where she wore only green-coloured clothes, and for food, according to the *Gentleman's Magazine* for 1780, 'a fricasse of frogs and mice is her delight. Loves beef and mutton that is flyblown; when a child she used to be found eating small coal, and at night if her mother left her in her room by herself, she was seen to dispatch all the contents of the candle snuffers'.

The hangman, that figure who hovered perpetually in the background of eighteenth-century life, often did his work in disguise. He might wear a mask, or fit his back with a hump made out of a wooden bowl. Such concealment, which could be easily discarded, would help him escape from spectators who sought to pelt him after the execution of a popular criminal. Some administrators of justice dressed up specifically to give a surrealist air to a sinister occasion. The *Newgate Calendar* described a man who performed a whipping as 'highly grotesque . . . tall . . . in a grey coat with a huge wig and a large slouched hat . . . his face, completely covered with yellow ochre, strongly tatooed in deep lines of black'. In 1800 the executioner of six men condemned for murdering a Colonel Hutchinson wore 'a singular costume. From head to foot he was dressed in a uniform of bright green—the national colour—and around his waist was a broad buff belt on which was inscribed in large letters ERIN GO BRAGH'.

Familiars could be more respectable members of society. Some bucks qualified, although it was a hard time for dandies to stand out because of the brilliance of their dress. They had to outdo rich men like the Bishop of Derry who wore diamonds on his shoes, or Mr. Coote who returned from the Grand Tour in a startling outfit highlighted by the size of his feather hat and the brightness of his satin shoes with their red heels. Perhaps the most prominent of the bucks was the Sham Squire, Francis Higgins, the gutter journalist and government informer, who, during the last decade of the eighteenth century, was 'daily to be seen ... upon the Beaux Walk in Stephen's Green wearing a three cocked hat with fringed swansdown, a canary coloured waistcoat with breeches to match, a bright green body coat and violet gloves, the only buck in Dublin who carries gold tassels on his Hessian boots'.

Around 1770 Dubliners were entertained by the appearance of a mysterious Turk named Dr. Achmet Borumbad. His story is told at length by the diarist, Jonah Barrington. He was over six feet tall, and his imposing figure, invariably clothed in Turkish costume, was set off by a generous black beard which covered his chin and upper lip. After fashionable society welcomed him as a refugee from Constantinople, he managed to convince the College of Physicians that there was a need in the city for public baths —simple, medicated, cold, temperate and warm. These would cure 'all disorders whatever'. He even persuaded the Irish House of Commons to make him a series of annual grants to finance their construction in Bachelor's Walk.

The Doctor's requests for Parliamentary aid were accompanied by lavish parties which took place before every Session. During the last of these, when the festivities got rowdy, one of the more temperate guests excused himself and prepared to leave. On his way out he fell into the vast cold bath, and was followed by numerous other revellers, who had rushed after him trying to prevent his departure. Dr. Borumbad found 'a full committee of Irish Parliament-men either floating like so many corks upon the surface, or scrambling to get out like mice who had fallen into a bason!' Restored with brandy and mulled wine, large fires and oriental blankets, they were sent home in sedan chairs; but they gave him no more grants.

The Doctor then fell in love with a Miss Hartigan, whose family insisted that he should shave and become a Christian. He emerged from beard and robes as a plain Irishman, Mr. Patrick Joyce from Kilkenny—'the devil a Turk', he told his beloved, 'any more than yourself, my sweet angel'. He had spent some time travelling in the Levant, and following his experiences there, decided to make a business out of posing in Turkish costume. The Dublin Baths did not long survive the stripping of their proprietor's mysterious background, and in 1784 they were sold to the Wide Street Commissioners.

In 1816 a Dublin newspaper reported the detention in the House of Industry of a notorious individual known as Stack of Rags. 'His great care and anxiety to preserve every scrap of old rags, and his uneasiness when any person approached him gave concern of suspicion, and a search was made; seventy-five guineas in gold were found carefully sewed up among the rags, and receipts from a most respectable banking house in this city, for different lodgements amounting to fifteen hundred pounds.'

Stoney Pockets walked round the Dublin streets with a pronounced tilt to one side, keeping his right-hand pocket filled with stones to straighten himself up, or as he sometimes claimed 'to keep his head from flying away'. He was a friend and associate of one of Dublin's best-known characters, Zozimus the reciter.

Zozimus, who was born around 1794 as Michael Moran, became blind a few months after his birth. Probably this misfortune encouraged him to become a story-teller, which he did with great success, so that by the time he was twenty-two he was famous in the city as an itinerant reciter. He had taken the name of a fifth-century cleric who discovered St. Mary of Egypt when she was a hermit in the wilderness. The meeting of Zozimus and St. Mary, which had been written up by Bishop Coyle, formed one of his favourite recitations.

He wore a long frieze coat with a curious scalloped cape, an old greasy brown beaver hat, corduroy trousers and what were described as 'Francis Street brogues'. He always carried a blackthorn stick tied to his wrist by a leather thong. During the day his favourite stand was on Carlisle Bridge, but most evenings he wandered round the city on a well-known itinerary, giving his recitations, and stopping every few minutes to receive contributions from 'good Christians' of whom there were fortunately many. He did not like Protestants.

'Is there a crowd about me now? Any blackguard heretic about me?' Zozimus would begin, before launching off into a set piece.

> Gather around me boys, will yez,
> Gather around me?
> And hear what I have to say
> Before ould Sally brings me
> My bread and jug of tay.
> I live in Faddle Alley,
> Off Blackpots near the Coombe;
> With my poor wife, Sally,
> In a narrow dirty room.

Another opening was:

> Ye sons and daughters of Erin attend,
> Gather round poor Zozimus yer friend;
> Listen, boys until yez hear
> My charming song so dear.

The shake of his shoulders and a characteristic wriggling of his body accompanied an actor's ability to extract the last piteous ounce of pathos from his material, much of it patriotic, some of which he composed himself. It was usually effective, even if, as in a favourite ballad, *St. Patrick was a Gintleman*, it became meaningless doggerel:

> There's not a mile in Ireland's isle
> Where the dirty varmint musters
> Where'er he puts his dear forefeet
> He murders them in clusters;
> The toads went hop, the frogs went pop
> Slap haste into the water.

The verses would be accompanied by a barrage of asides:

> At the dirty end of Dirty Lane
> Lives a dirty cobbler, Dick McClane.

Dick McClane was a strong Orangeman. Sir John Grey, editor of the *Dublin Freeman's Journal*, once led Zozimus across Essex Bridge.

'Now, Zozimus, why is it you are always so hard on us Protestants? Here am I, a heretic, who have taken you safely over the bridge, when none of your faith was near to assist you, and yet you may say harsh things against us.'

'Sir,' Zozimus replied. 'Sir! Do you not know that we must somehow for their own good pander to the prejudices of an unenlightened public?'

During his lifetime he had numerous rivals and imitators. Immediately after he died on April 3, 1846, one of his companions set himself up as 'the real identical Irish Zozimus'.

A shortlived humorous periodical was named after him. For years photographs of him in his strange clothes were advertised for sale:

> Photographs of the great original Zozimus.
> Carte de visite 6d. and post free
> Cabinet size 1s. 6d.
> Large size for framing, 14 by 11 inches with
> quotations from Saint Mary of Egypt and Finding of Mary
> 2s. 6d. each and post free.

Although the best-known figures are associated with the city, where they are constantly under the scrutiny of their fellow citizens, they are found in rural areas as well. Robert Cook, all dressed in white, flourished late in the seventeenth century down on a farm in Cappoquin, Co. Waterford, where he stood out from the commonalty by reason of his startling white linen suits. An early vegetarian, he refused to eat flesh or wear the product of any animal; consequently he wore nothing but linen, so that he came to be famous as Linen Cook. He also refused to have any black cattle on his farm which was run with 'Phagorian Philosophy', and even his horses had to be the same unblemished white as his clothes.

'Whereas I cannot kill without wounding my conscience,' he wrote, 'rather than will I offend the innocent life within me, I refuse any food or raiment that may come from any beast or other animal creature. And wine and strong drink are hot in operation and intoxicating, and I think as needless to be as tobacco, and I, by experience, find that water for drink and pulse or corn and other vegetative for food, and linen and other vegetatives for raiment be sufficient . . .'

A fox which had the temerity to attack Cook's poultry was not killed when it was caught; first he gave it a dissertation on murder and then a sporting chance by making it run the gauntlet of his farm labourers armed with sticks. Like many cranks, he had a long and healthy life, dying in 1726 when he was over eighty years old. He was buried in a linen shroud.

Lord Howth, according to O'Keefe, always wore 'a coachman's wig with a number of little curls and a three-cornered hat with great spouts. When on the horses' box I never saw him without a bit of straw about two inches long in his mouth'. Later in the eighteenth century the antiquarian and bookseller Gabriel Beranger was to be seen in a long scarlet frock-coat, yellow breeches and top boots scrambling over the countryside looking for ruins.

J. D. Herbert in his *Irish Varieties* describes a rural scholar nicknamed the Knight of the Boyne whose farm in Co. Meath was crammed with books. He habitually wore 'a large cloak with hanging sleeves, a crimson silk handkerchief about his neck and head and a large leafed hat'. Another voracious reader was Mr. Henry Dodwell of Manor Dodwell, Co. Roscommon, who went about on foot, even walking from Holyhead to London with his pockets and bosom stuffed with books, reading every mile of the way.

Overhead in his balloon painted with the arms of Ireland Mr. Crosbie tried to cross the Irish Sea dressed in an 'aerial dress' he designed himself, consisting of 'a robe of oiled silk lined with white fur, waistcoat and breeches combined in one garment of quilted white satin, morocco boots and a montero cap of leopard skin'.

The Old Kerry Records mentions how 'eccentricity of attire was not rare in Tralee and its vicinity'. It goes on to describe a character known as Georgy Gay 'who down to the day of his death in 1838 wore the enormous ruffles and frill shirts of finest French cambric at a guinea and a half a yard, material which went out with the last century'. Georgy also had an eighteenth-century appetite; not long before his death he gave dinner parties with dishes which included twelve huge turbot as an entrée, Kerry mutton, barn-door fowl, mountain trout, lobsters and grouse, swallowed down by bottles of mountain dew.

In Cork the tailor known as Bothered Dan dressed in his cocked hat and home-made uniform complete with breastful of medals. Harry Badger paraded or lounged in front of the city courthouse wearing a pair of yellow buckskin trousers, a red coat and a brass helmet which he had ornamented with iron spikes against the attacks of small boys. He was universally regarded as a figure of fun and even his friends took advantage of his many peculiarities, including his indifference to what he ate or drank. When a mouse was dropped into his porter, he swallowed his pint without protest. His death came about as the result of another practical joke, after he had been given a dish of tripe made out of strips of leather from a huntsman's breeches boiled with milk and honey. Harry took two days to finish the meal—and died on the third.

Dublin familiars of this century have included Jembo-No-Toes, Old Damn and All-Parcels, the beggar lady who lived by collecting and selling waste paper which she accumulated in endless neat bundles. Tie-Me-Up used to stand at the Metal Bridge stripped to the waist cracking a big whip and shouting: 'Tie me up! Tie me up!' Someone would oblige, using a chain and perhaps a strait-jacket, whereupon he would manage to release himself within ten minutes or so to the cheers of the crowd. Specs was a figure of the suburbs, lean, lanky, over six foot tall, who used to tie a piece of cloth to the front wheel of his bicycle handlebars to catch the wind. He would peel an apple in one curling piece, throw away the apple and eat the peel. More recently Dubliners have noted Lino—who was always lying down—and Bang-Bang, well known for shouting 'Bang Bang you're dead!' at passers-by.

The Bird Flanagan was a practical joker whose exploits became city legends. His nickname arose from the occasion when he went to a fancy-dress ball as a bird. When he didn't get a prize, he pretended to lay the egg which he proceeded to throw at the judge. Another time he managed to get himself arrested by snatching a fowl from a poulterers' shop just as two policemen were passing. He had taken the precaution of buying it first and having a label with his name tied round its neck. Perhaps his most startling exploit was the theft of a black child from the Kaffir Kraal in Herbert Park during the Great Exhibition of 1906.

There are people today who remember Endymion clutching his swords and can testify to the accuracy of Gogarty's description of him. 'He wore a tail coat over white cricket trousers, which were caught in the ankle by a pair of cuffs. A cuff-like collar sloped upwards to keep erect the little sandy head crowned by a black bowler some sizes too small. An aquiline nose high in the arch gave a note of distinction to a face all the more pathetic for its plight. Under his left arm he carried two sabres in shiny scabbards of patent leather. His right hand grasped a hunting crop such as whippers-in use for hounds.' Sometimes he would be holding a fishing rod which he used to fish through the railings of Trinity College.

He had worked in Guinness, and the story had it that he went strange after falling into an empty vat and breathing fumes. When told that his condition was likely to get worse, he said: 'Endymion, whom the moon loved: a lunatic.' But in the National Library he signed himself James Boyle Tisdell Burke Stewart Fitzsimons Farrell.

He could be seen entering the library, saluting the clock at the ballast office with a drawn sword, or taking out his alarm clock and compass with which he set a course for his home, raising his whip hand to the north as he entered Molesworth Street. He was a harmless gentle old man, whose main interest, apart from his fanciful clothes, was in music. 'Dublin saw him', Gogarty wrote, 'only as a man gone "natural" and Dublin has outstanding examples in every generation.'

Hermits and Ascetics

THE Skelligs are three steep rock islands eight miles out in the Atlantic off the south-west coast of Kerry whose dimly-seen mountains and headlands bound their eastern views. The little Skellig and Washerwoman's Rock are inaccessible at most times; but on the Great Skellig or Skellig Michael landings can be made during the summer. Today lighthouse keepers live four hundred feet above the swell, relieved of their duties by helicopter. Their lighthouse is near the site of 'the most western of Christ's fortresses'.

Some time during the sixth or seventh centuries a small group of monks settled on Skellig Michael, which is dedicated to the archangel, like those other sea-girt mountains, St. Michael's Mount in Cornwall and Mont St. Michel in Normandy. Here they founded a sanctuary which for a few hundred years attracted a stream of holy men seeking to live apart from the vanities of secular life. They constructed six beehive cells and two oratories near the top of the conical mountain, using a beautiful technique of dry-stone walling which has survived fifteen hundred years of storms. Five of these cells are intact; they each contain an ambry or wall recess where the monks could store their scanty supplies and there is also the occasional stone projection which could have been used as a hook to hang garments on. Outside on the roofs there are similar stone projections which held in place insulating layers of turf, or perhaps tufts of the mat-forming sea pink which grows abundantly on the rock.

Stormbound for months on end the monks lived austerely. There were two wells near their settlement and plenty of seabirds and their eggs to eat. Fulmars and petrels nest on the Skelligs, as well as the more common ducks of the sea, puffins, razor bills and guillemots. The little Skellig is flecked in a perpetual snowstorm, since it is one of eleven gannetries around the coast of the British Isles. On calm days, the monks came down and caught pollock, and their diet may also have been varied by goat's flesh and milk, since there is just enough grass to support a small herd of animals. They may have brought the earth across in curraghs. Enduring the tempests and contemplating the sparkle of sun on the ocean, they were satisfied that apart from the occasional band of pilgrims— a pilgrimage to the Skelligs persisted until modern times—outside human contacts could not distract them from their vigil with God.

Sparse records have preserved the names of some of those who chose to spend their lives here. Before the monks came Skellig Michael seems to have been used as a stronghold by kings in Kerry and a place of refuge if troubles on the mainland got unendurable. Then a shadowy St. Finan may have been the founder of the monastic colony. *The Martyrology of Tallaght*, written at the end of the eighth century, mentions a Sweeny of the Skellig. There was an Elann, son of Cellach, abbot of Skellig, who died in 824; Balthmhac of the Skellig died sixty-eight years later. In 1044 died Aodh of Skellig whom the *Annals of Innisfallen* referred to as 'the noble priest, the celibate and the chief of the Gaedhil in piety'. The *Annals* also recorded an attack on the hermitage by some Vikings, during which a monk named Etgal of Skellig was carried off; he escaped, but died of hunger and thirst. On another occasion when the Vikings came in search of plunder, they again kidnapped a monk, Cormac the anchorite, son of Selbach. He, too, managed to escape: 'he it was whom the angels set free three times, though he was bound up again every time'.

It seems probable that the little community remained intact until the middle ages, since a chapel was added to the older buildings some time during the twelfth century. But by then pious people were less zealous about seeking out lonely discomfort. Giraldus Cambrensis mentioned that 'the situation of the abbey being found extremely bleak, and the going to and from it highly hazardous, it was removed to Ballinskelligs on the continent', in other words the mainland.

The early Irish hermits were pleased to emulate the excesses of the Desert Fathers in Egypt and Syria, but in a less accommodating climate. Monasticism was dominated by rigorous régimes of fasting and penance designed for sinners to attain 'a loving attention upon God'. Saints and wise men chose to become hermits, or at least to live in inaccessible places, and islands were particularly suitable for those who sought isolation. During the sixth and seventh centuries which heralded the dawn of Ireland's great age of monastic splendour islands all around the coast were snapped up by hermits or small anchoritic communities. They were ideal situations for the contemplative to view some of God's creation with a selective and pure vision:

> Delightful I think it is to be in the bosom of an isle
> On the crest of a rock
> That I may look there on the manifold face of the sea;
> That I may see its heavy waves
> Over the glittering ocean
> As they chant a melody to their Father
> On their eternal course.

St. Columcille, who spent his life bringing Christianity to islands, Tory, Iona and Eigg, spoke approvingly of his brethren seeking *destrum in pelago intransmeabilu*, a desert in a trackless sea. Calling an island or any isolated holy place a desert was associating it with the environment of the Desert Fathers, and place names like Dysert o Dea and Reendesert still recall the site of hermitages. It is possible that the monks of Skellig Michael made comparisons between their mountain and the pillar of Simeon Stylites. Contrasting the violence of storms with the peace of calm days was also a practice associated with the Desert Fathers, who saw the struggles between the forces of light and darkness in nature as paralleled within the soul.

Such ascetics, according to the ninth-century *Catalogus Sanctorum Hiberniae*, belonged to the third order of saints. The bishops, who received their *missa* from St. Patrick, were considered Most

Holy, the Presbyters Very Holy, the anchorites merely Holy. But some of the greatest names in early Christianity travelled across the sea in search of solitudes. The islands visited and transformed by Columcille became symbols of Christianity. Many went further than he; Cormac, Abbot of Durrow, sailed into Arctic waters before turning south and ending up on Iona. Brendan was looking for the perfect island when he set off on his voyages in search of 'Paradise'. The most famous of those he visited, the back of the whale, Jasconious, where he celebrated Easter Mass, may indicate that pure contemplative peace is not always forthcoming even with ideally austere conditions. Modern commentators have suggested that Brendan's was a genuine voyage undertaken in the spirit of exploration, presented to us through the bright eyes of the myth makers. The story has similarities to an adventure of Sinbad. Jonah's involvement with the ocean also shared the mysteries of the unknown, and perhaps Bede was thinking of Brendan's adventures when he stated that Jonah was swallowed by a whale. He was the first to do so; earlier accounts had merely specified 'a great fish'. Medieval chroniclers may have believed that Jonah and Brendan encountered the legendary Aspidochone which occurs in bestiaries, a sea creature with seven fins which sailors often mistook for islands.

Among the Magharees, islands off north Kerry, Illaunanil bears striking similarities with the whale island described in Brendan's *Navagatio*: it has no grass, very little timber and no sand on its shores. A landmark is even known as Coosarim or the 'creek of the spout'. There is a story in west Cork of how some fishermen discovered what seemed to be a dead whale floating in the waters of Bantry Bay. They sent the boat back to get help salvaging it, while a couple climbed on the animal's back where they lit a brazier to make tea; they woke it up.

Inland, the big monasteries also sought isolation. A great foundation like Clonmacnoise was surrounded partly by bog and partly by a swampy arm of the Shannon. Clonfert was similarly located on an island in a bog. Other less important monastic settlements were sited on the edge of lakes, or on the tops of mountains. But they only provided a degree of isolation, and it was difficult for the true hermit to withdraw entirely from community life and follow St. Columcille's edict: 'Be alone in a desert place, apart in the neighbourhood of a chief monastery if you distrust your conscience in the company of many.' Complete isolation was never easy to achieve. 'I wish,' bemoaned St. Manchan, 'O Son of God, eternal ancient king, for a hidden little hut in the wilderness that it might be my dwelling.' An anonymous monk longed to be 'all alone in my little cell without a single human being with me; such a pilgrimage would be dear to my heart before going to meet my death'.

Frustrated ascetics longed for 'a cold fearsome bed where one rests like a doomed man; food, dry bread weighed out, water from a bright and pleasant hillside'. The programme for the ideal hermetical routine included an unpalatable and meagre diet, reading and self-mortification. Discomforts included austere sleeping arrangements. St. Columcille had 'a bare rock for pallet and a stone for pillow'. St. Kieran also had a stone pillow, which seems to have been quite a common piece of furniture in hermitages. Mlle Françoise Henry has suggested that the two polished red stones she discovered in the sleeping-places of two excavated huts on Inishkea island might well have been pillows. Some hermits went as far as entombing themselves—again in imitation of the Desert Fathers—and various earth houses and souterrains, like an earthhouse in Killala church in north Mayo and another at Kilcolomcille in Co. Donegal, have been identified as places in which hermits chose to spend time. On Skellig Michael a neolithic souterrain may have been adapted as living quarters.

Hermits had to interpret in their own way the programme recommended by St. Jerome: 'Those who have devoted their lives to God should spend their nights like a tree hopper passing untiringly from one exercise of devotion to another.' St. Samathann, advising a monk who asked what method is best for prayer, interpreted this by recommending that 'we must pray in every position'. Self-mortification was an important aspect of many régimes of prayer. It usually included a schedule of fasting. The behaviour of the anchorite, Gorman, who lived on bread and water for a year was typical. Madeoc of Ferns went better and ate only barley bread with water for seven years. Other hermits used ingenuity in finding new disciplines. Some carefully tended worms and encouraged them to gnaw at mortified flesh. Another suspended himself for seven years from iron hooks. Maclaius spent six months in a marsh infested with mosquitoes. Ailbhe regularly kept a cross vigil, using a cross of stone which he had made himself, on which he stretched regardless of the weather, reciting the psalter. Findchu, who surrendered his place in heaven to a king of the Deise, got seven smiths to construct seven sickles with which he thrashed himself for seven years to win a new place above.

Extreme forms of self-denial were not, of course, confined to hermits; they were general throughout the monastic system. Over the centuries a number of elaborate lists of rules and penitential exercises were drawn up for holy men to follow. The earliest to survive, the Rule of Columcille, believed to date from the sixth century, has punishments for breaches of community rule that might have derived from a sadistic prep school: six strokes of the cane for the monk who speaks during the meal; ten for the one who makes cuts on the table with his knife. Giggling during holy office cost six, contradicting another monk earned the sinner fifty, while biting the chalice at Mass merited six.

Later rules, penitentials and martyrologies were more severe. 'Anyone who touches food with unclean hands, a hundred lashes are laid on his hand.' 'For being drunk to cause vomiting—let him do a penance for forty days on bread and water.' Such regulations came to be considered too severe by church authorities; the Penitentials were formally condemned by the Councils of Chalon (A.D. 780) and of Paris (A.D. 829). Peter Damien even recommended those who followed them to the fire of Gomorrah.

The strictest Rule was made up by a fanatical reformist sect known as the Culdees which was active towards the end of the eighth century. Under the Abbot Maelruin, the Culdees, friends and companions of God, instituted a fierce reappraisal of the tradition of austerity. There is a theory that the Rule of Columcille as it survives was redrawn by one of the Culdees. They were noted for their asceticism rather than for any artistic or intellectual activity, although it is fair to add that a Culdee environment created an atmosphere in which such a masterpiece as the Stowe Missal came to be written out. They had an important monastery at Tallaght—Tallaght and Finglas on either side of the Liffey, now bleak Dublin suburbs, were both centres of religous learning, once known as 'the two eyes of Ireland'. Tallaght's formidable Abbot Maelruin was a rigid disciplinarian, and his influence helped to formulate one of the harshest rules in church history. The lives of his monks ground inexorably around a system of prayer, strict fasting, penances and castigation. There was no relaxation. Once a well-meaning musician, Cornan of Desert Laigen, offered to play the pipes and make a little secular music for the monks. Maelruin admonished him: 'Tell Cornan these ears of mine shall not be delighted with earthly music until they are delighted with the music of heaven.' Food was distributed in accordance with the recipient's state of sin. Those whose sins were lightest received gruel floating on water; gruel between the water was given to the more disreputable, while gruel which sank to the bottom was reserved for hardened sinners.

The Culdees were responsible for a particularly severe table of penitential commutations. 'A commutation for rescuing a soul out of hell: 365 paters, 365 genuflexions, 365 blows of the scourge every day of the year and a fast every month rescues one soul from hell.' Another commutation 'of a black fast for grave sins for one who cannot read' demanded '300 genuflexions and 2,000 properly administered blows with a scourge, at the end of each a cross vigil until the arms are weary'. First commutations for laymen and women included 'spending the night in water, in nettles, or with a dead body . . . spending the night in cold churches or remote cells, while keeping vigil and praying without respite'.

The Penitentials were very largely devoted to punishments for carnal sins and lustful thoughts. Fasting was believed to reduce the amount of blood in the body, and from this would come a lack of desire. 'Seven days' penance on bread and water for any cleric who lusts after but does not speak with his lips . . .' Pollution in sleep exacted a punishment of singing seven psalms and living on bread and water throughout the following day. Taking a virgin required a three days' penance.

In general women and the lusts they inspired were abhorred. The monks of Inniscarthy island never allowed one to land there. 'What have women to do with monks?' a virtuous lady was asked as she tried to disembark. 'Return to the wicked world lest you be a scandal to us, for however chaste you may be, you are a woman.' St. Columcille would not even let a cow within sight of one of his monastery walls, because, as he explained, 'where there is a cow there must be a woman, and where there is a woman there must be mischief'. As late as the twelfth century Giraldus Cambrensis described a lake in Munster with two islands, the larger of which had a church. 'No woman or animal of the female sex is allowed thereon without dying instantly. This has been proved many times by examples of female dogs and cats perishing.'

Not all ascetics were as sensitive to the problems of carnal lusts as the Anchorite, Laisren, who lived quite naked and free from sin with nothing on his conscience, until he made the mistake of spending the night in a friend's cloak. For the first time in his life he had a 'carnal vision' and later he discovered the reason why; the cloak had belonged to a married couple. Saints gave a lead in efforts to suppress lustful thoughts. Amonius heated irons and applied them to his body to keep down desire. St. Oengus restrained the impulses of the flesh by constant scourgings, reciting the psalter every day, reciting the oratory under a tree, standing in a cask of cold water, and binding himself to a post with a rope round his neck. Women saints were not to be outdone; St. Derville of Erris put out her eyes because an unwanted suitor said they were the most attractive thing about her.

Saints were the popular idols of the day, and it was natural to assume that they should be pursued for carnal motives. Women lusting after saints became a persistent theme of medieval legends. St. Senan, according to an early poem, narrowly escaped being trapped on his island retreat by a beautiful maiden; had he given her any encouragement or allowed her to stay there overnight, she would have remained with him for ever. His plight was typical.

Such legends are closely associated with prominent figures of the
early church; St. Columcille and St. Kevin, both strikingly handsome, attracted persistent female admiration.

As a young man St. Kevin, whose name means the Fair Begot-
ten, had to flee the blandishments of a woman and run into a
forest where he stripped off his clothes and rolled himself in a
bed of nettles. (This was an easy and popular purgatorial exercise
which lingered on—it survived in one form up to this century,
when children used to go round on May Eve and May Day carrying nettles and stinging everyone they met.) When his pursuer
caught up with him, Kevin, recovering his presence, put on his
clothes and chastised her with the same nettles. She fell on her
knees and begged to become a nun.

St. Kevin, perhaps the most famous of hermit saints, belonged to
the great early period of Irish monasticism. When he decided to
become a contemplative hermit, he did not desert the dark valley
of Glendalough beside whose lower lake he had founded a monastery. He merely moved away into the forests on the chill north
side of the upper lake and obtained temporary accommodation
in the hollow trunk of a tree. In theory a hermit should have been
able to live comfortably off food gathered in natural surroundings
—'a clutch of eggs, honey, mast and hearthpease sent by God . . .
herbs and berries . . .' but probably Kevin's diet was supplemented
by visiting monks. From his tree he moved to a less exposed
hermitage, the famous 'bed' thirty feet above the black waters
of the lake. This little cave hollowed out of rock may have originally been a neolithic mine; there is one rather like it on the island
of Hoy in the Orkneys. Even today it is difficult to reach without the aid of a boat. Here he spent from four to seven years,
and here he was supposed to have been followed by another
female admirer.

Although the pursuit of St. Kevin by the fair Kathleen is usually
regarded as an invention of nineteenth-century guides for the
entertainment of visitors, it must derive from medieval legend.
'The blessed saint was layin' there, belike dhrayming o'Kathleen
for sure, there was no harm in that, and when he wake up an' seen
her settin' by his side, he thought his eyes ud lave him. "Kathleen,"

says he, "is it yourself that's in it un'me thinkin' I'd parted from you forever." ' Inevitably he discovered that she was the devil, so 'the blessed saint jumped off the ground and wid his two feet gave the ould rayprobate a thundering kick in the stummick . . .' and pushed her into the lake.

In spite of the harshness of their chosen way of life, most hermits were supremely happy. One result of living so near to nature was that they were trained observers. They possessed what Robin Flower has called 'an eye washed miraculously clean by continual spiritual exercise, so that they, first in Europe, had that strange vision of natural things in an almost unnatural purity'. They wrote many touching lyric poems testifying to their love of nature. 'A hedge of trees overlooks me; a blackbird's lay sings to me,' noted a monk of the ninth century, and found the bird's song a gentle substitute for the monastery bell calling him to prayer.

Like hermits everywhere they kept all sorts of animals as companions—foxes, badgers, deer, herons, even wolves. Marban had a white sow; the virgin, St. Cruinthereis, kept a lapdog which she fed on the milk of a doe. St. Moling of Ferns had a fly, a wren and a fox; St. Mochua a cock, mouse and fly. The cock crowed the hours of matins for him, the mouse would wake him by licking his ear, while the fly marked the passage in his psalter. When Mochua wrote to Columcille lamenting the death of his creatures, he got back the message: 'My brother, marvel not that thy flock should have died, for misfortune ever waits upon wealth.'

Perhaps the nature of this early cult of asceticism, its harshness and its compensations can be summed up by the story of St. Kevin and the blackbird. St. Kevin's behaviour may prompt a grotesque comparison with Indian fakirs holding up their arms for decades, and yet it is redeemed by his tender concern for natural life. Praying over a long period, perhaps during Lent, he was observed by a blackbird who chose to build her nest within his cupped hands. She was able to hatch her eggs and rear her fledglings before Kevin moved.

Parallel to the régimes of extreme self-denial by holy men there was a secular tradition of asceticism. It was a common form which lunacy took—the special and exhalted lunacy of legend associated with the word *geilt*.

The fullest account of *geilt* behaviour is to be found in the sagas and traditions relating to Buile Suibhne, mad Sweeny, a seventh-century king, whose madness was caused by the horrors of the battle of Magh Ragh in 637. After seeing visions of battle demons he began to fly. Many legendary lunatics could do this; their bodies became as light as air, and they flew 'with a sort of fluttering motion'. The ability to fly was recognized as a special form of battle fatigue; there are many references to warriors reacting strangely to bloody fighting and attaining magical powers. During the battle of Allen in 722 nine soldiers were regarded as having 'gone flying'. Similar accounts of *gealta* occur in medieval Welsh and Scottish traditions and also in early Norse literature. There is a Norse description of men stricken after battle . . . 'their swiftness is said to be so great that other men cannot approach them—for these men run along the trees as swiftly as squirrels'. Perhaps the Japanese soldiers who disappeared into the jungle for thirty years after World War II went *geilt*.

Sweeny escaped from the carnage by flight, hopping from shield to shield until he reached the sanctuary of the forest. There he lived like a bird, growing feathers to help him levitate and to protect him from the winter's cold. Moving through the forest, crashing in clumsy flight among the trees, 'shunning mankind, keeping company with wolves, racing red stag across a moor', Sweeny fled across the country, becoming a 'fantastical recluse'. In summer he lived in ivied treetops, eating 'apples, berries, beautiful hazel nuts, raspberries, haws of the prickly sharp hawthorn'. In the harshness of winter he was 'tormented by frost, falling from the tops of withered branches . . . walking through furze'. His diet of herbs, brooklime and 'everlasting green topped cress' was typical of this extreme type of asceticism; the word *geilt* may derive from the root *gel*, to pasture. Madmen were considered close to God, and many of the saints chose to have inspired lunatics as their companions. But Sweeny was rather special; sagas single out his behaviour in pushing a normal hermit's life to an extreme. Eventually he fell in with St. Moling of Ferns, the great Leinster saint, who became his friend and confessor, looking after all his austere needs. His cook was instructed to fill a cowpat full of milk daily for Sweeny, and this may have undermined his health for within a year he was dying in the saint's arms.

The desire for extreme self-denial was not confined to saints, contemplatives and madmen. Generations of sinners, ordinary men and women, have striven to purge their error here on earth. In a country where the ordinary struggle for survival was harsh, punishment for sin had to be correspondingly extreme. It is not surprising that one of the most astonishing places of pilgrimage in the Christian world, is still associated with extreme forms of penitence and punishment. The little island on Lough Derg in Co. Donegal with its small underground cave was renowned throughout Europe as St. Partick's Purgatory.

Lough Derg—Derg means red or blood-coloured—was said to have got its name from the blood of a monster who was killed there. This monster, collaterally descended from the thigh bone of a witch, was either killed with a silver arrow by Finn Mac-Canhaill, or by Coman Mal, who allowed himself to be swallowed before cutting his way out of its stomach. He lost his hair from the heat of the entrails, and was known afterwards as Coman the Bald. Such legends were good for tourism, and St. Patrick's Purgatory became something of a draw for pilgrims, many of whom were foreigners making the rounds of Irish shrines. Although their penitential excesses caused the pilgrimage to be banned, first by Pope Alexander VI and then by Pius II, the spate of visitors did not cease.

The penitent locked himself in the cave on Saint's Island where St. Patrick is supposed to have fasted for forty days and to have had a vision of the other world. Those who followed his example for a mere twenty-four hours would not only see Hell and Purgatory for themselves, but go straight to heaven after their death, avoiding any further contact with Purgatory at all. From the twelfth century onwards a stream of foreign sinners made their way over the boggy tracks of central Ireland to Lough Derg to combat nameless evil spirits in 'the last throw of the desperate

against the devil'. Clerical approval had to be obtained in order
to undergo the ordeal; and only after fifteen days of fasting was
the pilgrim, strengthened by Holy Communion, blessed with
holy water, 'naked except for rostetics and femoral', brought to
the door of the cave and locked in. If he emerged sane from his
experiences he received a certificate testifying that he had 'suffered
the attacks of unclean spirits'.

Some accounts survive of what took place. In 1353 George
Crissaphin had twenty-eight visions and was confronted with
3,000 devils in the shapes of animals which 'belched forth from
their throats a fierce and stinking fire'. Another pilgrim, Antonio
di Giovanni Manani, who came to Lough Derg in 1441, was found
after only five hours 'senseless and breathless, with my head resting
upon the cross which I had in my right hand'. Henry of Salthry's
Tractus de Purgatorio S. Patrici, which told of the confinement of a
knight named Owen to relieve his conscience after a life of
crime, became something of a best-seller.

In 1632 the cave was closed by James Spottiswood, the Protestant Bishop of Clogher; it was described then as 'a poor beggarly
hole made with some stones laid together with men's hands without any art, and after covered with earth'. But closure did nothing
to stop the pilgrims any more than the Popes' interdict. Today
they travel to Lough Derg, fasting from the time they leave their
homes. They stay two nights on the Station Island, one sleeping,
one keeping an all-night watch at the basilica. During the day they
do a pattern barefoot, circling the basilica and visiting the crosses
of St. Patrick and St. Brigid, and the remains of ancient monastic
cells or 'beds'. Their hardships have eased a little since the time
of William Carleton, who wrote that the experiences of pilgrims
were 'such as no man with flesh and blood capable of suffering,
and gifted with a good memory could readily forget'.

The outlawed church, which flourished in secret after the enact-
ment of the penal laws, had links with the shining dawn of Celtic
Christianity. Priests turned outdoors to perform their work secretly
must have felt affinity with those early hermits and saints who
had gained their strength by comparisons with the state of nature
and the state of their souls.

One priest revived the anchoritic tradition vividly by living 'in eremitical solitude' on the island in the remote lake of Gougane Barra for nearly thirty years. By 1700 hermits had become less common, and his presence there was observed with some amazement. The Protestant Bishop, Dive Downes, who visited the area some time between 1699 and 1702, noted that 'at Gougane Barry in this parish lives Denis Mahoney, formerly priest of this parish, now a hermit, who has built 7 chapels there. He was ordered at Rome to undergo the penance of a Hermit, having been guilty of fornication'. The story is not substantiated elsewhere, and probably Bishop Downes was repeating some gossip that sought to explain Father O'Mahoney's strange behaviour.

He appears to have been a member of the Order of Calced Carmelites which was trying to re-establish itself in Ireland as a move of the Counter-Reformation. The order itself had been re-organized after the Reform of Touraine, which had reimposed strictness of rule upon the Carmelites. In its return to the principles of Carmelite doctrine, the order had urged the setting up of hermitages in remote places, and this seems to have induced Father O'Mahoney to take up residence in a distant part of west Cork. The lake of Gougane Barra was chosen because it was associated with Finbar, the patron saint of Cork, and here the hermit built an imaginative reconstruction of Finbar's oratory and cells which is still to be seen. His long years on the island were intended to increase the importance of the place as a pilgrimage in the saint's honour; but his own personality superimposed itself upon Finbar's, and for some time after his death—when he was over eighty—a cult seems to have been partly directed at himself. Twenty years after he died (the exact date is not known) it was reported that 'many of the faithful . . . foregather regularly at the same holy place . . .' and even today people throw coins on his grave. They tend to believe that the buildings he erected are the work of St. Finbar, forgetting that St. Finbar's monks would have been housed in wattle huts.

Charles Smith gives an account of his visit to Gougane Barra in his *Antient and Present State of the County and City of Cork*, published in 1751.

Before one arrives at [the lake of Gougane Barra] both man and horse must perform penance for two miles, over the rudest high-way that was ever passed . . . It was with great difficulty that I passed two miles of this causeway in two hours. *Gougane-Barra* signifies the hermitage of St. *Finbar* he having (as tradition says) lived here a recluse before he founded the cathedral of Cork . . . This place, since the time of St. *Finbar* has been frequented by many devotees as a place of pilgrimage, and to get to it, is little less than to perform one. In the island are the ruins of a chapel with some small cells, a sacristie, chamber kitchen and other conveniences, erected by a late recluse (Father *O-Mahony*) who lived an hermit in this dreary spot 28 years . . . Round part of the lake is a pleasant green bank with a narrow causeway from it to the island. That part of the island unbuilt upon, Father *Mahony* converted into a garden planted several fruit trees in it with his own hands, and made it a luxurious spot for an hermit. Opposite to this island on the continent is his tomb, placed in a little low house, on which is this inscription. *Hoc sibi et Successoribus suis in eadem vocatione, Monumentum imposuit Dominus Doctor Dyonisius O'Mahony, Presbyter licet indignus. An. Dom 1700.* He was not buried in it till the year 1728.

The word *Successoribus* in the inscription appears to indicate that Father O'Mahoney expected that others would follow his lonely example. An undated petition addressed to the Vatican discovered in the archives of the Dominican house of San Clemente in Rome, seeks to establish the Calced Carmelites at Gougane Barra in charge of the ancient pilgrimage. It stresses Father O'Mahoney's success in popularizing Finbar's hermitage. No reply to it has been found, but it was certainly unsuccessful. However, Father O'Mahoney did help to establish Gougane Barra as a major centre of devotion to St. Finbar.

It is unlikely that Lord Orrery had heard of Father O'Mahoney, when, round the date of that hermit's demise, he followed the fashion for constructing artificial hermitages by building a most elaborate one in his garden at Caledon in Co. Tyrone. He com-

pleted it even before his great house had been finished. Mrs.
Delaney was shown around during the summer of 1748 and admired 'about an acre of ground—an island planted with all the
variety of trees, shrubs and flowers that will grow in this country,
abundance of little winding walks differently embellished with
little seats and banks; in the midst is placed an hermit's cell, made
of the roots of trees, the floor is paved with pebbles, there is a
couch made of matting and little wooden stools, a table with a
manuscript upon it, a pair of spectacles, a leathern bottle; and
hung up in different parts an hour glass, a weather glass, and several
mathematical instruments, a shelf of books, another of wooden
platters and bowls, another of earthern ones, in short everything
you might imagine necessary for a recluse'. It seems wasteful that
the place was not occupied, although it was rather too luxurious
for a Calced Carmelite. Mrs. Delaney was so struck by the pretty
idea, that later, when she settled at Delville, she erected a faint
imitation of it, a mere 'beggar's hut' intertwined with branches
and furnished with a stone seat.

The ideal stimulated by Rousseau and others of seeking nature
in seclusion was seldom carried through; few were prepared to
go further than Lord Orrery in planning their hermitages as
summer houses. But in 1778 two ladies from Kilkenny began a
programme of rural retirement that brought them fame and a
little notoriety; they withdrew from the world and spent their
lives together in a carefully tended retreat in Wales.

Eleanor Butler, the elder of the ladies, was thirty-nine, and her
mother had hinted that it might be a good thing if her stout and
ageing daughter became a nun and entered the comfortable French
convent where she had been educated. But she thought differently
and eloped with her kinswoman, Sarah Ponsonby, who was
thirteen years younger than herself. Their departure from Kilkenny
was bitterly opposed and frustrated by their families, but eventually they had their way and crossed the Irish sea to Wales. They
came to Llangollen where they rented a little farmhouse named
Plas Newydd. Here they spent fifty years, deeply in love, beautify-
ing their seclusion, ignoring the fact that their disapproving
relations, although wealthy—Eleanor's brother became Earl of

Ormonde—allowed them very little money. No one with true taste—a quality as rare as perfect pitch—has much idea of economy. Their debts were enormous, but their house, altered to the Gothic style, lovingly planted garden and model farm set in a wild Welsh valley had a beauty that struck every visitor. Fashionable people liked to make inconvenient journeys over the mountains to go and see their hermitage and admire the advantages they found there, which included, according to Prince Pückler-Muskau, 'a well furnished library, a charming neighbourhood, an even tempered life without material cares, a most intimate friendship and community among themselves'.

They spent much of their time reading improving literature in three languages from the red-bound books stamped with their initials ranged in the gilded shelves of their library. In winter they would retire early to their dressing-room and play backgammon, Eleanor crying out 'Faith!' after a lucky throw. On summer evenings they would stroll through the shrubberies they had planted with syringa, lilacs, laburnums, white cherries and filberts and scented creepers, some of which enclosed a font they had taken from a nearby ruined abbey—about as near as they got to the monastic ideal. As time passed their taste faltered; the Gothic became too ornamental and carved oak encrusted their cottage like a fungus. By the 1820s, still devoted to each other, they had become a touching pair; two stiff old ladies with cropped white hair, invariably dressed in black riding habits and stocks that made them look like men. Charles Mathews, the actor, who saw them on one of their rare visits away from Plas Newydd at the theatre in Oswestry, mistook them for clergymen. 'As they are seated, there is not one point to distinguish them from men,' he wrote to his wife, 'the dressing and powdering of the hair, their well-starched neckcloths, the upper part of their habits which they always wear, even at a dinner party, made precisely like men's coats and regular black beaver men's hats.'

The ladies of Llangollen are a frivolous addition to the Irish eremitical tradition, and their story is an indulgent digression from consideration of the cult of austerity. Not for them were the hardships that for so many were integral to proper Christian behaviour. Devout people like William Carleton's well-loved father were commended for religious practices which bordered on the extreme. Carleton senior 'was perpetually praying; in fact his beads were scarcely ever out of his hands . . . He prayed even on his way to Mass when one would imagine he could have got enough of it . . . He prayed on his way to fair or market, and he prayed on his way home again also . . . He was in the habit of going during the winter nights—indeed during every night of the year . . . up to the parlour to pray. This was not common prayer; it was penance of the severest kind got from certain specimens of Butler's *Lives of the Saints*. He always brought a round rod, about as thick as the upper end of a horsewhip, on which he knelt, perhaps for a couple of hours, repeating rosaries and prayers to no end'.

There were many like him, or like the priest cited by Le Fanu, who always wore rope round his knees to prevent them becoming calloused through prayer. None have attracted the veneration of Matt Talbot, described in the prayer for his canonization as a 'model for penance', who suffered decades of solitary discomfort by patterning his day-to-day life on the disciplines of the ancient saints. He did so, not in any hermitage, but in the bustle of Dublin.

Born in Dublin in 1856, Matthew Talbot became a hodman, an affable worker who liked his drink and spent his wages on porter at tuppence a pint and whiskey at threepence a glass. Once he stole a strolling player's fiddle to pay for drink; at other times he pawned his boots. Then in 1884 when he was twenty-eight he abruptly took the pledge and began to read St. Augustine and the *Lives of the Saints*—with difficulty, since he was almost illiterate. He admired St. Catherine of Siena and St. Teresa of Avila—'grand girls'—and especially studied the latter's injunction as to how to pray. 'He was never off his knees in the evening—except if a visitor called.' He began fasting; his midday meal, taken at work, consisted of a mixture of tea and cocoa which he allowed to get cold and drank without milk or sugar. Following tradition he had a plank for a bed and a wooden block for a pillow. Later in his life, working in T. & C. Martin's timber yard creosoting wood, he took advantage of any lull to retire to a passage between the church-high timber stacks to pray. If it rained he would put a sack over his shoulders.

He fasted and held nightly vigils for forty years. Beneath his clothes he wore chains binding his body and limbs, a habit which was not discovered until he had collapsed and died during a heat-wave on June 7, 1925. When the two attendants in Jervis Street Hospital removed his spotlessly clean clothes, they found a heavy chain wound around his body, a lighter chain on one arm, another below the knee and a cord knotted around the other arm. They had worn grooves in his skin.

After his death his body, as so often happens to the venerated, was moved about, once in 1952, and again in 1972, when it came to rest in his old parish church in Gloucester Street where people pray at his tomb of Wicklow granite.

Miracle Makers, Rhymers, Witches, Giants and Oddities

ST. PATRICK's fingers were able to turn into lighted candles in the dark. St. Declan swallowed a threatening pirate fleet. St. Nauman miraculously rid a Connaught village of fleas. St. Brigid hung her cloak on a sunbeam. St. Gobnat commanded a swarm of bees to blind her enemies. St. Tigernach of Clones breathed alternately white, red and yellow.

It is difficult to know how far to allow Irish eccentricity to be tangled in legend. Lumbered with their strange miracles, inextricably linked with the mysterious strength of the pagan forces that preceded them, the behaviour and attributes of Ireland's saints can be very odd. On one side Christianity had to absorb many of the elements of the pagan past. On the other hand the imaginations of those who compiled their lives obscured the truth about them in outrageous tall stories. The medieval hagiographer has been compared to the modern novelist—someone who provided entertainment for the public whose preferences and tastes had to be considered.

Although Ireland's hagiography is possibly the most extensive in the world, it consists largely of names. When it comes to facts there is often not much to tell. A typical entry in a recent book on Irish saints reads: 'This is the feast day of three saints, and little is known about any of them. They were all monks and all men, and that about sums it up.'

A hundred and twenty saints have the name Colman; fifty-nine are called Mochua. At least eighteen have names that are derived from Fintan; thirteen from Finnan; sixteen from Comman; fourteen from Ciaran; eleven from Brigid and twenty-eight from Aiden. Scholars postulate several St. Patricks. St. Patrick himself was preceded in Ireland by a number of historical figures who permeated Christianity with the purity and strength of the early church. But among those who from their labours rest are wild creatures of legend. Some may have been ancestors of forgotten tribes and products of the dying practice of ancestor worship. It may be for this reason that a convention arose by which the more prominent saints were assumed to be of royal blood; Finbar of Cork, Molaise of Leighlin, Diarmuid of Inishclogran, Aiden of Kildare, Camin of Lough Derg and St. Patrick himself make up part of a long list of noblemen who became saints.

Ultan of Ardbracan was descended from the legendary hero of the Red Branch Knights, Conal Cearneach. Senan of Scattery had a genealogy which could be traced back for sixteen hundred years from A.D. 600.

There were ten speckled saints and eleven leper saints. Others more fantastical had attributes connected with ancient fertility beliefs. Many were prolific, like the female saint, Darerca, who had seventeen sons and two daughters. The sons all became bishops while the daughters remained virgins. A bisexual like Mochue Cicheach had remarkable breasts which 'fed babies of future eminence'. Other saints had three and even four breasts. Others were odder still, like Fer Caille, who had buttocks like cheese, one arm and one leg and a long enough nose to be looped around the branch of a tree.

A saint like Silan was more directly linked to mythology. He was the Christian counterpart of the legendary Formorian King, Balor of the Evil Eye. Balor, the Gaelic version of Cyclops, could kill anyone who looked at the eye in the middle of his forehead. It needed four men armed with hooks to raise the lid and one stare was enough to enfeeble an army. But for most of the time Balor was considerate, covering his eye with the skins of seven sheep. St. Silan's eyebrow was equally destructive to man or beast. 'For the nature of the hair was such that whoever saw it first in the early morning died straight way.' Prospective suicides used to wait at sunrise to encounter him. In order to relieve Silan, St. Molaise (which one is not clear since there were three) plucked out the fatal hair from the eyebrow and perished himself.

The wizardry of the Druids, skilled in 'idolatry, sorcery, the composition of bright poems, divination from sneezing and the voices of birds', became part of the saint's standard equipment. None of these talents helped the Druids themselves in the face of the new powers of Christianity. When they tried to make a show of strength against St. Caillia, they were seen to 'turn up their backsides, and their jaws moved angrily and they unjustly rebuke the clerics'. Caillia transformed them into standing stones. Other saints that followed took over the ungodly habit of cursing. A curse, once pronounced had to fall somewhere; Giraldus considered that Irish saints were more vindictive than those of any other region.

Legend and magical legacies blurred not only the deeds and attributes of the saints, but the reputation of secular miracle makers who performed their wonders outside the sanctity of the church. Even more than the saints, the bardic poets, 'rimers', were the direct inheritors of the Celtic *Druidi*, deriving from the *fili* or poets of early Ireland. The bards became a group of highly professional practitioners who organized their art on union lines. Poetry was treated as a skill which required a long period of arduous training; composing poems was an exclusive skill, confined to certain families like the O'Dalys. Amateurs were not admitted into their midst. The O'Dalys were a sect especially privileged because of its poetic gifts, and other chieftains would grant its members land in recognition of their importance. The places where they chose to study were always remote, because bardic composition required a régime of fasting and solitary confinement. In his memoirs published in 1772, the Marquis of Clanricarde described how aspiring bards were expected to do their compositions in the dark. 'The said subject (either one or more aforesaid) having been given overnight, they worked it apart, each by himself upon his own head, the whole next day in the dark, til at a certain hour in the night, lights being brought in, they committed it to the writing.'

The long apprenticeship brought benefits other than facility in composition. Like the Druids before them the bards were magicians. According to Cormac's glossary, written in A.D. 831, a poet could cast injurious spells; 'he chews a piece of the flesh of a red pig or a dog or a cat and puts them on the flagstones behind the door . . . he grinds the lobe of the person's ear between his fingers and the person on whom he performs the operation dies'. The poet dressed distinctly, 'like a bird . . . up to the girdle of the neck of mallards, and from his girdle up to his neck of their tufts'. He was a man to be feared. He could invoke cattle raids, and his satire was regarded as a terrible weapon, almost equivalent to the Church's excommunication. His poetry could cause death. In 1493 Cian O'Gara was killed by the power of rhyming; another victim was Sir John Stanley, Lord Lieutenant of Ireland, who was recited to death by the poet Niall O'Higgins after Stanley had plundered land belonging to his family.

The power and prestige of the rhymers continued well into the sixteenth century. Elizabethan officials in Ireland regarded them as a persistent nuisance. Thomas Smith categorized the different bardic ranks, listing as most tiresome the '*Fillis*, which is to say in English, a poet. These men have great store of cattle and use all the trades of the others, with an addition of prophecies. These are great maintainers of witches and other vile matters; to the great blasphemy of God and to great impoverishing of the commonwealth'. Suspicion of the rhymers did not prevent Elizabethans from using them to foment trouble among their enemies; Sir George Carew once employed an O'Daly, Angus of the Satires, to compose lampoons of ancient families, a betrayal for which he was stabbed to death by the chief of the O'Meighers.

Witches, like rhymers, were inheritors of ancient mysteries, and they, too, could rime men and beasts to death. Hags and witches were degenerate representatives of Celtic goddesses who trivialized the miraculous powers evolved from the traditional Druidic rule and shared by saints and bards. The Druids used wisps of hay to induce madness; Irish witches, according to Giraldus, could turn sheaves of hay or straw into red-coloured pigs which they sold dishonestly in the market place.

Naturally the practice of magic and witchcraft was condemned

1a.　Crazy Crow

1b.　Zozimus. From a sketch by H. O'Neill,
November 25, 1836

2a. Richard Crosbie

2b. Harry Badger. From a painting by James McDaniel

3.　　St. Brendan celebrating Easter

4.   Valentine Greatrakes

by the church. In the penitential of Theodore, composed during the eighth century, degrees of penance were enjoined on magicians and enchanters and those who dealt in charms. A penance, for example, was meted out to those who ate mouse droppings; any woman who actually killed someone by witchcraft was penalized for seven years. Such mild punishment reflects the fact that there was never any systematic persecution of witches in Ireland. Various reasons have been put forward to try to explain this; Ireland was remote; fear of witches was outside Celtic experience and associated with dourer national temperaments. European witches were more sinister. Although it must be said that they did sometimes find pieces of skin from a corpse or a dead hand—especially that of an unbaptized baby—useful prophylactics, the old women of Ireland with their charms and cats were largely ignored and their milk and butter magic tolerated.

Dame Alice Kytler, Ireland's most famous witch, belonged to a Norman family, and her practices have an aristocratic imported air, different from the usual folk magic. An attractive middle-aged lady at the time of her inquisition, she lived in Kilkenny where her house is still to be seen. In 1325 an inquisition under the control of Bishop de Ledrede of Ossory was set up to investigate seven counts of sorcery practised by a band of heretical sorcerers led by Dame Alice. (The distinction between witch-craft and sorcery seems to be one of degree; sorcery is the more sophisticated pursuit, since its practitioners seem to be rather masters of the devil than his slaves. Of course, the advantage is only temporary.) Dame Alice had married four times; her sons by her first three marriages accused her of murdering their respective fathers magically and accumulating the wealth she inherited from them in order to present it to her favourite son, William Outlawe. Her current husband had been 'reduced to such condition by sorcery and powders that he had become terribly emaciated, his nails had dropped off and there was no hair on his body'.

The coven she controlled parodied the power of the church by 'fulminating sentence of excommunication with lighted candles, even against their own husbands from the sole of their foot to the crown of their head ... and then extinguishing the candles, crying *Fi! Fi! Amen!*' Its paraphernalia included 'certain horrid worms, dead men's nails and the brains and shreds of grave clothes of boys who were buried unbaptized'. A sacrificial wafer with the Devil's name on it was found among Dame Alice's effects, together with the traditional broomstick 'upon which she ambled and galloped through thicke and thin, when and in what name she listed'. She swept clean the streets of Kilkenny between compline and twilight, shoving the dust and refuse towards the door of her son, William Outlawe, chanting:

> To the house of William my sonne
> Hie all the wealth of Kilkennie towne.

She sacrificed nine red cocks and nine peacock's eyes to her incubus, Art, or Robert, who had carnal knowledge of her in the shape of a cat, a black hairy dog, or in the likeness of a negro (Aethiops). More than two hundred years later, during the November sessions of 1578, two witches and a 'blackmoor' were sentenced and executed in Kilkenny after a trial of which no details survive. Perhaps this Negro died as a result of old memories and old associations.

During her inquisition Dame Alice managed to slip away with the aid of influential relatives. She escaped to England and was never heard of again. One member of her coven, Petronilla of Meath, was burnt in Kilkenny on September 3, 1325, the first record of a witch being burnt in Ireland. Others may have suffered too.

The fourth Earl of Desmond flourished a little later than Dame Alice; his disappearance in 1398 helped to confirm his reputation as a sorcerer, but the circumstances of the event are now obscured in robust legends. The Earl had a castle beside a lonely lake in Co. Limerick, Lough Gur, where he practised his magic arts. When he brought his new-wedded wife home for the first time, she asked him to put on a show of his powers. The Earl acquiesced, only stipulating that she must keep silent throughout the performance; otherwise the castle would sink into the lake. He turned himself into a giant vulture with a corpse-like smell, then a contorted hag, and finally a serpent, stretching himself on the floor until his length spanned the room. Who could blame his wife from screaming, with the result that the castle disappeared under water? Every ten years the Earl reappears together with his knights and their horses, and they can be seen galloping over the lake. His own horse's shoes are of silver and when these are worn out he will be able to surface for good and reclaim his vast possessions.

The behaviour of Dame Alice and other sorcerers may have expressed heresy, a denial of the authority of the church and a revolt against its jurisdiction. Heresy was an occasional problem. In 1327 Adam Dubh of the Leinster clan of O'Tooles expressed opinions out of his time and country, opinions that must have seemed eccentric indeed. His story is told in Holinshed. 'A gentleman of the family of the O'Toulies in Leinster named Adam Duffe, possessed some wicked spirit of error, denied obstinatelie the incarnation of our sauior and trinitie of person in the unities of the Godhead . . . as for the holie scripture he said it was but a fable; the Virgin Marie, he affirmed to be a woman of dissolute life.' He was burnt on Hogsy Green (later College Green) in Dublin in 1327. Others who were not tolerated were two men burnt in 1352 for 'offering contumely to the Blessed Virgin'. The links between heresy and sorcery were those that helped to establish the persecution of witches throughout northern Europe.

It is difficult to make out if Sir Thomas Bath, Lord of Howth, practised sorcery when in 1459 he was relieved of peerage and public office 'for having put out the eyes of one Master John Stackboll, a priest and doctor of four degrees, and cut out his tongue'. The tongue was restored by the intercession of the Virgin Mary. On surer but more pedestrian ground, we know that by the sixteenth century the invading English were confusing folk-magic with the sort of witchcraft that was condemned by James I. They saw witches everywhere, holding them especially responsible for the devastating wet weather that bedevilled their Irish wars during the 1590s. Sir Geoffrey Fenton wrote how it 'maketh me to think that if God hath given liberty to the witches of that country (which aboundeth with witches) they are all set on work to cross the service by extraordinarily unseasonable weather'. Sir George Carew blamed them for the storms in west Cork that interfered with his campaign of 1601, noting 'that the country of Beare was full of witches'. Half a century later in 1642 a section of the Cromwellian army had its tents blown down by a rainstorm. 'Yea, severalls of them dyed that night of meere cold. Our sojers and some of our officers too . . . attributed this hurrikan to the divilish skill of some Irish witches.' Old women were persecuted for eye-biting, afflicting cattle so that they became blind. Barnaby Riche thought that 'the Irish were wonderfully addicted to the prognostication of soothsayers and witches'.

During the seventeenth century orthodox witchcraft continued to be a rare import, the occasional indulgence of the new settlers. In 1616 an unknown clergyman was indicted for practising 'unhallowed arts'. In 1660 the Reverend James Shaw 'was much troubled with witches, one of them appearing in his chamber and showing his face behind his cloke hanging on the cloke pin'. Mr. Shaw, his wife and servant mysteriously sickened and died. Around this time a lady named Anastasia Sobechan was cured of magical spells by touching the holy relic at Holycross Abbey, after having the traditional girdle tied round her waist. 'Suddenly she vomited small pieces of cloth and wool, and for a whole month she spat out from her body such things.'

In 1654 Mr. John Browne of Durley lay dying; at the foot of his bed was a great iron chest filled with legal papers and fitted with three locks. His friends and relatives standing around suddenly saw the locked chest begin to open on its own, lock by lock, until the lid stood upright. Mr. Browne, who had not spoken for twenty-four hours, sat up in bed, looked at the chest and said, *You say true, you say true, you are in the right* (a favourite expression of his) *I'll be with you by and by*. He lay down and never spoke again. The chest slowly closed and locked itself and shortly after Mr. Browne died.

Only once during this period was there a witchfinding parallel in sensation to the excesses that took place in the rest of Europe and in America. In Youghal on March 24, 1661, Florence Newton was indicted for bewitching a servant girl named Mary Longdon by kissing her. As a result Mary Longdon became ill with fits and trances and vomited up 'needles, pins, horsenails, stubbs, wool and straw'. Even as she gave her evidence, the accused continued to bewitch her, 'peering at her between the bystanders and shaking her manacled hands while saying *Now she is down*'. Longdon had another vomiting fit and 'passed up several crooked pins and straw and wool in white foam-like spittle in great proportion'. While in prison Florence Newton was said to have bewitched one of her jailers to death by kissing his hand through the grating. No record exists of the outcome of the trial, but it seems likely, in spite of her assertions 'that there were others, as Goody Halfpenny and Goody Dod in town that could do these things as well as she', that she suffered the usual sad penalties of persecuted witches.

One of her examiners was Valentine Greatrakes, who became famous by the use of gifts that some might consider related to witchcraft. Greatrakes was an 'empiric' or faith healer, who discovered the gift of 'stroking' that brought relief to many sufferers.

He was the son of an Englishman settled in Affane, Co. Waterford, where he was born in 1629. He had a varied early career which included service in Cromwell's army, followed after the Restoration in 1660 by an early retirement during which he decided to give himself wholly to 'the study of goodness and mortification'. He took time off to go witchfinding; with Messrs. Perry and Blackwell he went down to Youghal to test the imprisoned Florence Newton. The Mayor of Youghal disapproved of the old-fashioned water ordeal, so other tests were devised to find out if she were a witch. Her hands were pricked with a lance (no blood came), and she sat on a stool while a shoemaker tried to stick his awl into the wood. The tests were considered to be positive.

In 1663 the idea came to Greatrakes that he could cure the King's Evil. He concealed it for a time 'for the extraddiness of it', but eventually informed his wife who 'conceived this was a strange imagination'.

A print exists of Greatrakes performing one of his early cures; dressed in his buttoned-up coat and floppy collar, he is laying his hands on a scrofulous small boy who kneels in front of him.

Behind are three more patients, one of them on crutches. One of these must be William Maher, the first of his successes. 'Within a few days he saw the eye was almost cured, and the nose, which was almost as big as a pullet's egg, was suppurated and the throat strangle amended.'

Three years later Greatrakes progressed from scrofula, which any monarch could cure, to general practice. 'God was pleased . . . to discover unto me that he hath given me the power of healing. This impulse I had the Sunday after Easter Day, the 2nd of April, 65.'

The first patient on whom he tried out his wider powers was the colonel of his old regiment. Colonel Phaire was a regicide, and had retired to live very quietly in Cahirmore, Co. Cork. Greatrakes stroked away his agonizing gout within a few minutes. From that time his fame began to increase, so that people came to him with their diseases from all over Ireland. He stroked away their complaints. 'He would drive the morbific matter into some extreme part, suppose the fingers, and especially the toes, or the nose and tongue into which parts he had forced it. It would make them so cold and insensible that the patient could not feel the deepest prick of a pin; but as soon as his hand should touch these parts or gently rub them, the whole distemper vanished.'

Crowds descended on his house in Affane 'so that my stable barn and malt house were filled with sick of all diseases almost'. Like many who genuinely believe that they have been specially selected by God to administer His gift, he refused payment for his cures. He complained bitterly about the onerous nature of his dedicated life, how he was obliged 'to cast all worldly pleasures and delights behind his back, to run himself into the midst of all diseases . . . to run the hazard of his liberty and life by the crowds, pressings, streams and stinks of the multitudinous and ulcerous persons . . . '

In 1666 he toured England, treating large numbers of sufferers. He had mixed success; in London, for example, he 'failed at Whitehall before the king and his courtiers'. He became the object of controversy. Already in Ireland the Dean and Bishop Ordinary of the Diocese of Lismore had tried to stop his career because he did not have a medical licence. Joseph Glanvil in his *Saduticimus Triumphatis* diminished Greatrakes' successes, claiming that 'his patients often relapse, he fails frequently, he can do nothing where there is any decay in nature, and many distempers are not obedient to his touch'. A doggerel ballad entitled *Rub for Rub, or an Answer to a Physician's Pamphlet styled The Stroker Stroked*, accused him of most medical crimes including taking advantage of his women patients.

> Her stockings off, he strokes her lily foot;
> What then? The doctor has a minde to do it.
> Her legs, her knees, her thighs, a little higher . . .

But he could afford to ignore criticism and libel. Some of his cures had been certified by the newly formed Royal Society of Medicine, which considered that his healing powers derived from 'a sanative contagion in his body which hath an antipathy to some particular diseases and not to others'. He had many fervent admirers, among whom was Mr. Henry Stubbs, whose eulogy of the Stroker, entitled *The Miraculist Conformist*, made a comparison between his cures 'and those of Jesus Christ and his disciples'. This was too much for the Reverend David Wright, who replied in a furious pamphlet entitled *Wonders No Miracles*. 'Sir, the man, it seems, being bred up in loose times and in a more loose way, a soldier, [has] prostituted his understanding to a variety of opinions and errors . . . '

After returning to Ireland Greatrakes seems to have given up healing. Perhaps the strains and disappointments of his English tour discouraged him, or he tired of the notoriety and the legions of sick that followed him wherever he went. Until his death in Affane in 1683 he lived the life of a country gentleman on an income of a thousand a year. Occasionally he was called in for help by a neighbour. One of his last cases was a butler who was tormented with spirits. He was confined in a large room where he was under observation by a distinguished group of spectators that included two bishops and the Earl of Orrery. In the afternoon he was seen to rise from the ground. In spite of the efforts of Greatrakes and another man to hold him down, 'he was carried in the air to and fro over their heads, several of the company running under him to prevent him receiving hurt if he should fall'. He must be considered another of Greatrakes' failures; all the Stroker could do was to help catch him when he eventually came down.

Recently Finbarr Nolan has demonstrated that faith healers can attract as wide a public as they did in Greatrakes' day. The seventh son of a seventh son has traditionally been able to heal psychological conditions such as eczema and asthma. Finbarr, who has the requisite number of uncles and elder brothers, treats a far wider range of diseases since the time when, still in nappies, he put his infant hands on another child and cured it of ringworm. He claims that roughly seventy-five per cent of his patients are improved or cured after he has laid hands on them; this is about the same percentage of patients relieved by placebos provided by their doctors. People flock to his remote home in Co. Cavan, just as they gathered at Affane three hundred years ago. He has also visited England, where he appeared on television. His publicity agent, Fred Hift, has worked for Julie Andrews and Raquel Welch. He has administered to mass audiences. His method is simple; he merely touches the afflicted spot, since he has been discouraged by the Catholic Church from praying and sprinkling holy water during healing sessions. He believes that rheumatism and arthritis start from a worm in the spine. When he was two, his mother put a worm in his hand and it died. Any worm put in the hands of a faith healer should die. However, when Finbarr handled some in front of television cameras, it was noted that they survived the experience. He charges nothing for his services, and grateful patients usually leave him a donation in an envelope. Tax men would like to know how much. He has stated that his greatest happiness is healing people.

*　　　*　　　*

The giants who strode so confidently through Irish mythology lingered forlornly in history for men to stare at. Corney Magrath and Charles Byrne were the enfeebled successors of Balor and Finn McCool. Finn McCool is best described by Flann O'Brien:

'Though not mentally robust he was a man of superb physique and development. Each of his thighs was as thick as the belly of a foal. Three fifties of fosterlings could engage at handball against the wideness of his backside, which was large enough to halt the march of men through a mountain pass.'

Belief in giants could colour eyewitness descriptions. 'Once a drowned giantess was cast upon the shore. She was fifty feet tall, that is, from her shoulders to her feet, and her chest was seven feet across. There was a purple cloak on her. Her hands were tied behind her back and her head had been cut off; and it was in this way that the woman had been cast up on the land.'

A giant belonging to a similar category was exhibited in the Trinity College Museum, whose bizarre collection (including 'the skin of one Ridley, a notorious Tory which had long ago been executed . . . tanned and stuffed with straw . . . mice had eaten up much of his face . . .') was written up in 1699 in the *Dublin Scuffle*. 'We saw on a table the thigh bone of a giant, or at least of some monstrous overgrown man, for the thigh bone was as long as my leg and thigh, what is kept there as a convincing demonstration of the vast bigness which some human bodies have in former times arrived too.'

The remains of a giant found by two labourers in Leixlip grave-yard in 1812 were exhibited a few years later in Kirby's Wonderful and Eccentric Museum. The skeleton, ten feet in length, said to belong to one Phelim O'Toole, had a tooth as big as an ordinary finger. Later this was said to be a mammoth bone.

The *Strand Magazine* for December 1895 reported a fossilized Irish giant who had been left in the Broad Street goods depot of the London and North-Western Railway. This giant had been in the possession of a showman named Dyer, who said he found him while prospecting for iron in County Antrim. He was put on exhibition at a charge of sixpence a head in Dublin, Liverpool and Manchester, and had been sent from Manchester to London by rail in 1876. He had never been collected, and the charge for carriage, four pounds, two shillings and sixpence, had never been paid. The artist of the *Strand Magazine* sketched the vast mummi-fied figure, which weighed over two tons and had to be hoisted into position with a crane and the help of six men. When erected it stood over twelve feet high with a breast span of six feet six inches. To add to its interest the right foot had six toes.

Real-life Irish giants were common enough, especially during the eighteenth century. In 1682 Dr. Molyneux had made an examination of 'Edmond Malone, born in Ireland at Porchester in County Meath . . . when he stood on the bare ground with his shoes off he measured full seven feet seven inches in height—that is, above two feet taller than a man of common size'. A few decades later the Munster giant, Cruathair O'Carevaun, was reputed to be over eight feet high and strong in proportion. Once in Cork harbour he lifted up a ship's anchor which the whole crew had been unable to budge, even with the aid of a windlass. He retired to his native island of Cape Clear, where he lived a hermit in the ruined castle of Dunanore.

The most famous giants of the period, who had brief tragic lives and grotesque ends were Corney Magrath and Charles Byrne. Both became victims of resurrectionists and both are still to be seen.

Corney Macgrath was born in 1736 in Silvermines, Co. Tipperary, a remote mountainy district that had been the haunt of rapparees. While still a boy he made his way southwards to Cloyne in Co. Cork, where he was given employment by Bishop Berkeley. Berkeley, who dabbled in quack medicine, was later credited with being responsible for Magrath's great size. Watkinson in his *Philosophical Survey of Ireland* considered that 'the Bishop had a strong fancy to know whether it was not in the power of art to increase the human frame. An unhappy orphan appeared to him a fit subject for trial. He made his essay according to his preconceived theory, whatever it might be; and the consequence was that he (the orphan Magrath) became 7 feet high in his 16th year'.

It was true that after Magrath left Berkeley's employment and arrived in Cork in July 1752, his remarkable height attracted crowds who followed him around. He was persuaded to go on exhibition. An advertisement appeared in the *Daily Advertiser* on August 4, 1752. 'Cork, July 24th—there is now in this city Cornelius Magrath, a boy of 15 years 11 months old, of a most gigantic stature, being exactly 7 feet 9 inches three quarters high, he is clumsy made, talks boyish and simple, he came hither from Youghal where he had been a year going into salt water for rheumatic pains which almost crippled him.' (Perhaps these baths were prescribed by Berkeley.) A clinical observer noted that he had a pale and sallow complexion, his hand was as large as a middling shoulder of mutton, his pulse rate was sixty-two times in a minute and in only one year he had grown from five to seven feet.

He was taken up by an impresario who brought him to England and then to the Continent. In London he was described as 'the most stupendous and gigantic form (altho a boy) and is the representation in the world of the ancient and magnificent giants of the kingdom'. In Italy he was examined by an Italian doctor who wrote a treatise about him. But he became ill, developing a fever in Flanders, and came back sick to Ireland. 'His complexion was miserably pale and sallow; his pulse was quick at times for a man of his extraordinary height; and his legs were swollen.' He died at the age of twenty-three at the Sceptre and Cushion after a fall. One version of his death claims that he was performing in a play called *The Giant Queller*. Another has a student darting between his legs, making him tumble like Goliath.

His body was eagerly sought for by Trinity College, and the struggle between the anatomists and Magrath's friends aroused public interest. In Trinity, the Professor of the Anatomy School gave his students a lecture. He advised them not to try to snatch the body, but if, against his wishes, they happened to do so, they must remember to strip it naked, as was customary among grave robbers, in order to avoid any prosecution for theft of clothing. Four students took the hint and went to Magrath's wake, where they managed to dope the whiskey with laudanum. Soon the giant's huge corpse was being heaved over the unconscious forms of the mourners lying on the floor and carried out into a waiting conveyance which took it to Trinity. Next day when the mourners applied to the Provost, they were told that the eager Anatomy School had already dissected their friend. They were paid compensation, after which Dr. Robinson, the Anatomy Professor, was heard to say: 'Divil a knife's in him yet!' In due course he gave a public lecture on Magrath's body.

The skeleton is preserved in Trinity's Anatomy School beside the Ossified Man, William Clark. Behind the giant is a poster showing him fashionably dressed, holding his arm above a Prussian grenadier. Magrath measured seven feet two and a quarter inches—contemporaries had grossly exaggerated his height. For years his remains were badly treated. Bones were lost and replaced by ill-fitting spares, while the whole skeleton was covered with paint and varnish. At one time it was hung from the ceiling beside the skeleton of an informer, Jemmy O'Brien. A visitor to the 'Natomy House' described how 'by some mechanical contrivance or perhaps a simple pulley by the man in charge, the fleshless forms commenced to sway above us with an easy undulating kind of motion, as if dancing to slow music'.

In London the long brown bones of Charles Byrne, filling up a glass case in the College of Surgeons, are one of the few surviving exhibits from the collection of human oddities gathered together by the famous surgeon, John Hunter. Nearly all the rest of it was bombed during the Second World War.

Byrne also had a tragically short life, dying of tuberculosis. He was born in 1761, two years after Corny Magrath died, in Littlebridge near Derry. The district bred giants, for five miles from his birthplace there were two others named Knife. According to local rumour, the Knife brothers and Byrne were all conceived on top of a haystack.

From an early age it was clear that Byrne was simple, and the tumour on his pituitary gland that stimulated his unnatural growth affected his intelligence. Symptoms of consumption also showed early and he took to drink. By then he was well over seven feet in height and his hands were eighteen inches long from the wrists to the middle finger.

He went to London where he teamed up with Count Joseph Borulwaski, a three-foot Polish midget, who arranged his first appearance before the London public in April 1782. The *Morning Herald* made an announcement about 'the Irish giant, to be seen this and every day this week in his elegant room at the cane-shop next door to Cox's Museum, Spring Gardens: Mr. Byrne, the surprising Irish giant, who is allowed to be the tallest man in the world'. The showing of Charles Byrne attracted wide publicity. People flocked to pay their money and see the pathetic shambling figure dressed in a cut-away coat, cravat, and tricorn hat, 'not well built, his flesh loose, and his appearance far from wholesome . . . he is an ill-bred beast, though very young'. On one occasion he appeared with two other giants of minor stature. At the Haymarket a pantomime named *Harlequin League or the Giant's Causeway* featured a giant in its cast. Elsewhere in London Dr. James Graham, who with the aid of the fair Emma, later Lady Hamilton, did business with his celestial bed, offered the use of it free of charge to the young giant, together with a female companion. Byrne declined, on the ground that he was 'a perfect stranger to the rites and mysteries of Venus'.

By this time he was dying of tuberculosis and alcoholism compounded by melancholia. The news that a rival Irish giant, Patrick Cotter O'Brien, was appearing in London with the claim that he was eight feet three and a half inches tall and a descendant of Brian Boru, sent him spinning on the bottle.

He had a dread of dissection so that the advances of John Hunter, who coveted his body for his museum, filled him with particular horror. After Hunter offered him a large sum for his body, which he passionately refused, the surgeon hired a man called Hewison, who began to follow him everywhere. Meanwhile he was making elaborate arrangements to cheat the body-snatchers. He ordered a lead coffin and found ten Irish friends who swore that when he was dead they would put him inside and sink him at the mouth of the Thames. A group of Hunter's students heard of this plan and said that they were constructing a diving bell to fish him out of the muddy estuary.

The sudden loss of his savings of £770 started Byrne on a bout of gin which killed him. He died in May 1783, at the age of twenty-two. Throughout his final illness Hewison had been shadowing him, and on the night he died the surgeon's man approached a member of the undertaker's guard, one of Byrne's friends, who sat drinking in a tavern while off duty. He offered

him £50; the Irishman, after consulting his mates, demanded
£100 and Hewison instantly agreed. The price was afterwards
raised to £500 which was said to be the highest ever paid for a
body.

Byrne was removed at dead of night, first by hackney coach,
and then transferred into Hunter's private carriage and taken to
the surgeon's residence at Earl's Court. Here Hunter was waiting
with a large copper cauldron filled with boiling water. The speed
with which he boiled away the flesh turned the bones brown.

Hunter's success in obtaining the corpse was kept a closely
guarded secret. The *Evening Courant* was led to report that 'yesterday morning the body of Byrne, the famous Irish giant (who
died a few days ago) was carried to Margate in order to be thrown
into the sea, agreeable to his own request, he having been appre-
hensive that the surgeons would anatomize him'. Not until two
years had passed did Hunter admit his acquisition, when he
wrote to Sir Joseph Banks, the President of the Royal Academy:
'I lately got a tall man . . . but at that time could make no particular observations. I hope next summer to show him.' In due course
Byrne was mounted in a glass case beneath a painting of his
friend, Count Borulwaski.

The giant whose rivalry Byrne had feared was born plain Patrick Cotter near Pallastown, Kinsale, in 1760. He became a stone-
mason who could plaster the ceilings of a room without ladders.
A showman bought him from his father for £50, took him to
England and exhibited him with the appellation of an Irish king.
'Just arrived in town in a commodious room at No. 11 Haymarket,
nearly opposite the Opera House, the celebrated Irish giant,
Mr. O'Brien of the Kingdom of Ireland, indisputably the tallest
man ever shown. He is a lineal descendant of the old puissant
king, Brien Boreua, and has in person all the similitude of that
great and grand potentate. It is remarkable of this family in
point of form and alliance, the lineal descendants thereon have
been favoured by providence with the original size and stature
which have been so peculiar to their family. The gentleman
alluded to measured more than nine feet high. Admittance one
shilling.'

O'Brien retired to Hotwells near Bristol, where he died in September 1801. When his coffin was accidentally opened in 1906 it was found that like other giants his height had been exaggerated. He himself had claimed that he was 8 feet 7¾ inches tall at the age of twenty-six. But Dr. Edward Fawcett, the professor of Anatomy at the University of Bristol, measured his long bones and calculated his height as 7 feet 10·86 inches. This was more than a foot shorter than the American, Robert Wadlow, the tallest recorded man, whose height was 8 feet 11·1 inches. Even so O'Brien is the tallest Irishman whose height has been officially recorded.

Other giants include Patrick Murphy, born in Co. Down in 1834, who claimed to 8 feet 1½ inches tall. He had the usual short sad career, exhibiting himself on the Continent. After he died in Marseilles in 1862 his embalmed body was brought back to his birthplace in Kilbroney, Co. Down. Big Magee was a neighbour of William Carleton, in Monoghan in the early 1800s. Thirty years later Carleton encountered him again at Maynooth College where he had retired after exhibiting himself all over the world. 'I knew him well, because he was the son of a man and woman, both under the middle size, in my native parish of Clogher, whose residence was not more than three miles from my father's. He was a most ingenious man, and his constant occupation was the invention of clocks and watches of original and strange construction . . . He was the largest object in the shape of man and the most symmetrically made I ever saw.'

In contrast Mrs. Katherine Kelly who died in childbirth in 1735 at Norfolk was thirty-four inches tall and weighed twenty-two pounds. She was known as 'the Irish fairy'.

The reputation for longevity was often due to the slip of a scribe's pen, but also to ancient life forces. The Hag of Beara, who embodies so much that was symbolic of fertility, witchcraft and mystery, was very old. Since she experienced seven periods of youth, her life passed slowly enough until she reached her four hundredth birthday. Crowds came from all over Ireland to see her and find out the secret of her great age. She told them that she had always covered the top of her head, had never touched the earth with the soles of her feet, and never slept until she felt sleepy. Saints followed her example and lived long. Sinheall, abbot and bishop of Killogh, died in A.D. 549 aged 260 years. Fintan, patron of Doone and Coona in Co. Limerick died, in A.D. 561 at 260 years. Cathdubh, a bishop in Antrim, was 150 years old at the time of his death in A.D. 555. No Chaemhoch, a disciple of St. Kevin, departed the earth more convincingly in A.D. 656 aged 105.

More recent old people have included the blind harpist, Denis O'Hempsey, who is said to have lived from 1697 to 1807—a hundred and ten years—on a diet of milk, water and potatoes. He played the harp at Holyrood before the Young Pretender and later performed at the great meeting of harpers in Belfast in 1793. He married at eighty-six and fathered a child. On his deathbed he played the harp for the Rev. Hervey Bruce. Tuckey's *Cork Remembrancer* mentions 'a poor labouring man' who died early in the nineteenth century near Ovens at the age of 127. 'He walked four months before he died without the help of a stick or crutch, could see without spectacles, retained his senses and appetite to the last, and was followed to the grave by his descendants to the seventh generation.'

Two noble old ladies of Norman descent tried to approach the life span of the Hag of Beara. Catherine Fitzgerald, the spry Countess of Desmond, was supposed to have lived to be a hundred and forty. According to legend she danced with Richard III, met Sir Walter Raleigh more than a century later, and died in the early 1600s having lived through the reigns of nine English sovereigns. A few years before her death she is supposed to have walked from Bristol to London to make a personal appeal to King James for her property which had been confiscated. Robert Sydney further embellished her story when he wrote: 'She had a new sett of teeth not long before her death, and might have lived much longer had she not climbed a nut tree to gather nuts; so falling down she hurt her thigh, which brought fever, and that fever brought death.' Others said that she fell out of a cherry tree or an apple tree.

Alas, some historical details cut down her age by forty years or so. Catherine, a Fitzgerald of Dromana in Co. Waterford, married as his second wife the 12th Earl of Desmond in 1529; a few years before his death she gave birth to a daughter who later married Philip Barry Oge. Her jointure after the Earl's death was the manor of Inchiquin, five miles from Youghal; in 1575 the 14th Earl persuaded her to make it over to him. Her encounter with Raleigh took place in 1589 and her name is mentioned on a deed dated a year later. Fynes Moryson was told that she was 'able to go on foote four or five miles to the market towne, and used weekly soe to doe in her last years'. It is thought that she died in 1604 aged about a hundred. None of the eleven or so portraits of her has been authenticated, certainly not the one hanging at Knole inscribed: 'Catherine, Countess of Desmond appeared at ye court of our sovereign James in present A.D. 1614 in the 140th year of her age.' Referring to this portrait, Vita Sackville-West wrote of 'a very old lady in a black dress and a white ruff with that strange far-away look in her pale eyes that comes with extreme old age . . . It is rather a frightening portrait . . . if you go into the gallery after nightfall with a candle, the pale far-away eyes stare past you into the dark corners of the wainscot, eyes either over-charged or empty—which?'

The Honourable Katherine Plunkett was born on November 22, 1820 and died in her great house in Co. Louth on October 14, 1932. 'She took her breakfast as usual yesterday morning, and then passed away peacefully at her house without any apparent illness.' She had remembered sitting on Sir Walter Scott's knee at the age of five. 'Her mind remained unimpaired to the end and she took a deep interest in current affairs, having the papers read to her every day.' Until she was a hundred she was driven every Sunday to church in a carriage drawn by four white horses. For years King George V and Queen Mary had been sending her birthday telegrams.

She lived for a hundred and eleven years, three hundred and forty-two days. Of all the legendary old men and women hers is the oldest Irish life span to be proved with documents; it is the fifth oldest age ever recorded. As yet, humans have not been proved to live much longer.

John Perrot

EARLY in the seventeenth century a Bishop of Derry died a lingering death as the result of an accident arising from his unsuccessful attempts to burn a statue of the Virgin Mary. A Catholic priest, Henry Fitzsimon, tried to woo Protestants by hiring an orchestra with lutes and organs. While Puritans burnt and killed, books and pamphlets fulminated against the church of Rome: *The Hunting of the Romish Fox*, *The Great Folly, Superstition and Idolatry of Pilgrimage*, or *Methods Employed to Prevent the Growth of Popery* underlined fears of the Counter-Reformation. Religious antagonism in Ireland, as always, was comic, violent and, above all, divisive.

The converted often became over-zealous in trying to impart their newly discovered doctrines, and this was the case with the earnest Quaker missionary, John Perrot, who in due course tried to convert the Pope. Seventeenth-century Quakers were noticeable for their fanaticism. Later they acquired a peaceable image, but in early days 'Friends' seemed to be an unsuitable term with which to describe themselves. Since they were persecuted constantly, it might be imagined that in Ireland, a country particularly poisoned by religious differences, they would be natural allies of the oppressed Catholic majority. But this was not so. From the very beginning they demonstrated special antagonism to the church of Rome. They staged incidents—like the Friend who interrupted a Mass by walking before the altar carrying a piece of brimstone on his head, or like Solomon Eccles in 1670, who got up during another Mass and denounced a priest with the words: 'What shall be done to the man that makes ship-wreck of a good conscience?' He was accused of being a vagabond, sent to prison for ten days and whipped along the streets of Cork from North Gate to South Gate, receiving about ninety stripes, and then expelled from the city.

Quakers in Ireland were generally of English descent or, like Eccles, Englishmen who came over as missionaries. Imprisonment was their common lot. William Penn endured an eight month stretch in an Irish prison. An associate of his, John Exham, originally a soldier of Cromwell, suffered a long imprisonment after he had walked through the streets of Dublin, his head covered with sackcloth and ashes, preaching repentance. Undismayed, he continued to behave in this way for the rest of his long life; one walk through Cork occurred in 1698 when he was seventy, and he was still putting ashes on his head at the age of ninety.

William Edmundson has left a description of Cavan jail, where he was lodged with common prisoners. 'In the day we had the benefit to look out through an iron grate, but at night the door was closed shut, and then we were as if we had been in an oven; in the day the prisoners would beg turf, and at night when the door was close shut they would kindle a fire which filled the dungeon with thick smoke, there being little air, this annoyed me much, but they could endure it, being used to the like in their cabins.' Such experiences were known as Sufferings.

No Quaker endured a greater range of Sufferings than John Perrot—discomforts that came about as a result of his own enthusiastic contriving. Perrot joined the movement very early, soon after it had first been propounded by George Fox. In *Rutty's History of the Quakers in Ireland* he is mentioned as being 'convinced' in 1655. He was in Limerick where together with a number of other people he was persuaded by the eloquence of an Englishman named Edward Burrough, who was conducting an early missionary tour of Ireland, and had achieved some successes among the Cromwellian garrisons in Cork, Waterford and other centres.

Before Burrough's mission Perrot's life is a mystery and his origins are unknown, although he was living in Ireland at the time of his conversion. He had a wife and children in Waterford, who remained there through most of the period of his adventures. The names Perrot and Parrott were to be found in several parts of England and Ireland during the seventeenth century. A tradition claims him to be a blacksmith from Sedbergh distracted from his profession like the tinker from Bedford. Another more colourful story makes him the son of Sir John Perrot, Lord Lieutenant of Ireland, himself a possible bastard of Henry VIII. Sir John, a flamboyant character with a temper as fiery and unpredictable as that of his reputed father, quarrelled with Queen Elizabeth, who may have been his half-sister, and died in the Tower of London in 1592. If he were John Perrot's father, this date would have made the Quaker at least sixty-three years old when he began his arduous career as a missionary. So advanced an age is very unlikely in a personality whose vigour and stamina were remarkable even by Quaker standards. Could he have been Sir John's grandson? He seems to have had mysteriously close links with Charles II, who was to befriend him in strange circumstances.

For nine years after his conversion by Edward Burroughs he displayed to an extreme degree those qualities cultivated by missionaries and some saints—bravery and vanity fortified by a conviction of righteousness. He was a successful orator and prolific writer of hortative tracts, missives and letters. His contemporaries considered him something of a mystic, but odd in his ways, 'a man of great natural parts, but not continuing in true humility, who ran exorbitant imaginations'. Like many early Quaker missionaries he had the knack of making enemies wherever he went, and in time, too, he made enemies of Friends.

He toured Ireland between 1655 and 1657, a sombre figure in wide-brimmed hat and buttoned-up tunic unadorned with so much as an enamelled button. His approach to the unconverted was brutally direct: 'Wexford, The Towne within Thy walls is measured and it is found Shorte of the breadth of the holy Citty. A Stincke is within Thy Streetes and loath Somenesse is within thy dwellings . . . Rottennesse hangs upon they Skirts . . .'

Understandably he annoyed local authorities, and within two years he had been imprisoned in Kilkenny, Waterford, and twice in Limerick. The jail in Kilkenny was crammed with 120 Catholics who were due to be shipped to the Barbados as slaves. When he was released, he returned to the town to plead their cause and, after approaching the governor and commissioners of the city, succeeding in having them set free. The released men fell down on their knees before him in the open street, 'worshipping' him, a posture he disliked, for, as he later wrote to the Pope, he remembered 'the words of Christ and of the Angel that said: Thou shalt worship God and Him only shalt thou worship'.

After a further period of imprisonment in Dublin he discovered that his Irish mission was not to continue. His trials in Ireland had been a brief prelude to the greater tasks which the Lord wished him to undertake. On August 17, 1656, 'about the first houre of the latter parte of the day', the word of the Lord came to him. He was commanded to desert his wife and family, to give up the ministry for which he had suffered and to go abroad. There he was to turn his attention to two particular cities; one of them seems to have been Smyrna, or possibly Athens. The other was Rome. 'Two Cittyes before thy face I have Sett,' the Lord told him, 'wherein thou shalt cry: The Prophet of the Lord . . . is arisen, the word of whose mouth is the Sword of Jehovah's wrath.' In Rome he was to confront the Pope.

He went to England where he got in touch with the mainstream of the Quaker movement which took his mission seriously. He was not the first Quaker to receive divine instructions of this nature; there were others spreading the truth abroad. In the same year, 1656, George Robinson was arrested for preaching in Jerusalem. Two women, Katherine Evans and Sarah Chevers, were held prisoners of the Inquisition in Malta from 1659 to 1662. One of Perrot's companions on his journey abroad was to reach Constantinople and have a personal interview of the Grand Sultan of Turkey.

The little group started out with the full authority of the Quaker body which paid its expenses to undertake the most ambitious mission possible. Its members were to attempt the conversion of the Sultan and of the Pope . . . or, if this were not feasible, to vanquish them with righteous eloquence.

Perrot's travelling companions were of the same stamp as himself. The formidable Mary Fisher was one of the leading Quakers in America, who had been recently expelled from Boston. The two other women who accompanied her were Mary Pierce, another exile from Boston, and Beatrice Beckley. The three men in the party were Irish; besides Perrot himself were his comrade, John Luff (Love) from Limerick, who was to die in Rome, and John Buckley, a native of Kilkenny.

They reached Leghorn on July 29, 1657, and immediately began to distribute books in French, English and Latin, and to hold a series of daily services lasting for fourteen days, directed towards 'the English Merchants, Factors, Jews, Papist priests, Italians and Irish' who thronged the busy port. The Quakers could claim some success and Perrot reported that the English Agent was 'truly stricken and convinced', and so was a French merchant. One of his bombastic pamphlets offended the Jewish community, but later, after he had been permitted to speak in Latin in the synagogue, a number of Jews came to see him. They had discussions 'part in latine, part in Italian, parte by interpretation, and one of them did openly confesse the truth, and many of them said they were obliged to us in our travells and service'. Soon after, Perrot had a favourable interview with the Governor of Leghorn.

But their activities were arousing antagonism. 'Satan grew quickly into soe high a rage that there were certain conspiracyes between the Vaggabond English, Irish, Italians and priests to take our lives.' Perrot's first bout with the Inquisition led to his arrest and rigorous questioning by its servants. After they released him, the party, which was in increasing danger from Leghorn's foreign community, was allowed to leave. No doubt the governor and the Friars of the Inquisition were glad to foist it on to the Turks.

The missionaries went to Greece which was then part of the Turkish empire. They split up, probably from motives of safety; Perrot and John Buckley crossed the Morea and visited Corinth and Athens before rejoining the others at Smyrna. The journey was hard. 'Crueltyes and fraud and robberyes by Turkes and those called Christians, almost in all places bonds did hold us, yet the word of God thorow all had a free course and passage.'

Perrot's original plan was to seek an audience with the Sultan of Turkey before going on to see the Pope. But the difficulties the group had experienced led them to divide once more; Perrot, confining himself to a letter directed to 'the great Turk', left Mary Fisher to begin her famous mission to Constantinople while he himself, together with John Luff, set out for Venice and Rome.

During the voyage to Italy they antagonized the captain and crew, whose irritation progressed from preventing them using the 'cook room' to dress their provisions, to threats of abandoning them on a barren island or having them burnt when they reached Venice. However before they made port the Quakers considered that they had won every argument. God demonstrated that he was on their side when the ship was struck by lightning which 'burned holes in the Sayles' and killed three sailors and two passengers, one Turkish and one Armenian.

In March 1658 they arrived in Venice where they spent two months. Perrot attempted to see the Doge. It is uncertain whether he actually had an interview, but he certainly left a pile of books and pamphlets at the Palace for the Spouse of the Sea to read. Then he prepared himself for his main task. 'God sends me to Rome to batter in it, if not through it.'

Contemporaries compared the entrance of Luff and Perrot into the holy city on June 6, 1658 to Daniel going into the lion's den. The Pope whom they wished to confront was Alexander VII, the enlightened patron of Borromini and Bernini. But instead the Inquisition awaited them.

On the advice of an English Jesuit, Thomas Courtney, Perrot sought out a fellow Irishman, John Crewy, who was a chaplain to the Pope. During the subsequent interview he revealed his aims in coming to Rome 'as an unfolded sheet upon a smooth floor'. The consequences were immediate and disastrous. On June 8, which seems to have been the same day that he saw Crewy, he and Luff were arrested. 'I was (by the Chief Marshal of the City and by his Guard) taken out of Bed in my lodging at the Sign of the Cock in *Piazza Formase* and stripped of all things except the apparel which I wore; and so at a late hour of the night was led bound to one of the New Prisons.' Six days later he was 'bound in a Coach' and taken to the special prison reserved for the Inquisition. During the eighteen weeks he was confined there he was questioned closely by official Inquisitorial interrogators and given pen and ink with which he wrote 'a naked explication of the words of Righteousness in sundry manuscripts, and an epistle general to the Romans'. The Inquisitors came to their own conclusions. They had him bound again and put in another coach to be transported to the Carcere dei Pazzi—the Roman version of Bedlam.

There may well have been a wild light in Perrot's eye as he talked to his captors. Sewel, William Sewel, the Quaker historian, reported upon his 'rare power of fascination' which was combined with an 'imbalance and rhapsodical mysticism'. The Inquisitors, suspicious enough of orthodox mystics, were unlikely to be affected by any demonstration of heretical ecstasies. The nature of his mission reinforced the conclusion that he was mad. Perhaps it saved his life, for if those cool and rational Roman priests did not believe him insane, they could well have burnt him.

The cell in which Perrot was confined measured nine feet by fourteen, but for a long time he could take little advantage of its dimensions. First he was chained by his neck to the wall in such a way that he was just able to stand up straight, sit and lie full-length. Later another, slightly longer, chain was attached to his leg, and he wore it during fourteen icy weeks of winter. When it was removed he found that the leg had shrivelled. He was stripped and beaten regularly, probably as part of an established routine for patients. The beatings were so severe that he was usually left 'black and bloody' from head to foot, while the instrument with which he was tortured, '*a dryed Bull's Pizzle*', often got broken. He was reviled, mocked, and threatened with galley slavery, burning and poison. Very often he was beaten while he was kneeling in prayer or 'walking Praises and Thanksgivings unto God'.

Sometimes his treatment took a different course and he was 'tryed with wine, proven with women, tempted with riches and honour and all the Pleasures that ever my heart could desire'. 'If they judged me to be a madman,' he wrote, 'they seemed to me to be nigh senseless to seek me by temptation and cruelties and pleasure to turn to them by sinning against the Lord of Righteousness.'

By the end of 1658 he did not have the consolation of knowing that Luff was a fellow sufferer. Luff died in prison some time towards the end of the year. It is not clear if he was in the same establishment, but probably he was. The official explanation for his death was that he went on hunger strike. There were other stories. Sewel, accepting that he died of hunger, qualified the supposition by adding, 'yet some nuns have told that he was dispatched in the night for fear he should annoy the church of Rome'. Others, including Perrot himself believed that he had been hanged.

After his release Perrot published two accounts of his experiences, *Battering Rams against Rome* and *A Narrative of some of the Sufferings of J.P. in the City of Rome*. They contained passages suggesting the delirium induced by the horrible conditions in which he was confined.

'When the wrath of Hell gaped as a gulf to swallow me in her belly of envy; when nets of Iron were spread about my habitation; when Serpents creeped over my body and frogs danced on my face, when Scorpions ran over my head and Dragons spat fire in my face, when the Spirits of infernal places encamped about me and surrounded me with their dreadful flames; when they pierced me with Speares in my side . . . then did I water my Couch with my tears and sow them as seed upon the ground . . . '

Part of the *Narrative* seems to have been written while he was actually in prison. Gradually the conditions in which he was confined became easier. He was allowed pen and copious paper, and set about composing a spate of pamphlets and letters variously addressed 'to the Pope', 'to the Governor of Rome' or 'to a Franciscan of the Irish Convent in Rome' (probably the unfeeling Father Crewy). The letter from 'John the lowly Lamb in the Life of Jesus the Son of God to the Pope of Rome' described those times in life when he had befriended Roman Catholics . . . 'not one of thy children can say he came to my Door for an Alms and went away empty handed'. He dwelt in wistful detail on the episode of the release of the Kilkenny prisoners; his part was inspired, he hinted, by the 'mercies, Pities and Compassions that God had put in my soul, beholding them *a bleeding People*.' None of his appeals to the rulers of Rome merited a reply.

These letters and others he sent to a wide variety of people in England and Ireland were signed simply with his Christian name, or with the variation 'John, the Servant of God'. 'To all the People on the Face of the Earth' was signed by 'John, the Suffering Servant of God'. He modelled himself on the author of Revelations, consciously imitating his language. Echoes of Revelations are frequent throughout the body of his writings, but in his address to the Pope he went further and opened with a paraphrasing of passages in St. John's Gospel. 'God is light, and in him is no darkness at all, who hath sent his Son as a Light into the world that all that believe in him who is the light of the world may have everlasting light.' The message continues with a call to repentance and conversion. 'Unto which light thou must bow, and oughtest to lay down thy crown at the feet of him who cometh in the clouds through the bleakness and darkness of the black and gloomy day.'

Some of his pamphlets were far less rational, and may have reinforced the decision of his captors to keep him where he was. One, which later invited the sneers of his critics in the Quaker movement, ran to forty-four pages of confused mystical verse divided under such headings as: To the Congregation of the valley of Megiddon . . . To the Seeds of the Kingdom, plants of the Paradise of God . . . To the Apostatized. Composed in prison, it was entitled *A Sea of the Seed's Suffering, Through which Runs a River of Rich Rejoycing*. Another pamphlet was called *A Wren in the Burning Bush Waving the Wings of Contraction to the Congregated Clean Fowls of the Heavens in the Ark of God, Holy Host of the Eternal Power, Salutation*.

But he could be vivid, if not concise, and *Battering Rams* and *Narrative* ('written in Rome Prison for Madmen—John') together gave a moving account of his experiences. Soon after they were published two anonymous writers were inspired to publish their own versions of his adventures. Perrot's non-Quaker contemporaries were eager to regard his sufferings as a joke, and both the *Account of the Quaker Proceedings and Entertainments at Rome* and *Perrot against the Pope* made capital out of them. The latter opens jauntily. 'Some sober persons will not easily believe . . . that the phanatick spirit of enthusiasm had in the year 1658 so far possessed John Perrot, an English Quacker, that whilst (to use his own phrase) he stood in the gap for Rome, he must needs go thither to convert the Pope.'

In this account Perrot's audience with the Pope is refused, because, since the Pope spoke no English and Perrot no Latin, there could be no dialogue between them. However, an interview is promptly described in which Perrot insists on wearing his hat and talking to 'Mr. Pope'. His Holiness gives him the choice of leaving the country at once ('seeing the sad effects of Quackerism') or being locked up. After choosing imprisonment, Perrot writes a challenge in which he will take on a hundred chosen Jesuits and chief doctors of divinity with whom to argue the fundamentals of the faith and to whom he could point out such errors that arose from the doctrine of remission of sins and the worshipping of images. In his reply to 'John Quacker' the Pope writes: 'Truely John, though deservest for these lines of nonsense at least three months more of the Pazzerella, too little learning, I see, hath made thee mad.' Instead of Perrot's proposed grand contest, the Pope nominates a solitary Jesuit to dispute with him. 'He shall be armed with the dreadful weapons of excommunication, and with bell, book and candle deliver thee to the devil for the destruction of thy fleshy body, and thy spirit may be saved.'

Before this satire was published Perrot after enduring the Roman madhouse for exactly three years, had obtained his release. News of his imprisonment had made a stir among his fellow Quakers in England. Very soon after his arrest, or perhaps at the same time, two Quakers happened to be in Rome on an evangelical mission. Samuel Fisher and John Stubbs do not seem to have made any effort to help their imprisoned colleagues, and it is likely that they wished to dissociate themselves from their predicament. They were allowed to leave Rome without trouble and probably brought the news of Perrot and Luff's position back to England.

After Luff's death a brave Quaker went specifically to Rome on Perrot's behalf. He was able to see him and advise and comfort him, 'God raised up his little babe, my dear brother *Thomas Hart* to set his tender soul nearer unto my sufferings and made him take my burthens on his back and the yolk of my Tribulation on his neck . . .'

Hart was also allowed to depart, and two years passed before two more 'babes', Jane Stokes and Charles Bayley, felt the call to go to Rome and rescue Perrot. One cannot help admiring their courage. They set out in 1661, journeying through France. Like Perrot, they were the sort who made enemies and only arrived in Rome after a trail of persecution. They were immediately arrested and interviewed by an exasperated Inquisitor General. Bayley (who later became the first governor of the Hudson Bay Company) told him that he had come from England to see his brother, John Perrot, and was prepared to take his place in prison. But there was room for all there, and soon both he and Jane Stokes were dispatched to the same madhouse.

On its way from the Inquisitorial prison to the Carcere dei Pazzi, Bayley's escort actually encountered the Pope. This seems to have been the nearest that any of these early Quakers got to the Pontiff, who sat in the *portantina*, his travelling litter, which was covered with scarlet and gold draperies and borne along by ten white mules. 'I met him towards the foot of a bridge when I was something nigh him, and when he came against me, the people being on their knees on each side of him, I cried to him with a loud voice in the Italian tongue "to do the thing that was just and release the innocent".'

In vain. Inside the madhouse Bayley went on a fast which lasted for twenty days, one more than the length of time it was supposed to have taken Luff to perish. He declared that his fast was a token of the Church's guilt for Luff's death. For Perrot his new companions' presence brought immense comfort. 'The everlasting mercies of my God did stir up the bowells of another two of his tender babes named in the tent, Jane Stokes and Charles Baylie, to come and visit me whilst I was foresaken of all men.'

Suddenly the authorities had enough. Realizing that Perrot's symptoms were not unique, and tired of the whole protracted episode, they released all three prisoners at the beginning of June 1661, warning the men that they would be condemned to perpetual galley slavery if they ever returned to Rome.

It is just possible that Perrot owed his freedom to the intervention of Charles II. During 1660, as he sat in his cell scribbling his missives and pamphlets, he did not fail to send some advice to the newly restored monarch, admonishing him 'as a true and unfeigned lover of thy soul' on the proper conduct of his office. Charles, who during the opening years of his reign, was favourably disposed towards Quakers, had an interview with Richard Hubberthorne in June 1660, when the following exchange took place:

KING: Are any of your friends gone to Rome?

R.H.: Yes, there is one is Prison in Rome.

KING: Why did you send him thither?

R.H.: We did not send him thither, but he found something upon his Spirit from the Lord whereby he was called to go and declare against Superstition and Idolatry, which is contrary to the will of God.

Charles Bayley's family had been connected with the Court in Charles I's time, and his son may have had some contact with him. Or it may even be that the king intervened on behalf of a distant cousin—supposing Perrot's relationship to Sir John Perrot to be a fact. Certainly on his release, before he started back to England, he wrote a letter ahead which proclaimed: 'Israel hoste of the most high God, his majesty having fulfilled the vision of my head unto me . . . hath now lastly delivered me and the two Babes with me out of our Captivity . . .'

Less obscure is a letter dated almost precisely three years later on May 10, 1644 from Thomas Modyford, the Governor of Barbados, to the King. (By this time Perrot was one of the more notorious inhabitants of that colony.) Modyford emphasized Perrot's loyalty to the Crown, and stated that he had been heard to declare many times that he would lay down his life 'for the King to whose letters when he lay a prisoner in Rome he affirmed to owe it'.

The three Quakers could now make their way back to England. They travelled slowly. In France, Bayley was briefly imprisoned in Bourg de Ault 'for speaking to a Cupell of priests that bowed to an Image as they passed the streets'. Perrot, dazed, limping and emaciated, was subdued by the discomforts of the journey. But his remarkable stamina and powers of recovery soon enabled him to resume preaching, and once he had crossed the Channel he was back on form. At the end of August 1661, three months after he had left Rome, he was arrested in Canterbury with eight other Friends. Two months later he was active in East Anglia, once again a travelling missionary. This inevitably meant more imprisonment. In late 1661 he was rescued from Newgate as a result of intervention by the king, an episode that seems to confirm the truth in the supposition that Charles took a direct interest in Perrot and his predicaments. A letter from a Quaker, J. L., written at the time, described how Perrot 'was sent for out of prison before the Kinge (whether he had a desire to see him or noe, I know not) & pretty much discourse they had. He was very loveing to John and gave order for his release & all with him'.

Not until January 1662 did Perrot make his way back to Ireland and to Waterford where he had a very brief reunion with his wife and family whom he had not seen for five years. But he wasted no time in returning to England to travel and preach. Several spells of prison resulted. One was the aftermath of the famous Bull and Mouth meeting in June 1662, when he was taken with other Quakers before a magistrate named Richard Brown. Sewel described how Brown took the name of the prisoners, 'and hearing that of John Perrot said, "What, you have been at Rome to subvert—" but recalling himself, said "to convert the Pope?" On which Perrot told him "He had suffered in Rome for the testimony of Jesus." Whereupon Brown returned, "If you had converted the Pope to your religion I should have liked him far worse than I do now." To which Perrot replied "But God would have liked it better." '

Perrot made the most of the aura of glamour which his Roman experiences bestowed on him. This, together with his natural eloquence, gave him a huge following. He was especially popular with female Friends. Once, four of them took a coach as far as it would go and then walked six miles in order to be with him. Many disapproving members of the Quaker movement thought that this circle of admiring women turned his head.

Not long after his return he began to create deep dissent in the Quaker congregation. He quarrelled with George Fox, who questioned his finances, alleging that his 'Expenses and Charge' during his voyage abroad were fraudulent. This was not merely petty irritation on Fox's part; the differences between him and his associates and Perrot and his admirers ran far deeper. Perrot had chosen this time to revive the controversy of the Hat. One of the tracts he had written while in Rome had advocated that the removal of the hat during prayer was a meaningless formality. On his return to England he attracted an increasing number of supporters to this heresy which had already divided and distressed Quakers. The Hat, its removal or non-removal, became an issue of enormous importance in subsequent bitter disputes. Perrot's friends published their views in a book called *The Spirit of the Hat*. Fox for his part claimed that, by refusing to remove their headgear during prayer, Perrot and his allies showed no more reverence to God than to a horse.

In late 1661 the yearly meeting of Friends presided over by Fox recommended Quakers to beware of printing and publishing or spreading the works of Perrot, and suggested that 'faithful and sound Friends' might inspect the manuscripts before they went to press. Perrot, meanwhile, was preparing to offend the Fox party still further; according to Sewell 'he made another extravagant step, and let his beard grow, in which he was followed by others.'

All the time this quarrel was taking place, Perrot, along with many other Quakers, was undergoing periods of imprisonment. When in 1662 he found himself yet again in Newgate, he made a bargain with the authorities in order to gain his freedom. He promised to go into voluntary exile in Barbados. He embarked at Gravesend, pursued by a group of Fox's supporters who followed him on board to read out a letter of condemnation written by Fox. Before the ship sailed Perrot had composed a reply stating that Fox was wrong in many things, and this he read out to the little group of Quaker exiles which was travelling with him.

Barbados had an active Quaker community which had been in existence for six or seven years when Perrot arrived. Barbadan Quakers had first introduced the movement to the American continent when Elizabeth Harris went to Maryland in 1656 and Mary Fisher and Ann Austin appeared in Boston during the same year. The Hat controversy was already hot news on the western side of the Atlantic. Perrot, with his compelling combination of energy, conviction and fame, had an easy success in spreading discord among Quakers in Jamaica, Virginia and Maryland. He went further in simplifying form and ceremony; his followers, who kept their hats on when they prayed, were now instructed not to hold prearranged services at all. Meetings were only to take place when the Spirit moved people to gather, and there was no need for a Quaker community to have a special Meeting House. His ideas attracted many converts from among Fox's followers. From Maryland Mary Tomkins and Alice Abrose described to Fox how many had been leavened with Perrot's unclean spirit. He had done 'much hurt' which made 'our travells hard and our labors sore'. The whippings they had received from the Chesapeake magistrates hurt them far less than what they had 'boren and suferd consarning him'.

Early in 1664 Perrot, having completed a brilliantly successful ministry among Quakers on the American continent returned to Barbados. Here he made the doctrinal decision which offended his brethren for ever, and in one move alienated all those who had joyfully agreed with his ideas. Quakers had always advocated that form and ceremony were unnecessary to worship, and Perrot had already taken this precept to its extreme. But if worship was to be totally informal, why should there be rules concerning secular ceremony, occupation and dress? He began wearing 'a velvet coat, gaudy apparel and a sword'. Even worse, he became an exactor of oaths, a position abhorred by Quakers. His followers deserted him.

'John Perrot, the power of God is turned against thee,' thundered George Fox triumphantly, 'and all thy vain prophecies and fained shews and carriages and fained love . . .' Another critic used that unpleasant image that re-occurs in contentious religious argument. 'That Sect-master returned with the dog to vomit, to swaring [exacting oaths], fighting, fine cloathes, cap and knee to men [while he] could sit on his B— with hat on his head while he prayed to the Most High God.'

Those outside the movement were gleeful, reporting that 'John Perrot had altogether renounced his faith and aimed at nothing but his profit'. In his letter to the king, Thomas Modyford reported: 'And really Sir, it may take off much of the rude roughness of that sect's temper, when they shall find in the Newes Book that John Perrot . . . was content for his Majesties service to appear in a satin sute with a sword and belt and to be called Captaine . . .'

And yet Perrot keenly felt his separation from the movement. He longed for conciliation, but only on his own terms. He alone was right. While advocating love and forgiveness and turning the other cheek, he wrote out a strongly worded case that his own precepts were the correct ones. Those for whom he had struggled and suffered and who now rejected him would regret their mistakes. Shortly before his death he declared:

'Woe! Woe! unto the Sanctuary of the Lord, for it is Polluted! Woe to the Mountain of the Lord, for it is at Ease! The Habitation where the God of Jacob should Dwell is become the Habitation of Devils. The Day is coming that it shall be Plowed like a Field: and the Families of the Mountain shall worship apart, yea, everyone apart, and their Wives apart.'

Meanwhile he worked for the Government as diplomat and businessman; he also gained a licence for shipping passengers from Barbados to America. His family, which had been separated from him during all the years of his ministry, eventually joined him from Waterford. He died suddenly during the first week of September 1665. In his will he left his goods to his 'dear wife Elizabeth' and remembered his younger children, Blessing and Thankful.

John Taylor described his death in *A Loving & Friendly Invitation to All Sinners to Repent, and a Warning to all Backsliders to Return unto the Lord while they have Time and Space given them.* This pamphlet had a special section about John Perrot. 'He ended his days miserably. For soon after he was dead and buried in an old Popish mass-house, all that he had left, which was not much, was seized on for debt; yea the bed that was under his wife, when she lay sick upon it . . .'

But another Friend, perhaps Robert Rich, recalled the inspired preacher rather than the embittered schismatic:

> In Memoriam Johannis Perrot:
> Sweet was thy Voice and ravishing thy Strain
> Thy Silver Trumpet sounded not in vain . . .
> Patience and holy Zeal did overcome
> The Cruelties of Anti-Christian Rome . . .
> In Shilo's holy Ink thy learned Pen
> Was dipped, which ravished the Sons of Men . . .
> Thou Heaven born Seed, blest let thy Memory be,
> The Love of Men and Angels honour thee.

John Asgill and Dean Swift

AFTER the rebellion of 1641 many estates of old Catholic families were forfeited and handed over to new waves of English emigrants. These Cromwellian settlements were shaken up in their turn when James II came to the throne; for a short time Ireland was once more a Catholic country. The victories of William of Orange immediately reversed this situation, and there were more lands to become forfeit. Throughout a turbulent fifty-year period, lawyers benefited as much as anyone. They flocked over from England to take advantage of the turmoil of land distribution. It was a particularly rich period of litigation, which has always flourished on Irish soil.

Among those hoping to make a few pickings was an unsuccessful barrister named John Asgill. Just before he set out for Ireland he worked out a theory that people need not die. The idea came to him while he was rusticating after a 'financial misadventure', voluntarily confining himself in his chambers in the Temple. Here, together with some books of law, he studied the Bible. He paid particular attention to the Gospel of St. John, Chapter 11, verses 25 and 26: 'I am the resurrection and the life; he that believeth in me, though he were dead, yet shall he live: and whosoever liveth and believeth in me shall never die.' Asgill chose to read this passage literally.

In the Gospel Jesus was addressing Martha, who had been bereaved by the death of her brother. Later He saved Lazarus at the last moment. Asgill believed that Lazarus' predicament was avoidable and that he or any Christian could avoid death much more easily. He interpreted the relations between God and man by ordinary English law. Thus, as death was the penalty for Adam's sins, and as Christ had suffered this penalty, death could no longer be inflicted on those who claimed their rights. 'Man died simply because he wanted perspicuity to see, courage to rely on it as all sufficient, and wisdom to plead it against the common enemy, death.' He himself expected to make his discharge or exit 'by way of translation'.

He set forth his beliefs in a book which he called *An Argument proving that according to the Covenant of Eternal Life revealed in the Scriptures, man may be translated into the Eternal Life without passing through Death.* While it was being printed the printer complained that it was a little crazed. On publication it was immediately attacked as blasphemous and became the subject of lampoons such as *An Account of Mr. Asgill's strange and wonderful Translation* and *The Way to Heaven on a String.*

The same year that the book was published, 1700, Asgill arrived in Ireland where he hoped to mend his fortunes. He did, indeed, do rather well, and not merely by collecting lawyers' fees. He married Lord Kenmare's daughter who, although nominally a Catholic, had been brought up as a Protestant by her grandmother. Lord Kenmare had been a supporter of James II, and as such his estate was forfeit. In 1703 Asgill was able to buy up a life interest in it.

But meanwhile he was haunted by his book. He complained that it 'was in Ireland almost as soon as I was, making a noise after me, that I was going away mad'. The uproar increased until on September 1, 1703, the Irish House of Commons passed a resolution. 'Resolved, nemine contradicente, that the said book [*An Argument, etc.*] contains in it several heretical and blasphemous doctrines and positions contrary to Christian religion and the established doctrine of the Church of Ireland and destruction of human society. Ordered that the said book be burnt by the hand of the common hangman before the gate of this house on Wednesday next at twelve of the clock, before the Tholsel at one of the clock the same day, and that the Sheriffs of the City of Dublin be required to see the same done accordingly.' (Burning books ceremoniously was still part of the duties of hangmen in Dublin. Another contemporary expression of censorship had occurred six years earlier in 1697, when the deist John Toland's *Christianity not Mysterious* had suffered the same fate.)

It was unfortunate that Asgill should choose the same month, September 1703, to enter politics. Probably through financial interest, he had been elected to the Irish House of Commons as a Member for Enniscorthy. His parliamentary career was unusually brief. After sitting for only four days in early October, he was expelled on account of his blasphemous book. The Parliamentary Records describe how the subject was brought forward on Monday, October 10, 1703. 'Resolved, nemine contradicente, that John Asgill esq., a member of this House, be expelled this house and be ever hereafter incapable of being chosen, returned or sitting a Member in any succeeding Parliament in this kingdom.'

He left Ireland soon afterwards. His Irish adventures had been financially successful, and he managed to hold on to the Kenmare estate in spite of a petition from the guardian of Lord Kenmare's other children that he should be relieved of it. He had developed a liking for Parliamentary debate, and decided that if College Green would not have him, he would do better in Westminster. With the aid of his new fortunes he got himself elected to the English House of Commons. But the reputation of his book followed him. In 1707 it was investigated by the House and Asgill was obliged to defend it.

'I know no business I have with the dead,' he declared, 'and therefore do as much depend that I shall not go hence by returning to the dust—which is the sentence of that law from which I claim a discharge—but that I shall make my exit by way of translation, which I claim as a dignity belonging to that degree in the science of eternal life of which I profess myself a graduate, according to the true intent and meaning of the covenant of eternal life revealed in the scriptures . . . and if I die like other men, I declare myself to die of no religion.'

These words were taken as blasphemy, and book and parliamentary career followed the same course as they had in Ireland. Asgill himself was continually startled at the savage reaction to his work. Others could not believe he was serious. One German traveller thought that *An Argument* was written as a result of a lady's challenge to show his skill in maintaining paradoxes.

Later criticism was less hysterical. Coleridge thought that Asgill's irony was often finer than Swift's. When the book was reissued in 1875, the Rev. T. D. Gregg wrote an introduction in which he considered that the argument as such was a fundamental principle of the Church.

After his expulsions Asgill seems to have lived quietly. He was translated in 1738 at the age of eighty.

*   *   *

Jonathan Swift's opinion of Asgill was contemptuous. In his *Argument against the Abolishment of Christianity* he describes his beliefs as Trumpery, and asks, 'Who would have suspected Asgill for a Wit or Toland for a Philosopher if the inexhaustible Stock of Christianity had not been at hand to provide them with Materials?' Swift had an uncle, who, like Asgill, came to Ireland to benefit from the profitable litigation arising from the division of forfeited estates. However, Asgill, although an Irish M.P., only lived in Ireland for a short time, whereas Swift spent most of his life there as schoolboy, student, clergyman, dean and patriot. It is difficult to assess how far his unflattering opinions of Ireland are equivocal; even at a time when grateful Dublin crowds were cheering him in the streets for the devastating impact of the Drapier letters, did he still feel himself an exile condemned to die 'in a rage, like a poisonous rat in a hole'? Dublin gave him its freedom and a gold box for Drapier, and eventually, it seems, he learned to love the mob which wanted to erect a statue to him in place of Marlborough. In 1734 he wrote: 'As to this country I am only a favourite of my friends the rabble, and I return their love because I know none else who deserve it.'

The English like to claim Swift as their own in the same way that liberal thinkers do, although he was a high Tory and a friend of hereditary and vested privilege. A typical recent claim by Bernard Ackworth describes him as 'a reasonable and uncompromising and therefore upright and fearless Englishman'. Bernard Shaw considered that this attitude began with Macaulay. 'Macaulay, seeing that the Irish had in Swift an author worth stealing, tried to annex him by contending that he must be classed as an Englishman because he was not an aboriginal Celt. He might as well have refused the name of Briton to Addison because he did not stain himself blue and attach scythes to the poles of his sedan chair.'

It might be argued that Swift was not Irish. It may also be argued that merely to include him in the tattered company of Irish eccentrics is to belittle his genius. This was not always the case; during the last century his reputation has undergone a transformation. 'I would rather have a potato from Goldsmith than a guinea from Swift,' Thackeray wrote. Victorians—Macaulay included—definitely considered him eccentric, and they used the word in a derogatory sense to cover a whole range of activity that differed from the normal. There was a good deal in Swift's personality and behaviour that was unacceptable to a prudish society. When Dr. William Russell, writing at a time when appreciation of the Dean was at its lowest, included him among his *Eccentric Personages*, he considered that 'the true solution of the enigma presented by the career of Dean Swift is, in my judgement, this—that he was in a certain morbid sense insane from an early age'. He added with some truth, 'There are innumerable anecdotes related to the Dean, all, or nearly all, exhibitive of a coarse, offensive nature. Nasty is the true word.'

Evolving theories about the mysteries of Swift's behaviour has become a cottage industry. In his own lifetime those who loved him tried to analyse him. Vanessa wrote, 'Could I know your thoughts which no human being is capable of guessing at, because never anyone living thought like you? Sometimes you strike me with prodigious awe, I tremble with fear; at other times a charming compassion shines in your countenance which revives the soul.' When she was dying the compassion faded from her vision of him, which was replaced by the sombre egoist who betrayed her. Every man can construct his own portrait of Swift, and there is plenty of material to make up a picture of Swift the Eccentric— his misanthropy, his obsession with cleanliness combined with his scatological visions, the bitterness of his satire—'last week I saw a woman flayed and you would hardly believe how it altered her person for the worse'—the secrets of his shadowed love for Varina, Stella and Vanessa.

His misanthropy and his illness were progressive, and it is plaus-ible that they were connected. The signs of Menière's symptom-complex began in his early twenties, when he suffered 'a giddiness and coldness of the stomach' which he thought was caused by 'a surfeit of fruit', This is just possible, since the condition may be derived from gastro-intestinal disturbances among other causes. The nausea and vomiting, the 'fitts' sometimes preceding loss of consciousness, were the result of a lesion of the labyrinth, leading to deafness in the left ear. The sufferer from Menière's symptom-complex is prone to depression, since he is generally afflicted by tinnitus, a roaring in the ears, and a giddiness which can so prostrate him that he is unable to work and may even contemplate suicide. Swift was sometimes attacked by giddiness during ser-vices at St. Patrick's.

Later his behaviour became startling. In her Memoirs Mrs. Pil-kington tells that the first proof of his madness was when he affronted the Lord Lieutenant at the Lord Mayor's table, because he had not paid his compliments to him in due form. He accosted him by the title of 'You fellow with the blue string'. 'Some little time after this he invited two clergymen to take the air with him, and when he got them into a coach, he did so belabour them and knock their heads together that they were obliged to cry out for assistance.'

Some students of Swift assume that he also suffered from syphilis which led to his final paralysis. He observed his physical deterioration closely:

> See how the Dean begins to break!
> Poor gentleman, he droops apace!
> You plainly find it in his face.
> The old vertigo in his head
> Will never leave him till he's dead.
> Besides, his memory decays . . .

The lesion in his ear contributed to the tortures of his last years that occurred between long periods of apathy. The agony he endured the night of April 29, 1740, he described in the famous simile: 'The whole of last night I was struck as if I had been in Phalaris's brazen bull, and roared as loud for eight or nine hours.' In *A Voyage to Laputa* he prophesied his terrible lingering old age when he made Gulliver describe the degradation of the Struldbruggs. The Struldbruggs, who lived among the Laputans, were doomed to immortality; they were marked out at birth with a red circular spot directly over the left eyebrow 'about the compass of a silver three pence'. 'They commonly acted like mortals till about thirty years old, after which by degrees they grew melancholy and dejected, increasing in both until they came to fourscore.' They were then afflicted with all the debilities which age can bring, loss of the senses, appetites and memory; their countrymen hated and despised them as 'they acquired an additional ghastliness in proportion to their number of years'. No merciful death overtook them, and Gulliver learned that, contrary to his ecstatic belief, eternal life was unbearable and death a release. In this deeply pessimistic passage Swift foresaw the prolonged conclusion of his malady that marked him out from his youth as different from others. When he was senile his manservant showed him to members of the public for a fee.

The Yahoos appeared to him early in life, long before they were described in *Gulliver*. His misanthropy began soon after his first giddiness assailed him, when he was already hitting out at Scotsmen and declaring his dislike for children. He first attacked the Scots when he was twenty-three in his 'Ode to King William': 'That discontented brood who always loudest for religion bawl.' His distaste was confirmed by his short experience among Ulster Presbyterians at Kilroot on Belfast Lough; and is to be seen in a furious pencilled note in Clarendon's *History of the Rebellion* which is on exhibit in Marsh's Library in Dublin. Beside an account of Covenanting ministers pestering Montrose before his execution Swift scribbled: 'Mad treacherous damnable infernal Scots for ever.' Honesty and courage, he considered in another note, were trifles to a Scot. Montrose himself was 'a perfect Hero, wholly UnScotyfied'.

His hatred of mankind was not comprehensive; he often gave

five pounds to a beggar and regularly supported old people, poets and young clergymen. He formed a fund of £500 for loans without interest with which he financed two hundred families to earn an independent living. But philanthropy did not overcome misanthropy and he came to regard most categories of the human race harshly. At the age of thirty-three he wrote among other resolutions 'when I come to be old', 'Not to be fond of children, nor let them come near me hardly.' In all his work it is hard to find an affectionate reference to a child. His dislike is more eccentric to us than it would have been to his contemporaries who regarded children as smaller, more culpable adults. They were more vulnerable too; we find the origins of *A Modest Proposal* in the child mortality of eighteenth-century Dublin. But even for purposes of satire perhaps it was unnatural to write: 'A child will make two dishes at an entertainment for friends, and when the family dines alone, the fore or hind quarter will make a reasonable dish, and seasoned with a little pepper and salt will be very good boiled on the fourth day.'

Gulliver rejected his children after his return from the Houyhnhnms. 'To this hour they dare not presume to touch my bread or drink out of the same cup, neither was I ever able to let one of them take me by the hand.' The female Yahoo who assaulted him when he was in the company of his gentle Houyhnhnm host and 'came running with all speed and leaped into the water within five yards of the place where I bathed' in order to embrace him, was 'not above eleven years old'. Glumdalclitch was much the same age. The two contrasting aspects of girlhood—the grotesque sexuality of one and the tenderness of the other—reflected his attitude towards Stella, whom he had known since she was a child of eight at Moor Park. Two decades later she was still essentially a child to him, and they communicated in stylized baby talk. 'Zoo must cly Lele and Hele and Hele aden. Must loo mimitate pafr, pay? Iss, and so la shall . . .' The pathetic young Yahoo, less unattractive than her red-headed sisters, was black-haired; Stella had hair 'blacker than a raven'.

He may well have feared Stella's latent sexuality since his relations with the women he loved were marred because of his horror of physical contact. Early in his life he lost the capacity for considering sex a natural function. 'I must likewise warn you,' he wrote to A Young Lady, 'strictly against the least degree of fondness to your husband before any witness whatsoever . . . This proceeding is so exceeding odious and disgustful to all who have either good breeding or good sense, that they assign two very unamiable reasons for it; the one is gross hypocrisy, and the other has too bad a name to mention.' Stella, Vanessa, and perhaps Varina whom he seriously contemplated marrying had their happiness destroyed, because although he loved them, his attitude towards womankind ('a sort of species hardly a degree above a monkey') made him an emotional cripple. From all his women he asked impossible things. Rejecting Varina, he doubted whether she would be 'ready to engage in those methods I shall direct for the improvement of your mind so as to make us entertaining company for each other without being miserable when we are neither visiting nor being visited'. He wanted her complete subordination to his wishes, knowing that she could not comply. In one of the prayers that he composed and used by Stella's bedside as she lay dying, he asked that she would be kept from 'both the sad extremes of presumption and despair', a phrase which also summed up his lifelong directive towards her love for him. These austere prayers, as well as conveying the stoical quality of his religion, speak of his very real devotion to her, just as much as his notes on the Death of Mrs. Johnson. But he could no more make her happy than Gulliver could his wife who 'took me in her arms and kissed me, at which having not been used to the touch of that odious Animal for so many years, I fell in a swoon for almost an hour'.

He made the Yahoos morally as well as physically unpleasant. His revulsion came to embrace all mankind in all its parts; humans were objects of disgust from head to toe. In *Directions to Servants in General*, that hilarious and revolting treatise on which he worked for a decade, he instructs the footman: 'Never wear socks when you wait at meals on account of your own health as well as of them who sit at table; because as most ladies like the smell of young men's toes, so it is a sovereign remedy against the vapours.'

Since the body and bodily functions affected so much of his later writing and wit, many of his admirers found themselves obliged to turn from the major body of his work and dwell on what he wrote with his eye to the privy door. Macaulay described 'a mind richly stored with images from the dunghill or lazar house', while William Eddy shuddered at 'a scatological ugliness that is nauseating to the most hardened cynic'. George Orwell called him a diseased writer. D. H. Lawrence explained Swift's preoccupation: 'Of course Celia s***ts! Who doesn't? . . . It comes from having taboo words, and from not keeping the mind sufficiently developed in physical and sexual consciousness.' Others have considered that the violent reaction of Strephon and Cassinus to Celia's habit not only mocked the conventions of Augustan verse, but also explained Swift's tragedy; their feelings were his own.

> His foul imagination links
> Each dame he sees with all her stinks.

But in portraying Swift the eccentric, it is easy to stress the abnormal aspects of his complex personality and to forget the genius and integrity that made him tower over his contemporaries and indeed over most of mankind. Perhaps William Eddy has defined Swift's true eccentricity in quoting Lord Chesterfield to his godson: ' "Learn to shrink yourself to the size of the company you are in. Take their tone whatever it may be." Chesterfield's advice . . . is the gospel truth for him who seeks to prosper. Only when man contracts his ideas and his ideals to the scale of his tribe will he find gratification in the world's applause and satisfaction with his own stature. In the meantime there will always be a few like Swift who cannot shrink—whose misfortune or preference it is to remain giants in Lilliput.'

Frederick Hervey, Bishop of Derry

SINCE Swift never succeeded in obtaining a bishopric he may have been prejudiced against Irish bishops. He contended that those who were newly appointed to Irish sees got caught by highwaymen as they crossed Hounslow Heath on their way west; the highwaymen thereupon stole their letters patent and came over in their place. This alone could account for the oddities of behaviour and the poor quality of Irish episcopal material. Swift's fancy underlines the fact that a majority of bishops appointed to the Church of Ireland were English. After his death during the period between 1760 and 1800 the ratio of English-born bishops to Irish was twenty-two to sixteen. Irish parsons had little chance of obtaining the highest offices, which were invariably reserved for members of influential English families. A cartoon of the period entitled *The Englishman in Dublin Gaping for Preferment* shows a clergyman on his knees gobbling up a cloth on which is written *Deanship—Bishoprick—Archbishoprick*.

Among the eighteenth-century English noblemen who obtained Irish Sees was Frederick Hervey, who became Bishop of Cloyne and later Bishop of Derry. His qualifications were of a minimum and he had enemies who believed that he was not even a Christian. He became an embarrassment to those who appointed him to his high office; George III who was one of his patrons came to regard him as 'this wicked prelate'. As he grew older his behaviour became odder. He had an aversion to the tinkling of bells. Once during his travels on the Continent, he paused in Siena for a meal, during which the procession of the Host passed under the window of his hotel. The Bishop leaned out of the window and threw a tureen of spaghetti at it.

He was a member of a singular family. His father, Lord John Hervey, the painted courtier, philanderer, father of eight children, was Pope's enemy, Sporus. His brother's matrimonial entanglements were astonishing and his nephew was hanged. Horace Walpole is generally accepted as being the illegitimate son of a Hervey. The life-styles of the Bishop and his relatives gave meaning to a contemporary aphorism that mankind was divided into men, women and Herveys.

Frederick Hervey entered the world on August 1, 1730. Later it was rumoured that his birth was a Caesarean delivery and that he was 'a man who should never have been born'. His christening took place in the distinguished presence of the Duchess of Marlborough, the Duke of Richmond and the Prince of Wales. Educated at Dr. Newcombe's private school in Hackney, Westminster and Corpus Christi, Cambridge, he took his M.A. as a nobleman in 1754 without having to sit an exam, He married early a girl without much money, and then became ordained at the age of twenty-four. There followed an unexacting period as clergyman and family man, punctuated by the financial difficulties that could beset the younger sons of noblemen. This situation changed suddenly in January 1767, when he became Bishop of Cloyne. He had no previous connection with Ireland, but owed his appointment to the elevation of his brother George, third Lord Bristol, to Lord Lieutenant. Lord Bristol held this powerful position for such a short time that he never actually visited Ireland at all. However, he had the opportunity of drawing three thousand pounds in travelling expenses for the journey, and making his brother-in-law an Irish baron and his brother an Irish bishop.

Frederick was consecrated Bishop of Cloyne in St. Patrick's Cathedral on May 31, 1767. His tenure at Cloyne lasted less than a year, during which he drained the surrounding bog, gained a place on the Privy Council, and waited for higher office. Cloyne was only a minor bishopric, and using all the influences he could muster, including the patronage of his brother, he angled for Derry, whose ancient incumbent, Dr. William Barnard, was slowly dying. Barely two days after his demise, Lord Bristol was canvassing the new Lord Lieutenant, Townsend, on his brother's behalf. 'My Lord, I am persuaded it is unnecessary for me to remind your excellency of the promise you made me to recommend the Bishop of Cloyne for his successor . . .' Three weeks later the promotion was obtained. According to tradition, Hervey learned of his elevation while amusing himself playing leapfrog with fellow clergymen in the grounds of his palace. He is said to have shouted to his companions:

'Gentlemen, I will jump no more. I have surpassed you all! I have jumped from Cloyne to Derry!'

He was thirty-nine years old, mercurial in temperament, charming and yet capable of demonstrating a curious callousness particularly towards his family. He had a taste for cruel practical jokes. The later eccentricities were not yet apparent, nor the liberalism and tolerance that would endear him to Irishmen. His passion for building and for collecting would develop as his wealth increased. Travelled, cultured, speaking a number of languages, he was a connoisseur of paintings and sculpture and an enthusiastic amateur geologist. His activities did not differ very much from those of other aristocratic gentlemen or even bishops. His predecessor, Dr. Barnard, also had a collection of pictures. Even the vagueness of Hervey's theology and his interest in Deism were not unique among ecclesiastical dignitaries. Robert Clayton, Bishop of Clogher and Cork, had been so advanced in his thinking that he opposed some of the fundamental teachings of the church. 'My Lord, quit writing, or you'll lose your Bishopric,' his demented wife is supposed to have told him. His unexpected death in 1758 saved him from this misfortune.

But Hervey managed to infuriate his contemporaries with his worldly preferences and a combination of vanity, arrogance and impetuousness which persuaded them that he had set himself above public morality. Above all they disliked his liberal ideas. He underwent that fierce metamorphosis that turns some Englishmen into Irish patriots. In a time of savage religious discrimination he openly supported the cause of Catholic emancipation. His great enemy, Lord Charlemont, blandly observed 'that he sometimes deviates into actions of a nature perfectly contrary which puzzles our judgement, and tends to show the astonishing contradictions that meet in the composite of a single man'. Walpole railed against 'that mitred Proteus, the Count Bishop . . . whoes crimes cannot be palliated but by his profligate folly'. Charles James Fox was one of the many who thought him mad. But many Irishmen came to like the generous broadminded prelate with a taste for popularity and an appetite for extravagance who believed that 'the rights of humanity demand a general and unlimited toleration at all times'.

One aspect of his behaviour was inexcusable in his calling. He was Bishop of Derry for thirty-six years, but nearly half that period was spent in travel outside Ireland. For the last thirteen years of his life he lived abroad and did not set foot in his diocese.

It was different when he first went to Derry. 'A true Irish bishop,' said Archbishop Bolton, 'has nothing to do than eat, drink, grow fat and rich and die.' Hervey started off with a diocesan stipend of £7,000 a year. By a different system of rating his parishes and more efficient methods of collection, he managed to raise this to £20,000 a year without rackrenting his tenants. With his increasing wealth he did not stagnate in the way Bolton described. He began to build. His tenure was notable for the way his building transformed his diocese, and for this reason—not for any other—he was known to his contemporaries as the Edifying Bishop. 'Though so few choose to live in it,' he said, 'I would fain make the County of Derry look like a gentleman; and nothing can give it that air better than a strutting steeple and spire with arms akimbo.'

He began a programme of improvement in which new mines were searched out and roads were made. One from Downhill strand across the Sperrin mountains became known as 'The Bishop's Road', and was described as 'rather the work of a Roman emperor than of an Irish bishop', He turned his attention to the material structure of the ecclesiastical buildings for which he was responsible. 'Let the church decorate the country, for it cannot receive it! Let its steeple and spire make it the visible as well as the established church.' By the end of his life, most churches in his diocese, had been given the appropriate spire. He laid plans for the first bridge to span the Foyle, which was finally constructed in 1790. He encouraged new methods of farming and 'introduced a very neat kind of gate, the bars of which are oak rounded'.

He built three great houses, two in Ireland and one in England. The first, Downhill, was perched on a high cliff above Lough Foyle. The position represented the extreme of 'sublime' landscape where nature at its most untamed blended with the classical proportions of man's constructions. Mrs. Anne Plumptre, who visited the area in 1817 long after the Bishop had died, considered it 'a most extraordinary spot for building a house . . . a noble seaview, it is true, and fine bold rocks rising almost perpendicularly above the water; but so miserably exposed to the turbulent north winds blowing around the coast, that one shivers involuntarily at the very idea of stirring without the door of the mansion except during a few weeks in the middle of the summer'.

Nevertheless, the Bishop delighted in his residence. He made it 'about the size of Blenheim with as many windows as there are days of the year'. The billiard room was decorated with a picture of Aurora and her handmaidens approaching the vast dome, whose representation of the sky surrounded a monster chandelier. The walls were painted with frescoes representing rustic scenery. The expanding library became famous, and so did the giant organ constructed in a corridor. Other corridors were lined with niches in which stood the busts the Bishop had brought back from Italy during his travels. Pictures included works attributed to Rubens, Murillo, Correggio, Raphael, Tintoretto, Perugino, Vandyke and Dürer. Hervey had an idiosyncratic approach to painting. He was more than a century before his time in his appreciation of Italian primitives, which formed one of his later collections. However, in general, Raphael and all Italian painters he classified as 'the minor Poets of Painting'. Michelangelo he considered 'mad, not sublime; ludicrous, not dignified. He is the *Dante* of painters as Dante is the Michael Angelo of poets. The picture of the Last Judgement is so tragicomical 'tis difficult to say which passion it excites most; and St. Barthlemé, all flayed, who folds up his skin as his ticket of admittance into Heaven, is worthy only of *Bartholomew* fair'.

Before Downhill was complete he began to build another house at Lough Beg a few miles away. The design of Downhill was long and rectangular; that of Ballyscullion was domed, so that it looked like the Pantheon. It contained an ingenious double corkscrew staircase and many features introduced by the architect Placidio Columbini that made its interior a delight. The two art galleries, intended to incorporate the Bishops' collections of Flemish and Italian pictures, never received them. He never lived in Ballyscullion, and although an army of workmen laboured for sixteen years at a cost of £80,000, the lovely building was never properly finished.

Hervey's third house, Ickworth in Suffolk, the family mansion which he reconstructed with even more elaborate plans than Downhill of Ballyscullion, was built under his distant direction, while he travelled about the Continent. His wife considered it 'a stupendous monument to folly'. Its development absorbed him to an obsessional degree throughout the latter years of his life; a letter to his daughter written from Naples in 1796 ends 'The House —The House—The House'. But his travels on the Continent prevented him from returning to see if his directions had been carried out, and he died before he ever saw his grandiose masterpiece.

For many years he kept his family impoverished in order to pay for his building programmes and his mania for collecting. His other lifelong passion was for travel. As a young man he visited Naples, witnessing an eruption of Vesuvius and venturing so close to the volcano that he hurt his arm with a falling stone. This gave him an interest in geology, enhanced by his observations of the patterns on the Giant's Causeway. Two years after he had been appointed to Derry he made geology the excuse for a long visit to Europe. The geological tour of Italy and Dalmatia was followed by other lengthy visits to the Continent. His favourite destination was Rome where *Milordo Hervey* or *Milor il Vescovo* was beginning to become a familiar figure as he went about annoying Vatican dignitaries by dressing in red plush breeches and a broad-brimmed white hat which made his appearance confusingly like that of a Catholic prelate.

In 1778, after a holiday in Italy which lasted for two years, he returned to England shortly before the death of his brother, Augustus. (This was not brother George who had been Lord Lieutenant of Ireland, but the next brother, notorious for having married the courtesan, Miss Chudleigh, with the ring of the bed curtain.) Hervey now found that he had inherited an earldom, £20,000 a year and the family estate in Suffolk. The world had its first Earl-Bishop since Odo, Bishop of Bayeux and Earl of Kent seven centuries before.

We have a glimpse of the Earl-Bishop around this time as guest of the Earl of Shelburne.

'To dinner,' wrote Jeremy Bentham, 'came a singular person, who not in the Falstaffian's sense, but in another sense, may be termed a double man. I mean the Earl of Bristol, also Bishop of Derry. He is a most excellent companion, pleasant, intelligent, well read, well bred and liberal minded to the last degree. He has been everywhere and knows everybody. Everyone seems to be agreed about two things, that he is touched in the middle and that he draws a long bow.' Today we would merely say touched; while 'to draw a long bow' meant to exaggerate.

About this time Hervey separated permanently from his wife; according to a servant they went out for a drive together, came back and never spoke to each other again. Lady Bristol remained behind in Ickworth while the Earl-Bishop went across the Irish Sea to Derry and Downhill where he resumed his pleasant and exemplary routine.

'You cannot imagine,' he wrote to his daughter, 'how satisfactorily I pass my time here—early hours, simple food, balsamic air, moderate company . . . I am now writing to you at 7 in the morning with an eastern sun dawning upon me and the magnificent ocean roaring in the most authoritative tone . . . how does my day pass? In acts of beneficence to the poor, of society with the rich and of benevolence to all. I improve my lands, enrich my tenants, decorate the country, cheer my neighbours, acquire health and good humour for myself and communicate wealth and comfort to others.'

'Oh, what a lovely thing it is to be an Anglican bishop or

Minister!' considered the French traveller, de Latocnaye, who was walking through Ireland around this time. 'These are the spoiled children of fortune, rich as bankers, enjoying good wine, good cheer, and pretty women . . . Lord Bristol, besides his bishopric, has a fortune of fifteen to twenty thousand pounds per annum. He is a man of talent, a learned man, but of singular habits. He travels nearly all the time in foreign countries, and spends his whole income on superb houses which are of use to the country through the money they cost.'

Hervey impressed others by his ability to converse in five languages on poetry, sculpture, politics, eloquence, natural history and painting 'with a knowledge and delicacy which announced the artist, but with a nobleness and impartiality which proved that he was not one'. (His enemies were less impressed by his general knowledge; Lord Charlemont said 'his genius is like a shallow stream: rapid, noisy, diverting but useless'.)

He filled Downhill with guests. Rich and poor, Catholics and dissenters were all welcome. So, naturally, were clergymen and men of God. One suite of guest rooms was known as the 'curates' corridor'. Wesley visited him and heard him preach 'a judicious useful sermon on the blasphemy of the Holy Ghost' and saw him administer the Sacrament with 'admirable solemnity'. He considered that 'the Bishop is entirely easy and unaffected in his whole behaviour, exemplary in all parts of worship, plenteous in good works'. Wesley was not asked to take part in the horse race between Presbyterian ministers and Protestant clergymen on the seashore at Magilligan Strand beneath Downhill. The Bishop's grooms assembled the best horses in his stables all saddled and bridled. 'The established clergy being generally rather portly men,' it was reported later, 'who were more accustomed to drive in their carriages than to ride on horseback, tumbled from their horses—while the Presbyterian ministers, being leaner men, kept their seats.'

Another race organized by Hervey had the fattest clergymen in his diocese competing for a particularly desirable living. He set them running against each other after he had entertained them to a lavish dinner. The course was fixed through a stretch of boggy ground in which the clerics floundered, not one of them finishing the course or getting the desired reward which was bestowed elsewhere.

High jinks were not confined to clergymen. An indiscreet lady guest had her sins discovered when the Bishop, like Daniel pursuing the priests of Baal, sprinkled flour outside her room to discover traces of her lover. It is not recorded if he came from the curates' corridor. The Bishop himself gave ground for great scandal by his admiration for the beautiful Mrs. Frideswide Mussenden, thirty years his junior. The little temple he dedicated to her still survives on the cliffs above Magilligan Strand. Almost certainly the brief flirtation conducted with her—the poor girl died when she was twenty-two—was an innocent one.

The Bishop's liberalism, so very unusual in a person of his rank and position, was growing to be a nuisance to those who governed Ireland. His enthusiasm for his adoped country began sensibly by his resolution never to appoint English clergymen to Irish livings. Soon he was opposing the penal laws and the tithe system by which clergy of the established church, including of course himself, drew the greater part of their incomes. He advocated the appeal of the Test Act.

'Can any country flourish,' he wrote to a friend in 1779, 'where two thirds of its inhabitants are still crouching under the lash of the most severe illiberal penalties that one set of citizens ever laid on the other?' 'As of any countries I have visited,' he told John Hely Hutchinson, 'I know of none in the remotest corner of Europe that stands so much in need of a liberal education.'

Irish bishops were expected to show a solid front with the government, which was one good reason why Englishmen got the appointments. But with his favourite toast 'The Irish Harp New Strung!' a clarion call among seekers of reform, Hervey threw himself into political agitations of the period which coincided with the formation of the Volunteers. Although there would have been nothing very startling in the Earl of Bristol becoming a Volunteer, for the Lord Bishop to be appointed Colonel of the Londonderry Corps was unsuitable, especially if the rumour was true that he had presented it with some guns whose barrels were engraved with the text, 'O Lord open thou our lips and our mouths shall show forth thy praise.'

His military début took place on September 8, 1783 at the great Volunteer meeting held in Dungannon which declared for a new parliament. 'Brought to notice,' Jonah Barrington recorded, 'a most singular personage, Frederick, Earl of Bristol, Bishop of Derry, who altogether adopted the view and avowed himself a partisan of the rights of Ireland. He was given a special vote of thanks for coming by the five hundred Ulstermen present, who resolved that a Grand General Convention of the Volunteers of all Ireland should be held in order to prepare the way for Parliamentary Reform.'

The Convention was opened in Dublin at the newly built Royal Exchange on November 10. Among the Volunteers who converged on the capital was the Earl-Bishop-Colonel, who travelled southward from Downhill, making a regal progress by stopping at Strabane, Aughnacloy, Caledon and Armagh in order to acknowledge a series of civic receptions. He was attended by a detachment of dragoons—'these being all dashing young fellows and gallantly mounted out of the Bishop's stud which was the finest in Ireland'. They were commanded by his nephew, George Robert Fitzgerald, who had recently been let out of jail.

On Friday, November 7 Hervey made a stately entrance into Dublin in the midst of his servants who rode on either side of his carriage in gorgeous liveries while the dragoons, in gold and scarlet, rode behind and in front. He sat in an open landau drawn by six horses caparisoned with purple ribbons dressed in a brilliant costume that was half military and half episcopal. His purple coat was faced with white and his colonel's hat hung with gold lace and surmounted by a cockade. He wore white gloves fringed with gold tassels and diamonds on his knees and shoes. The glittering little figure bowed to left and right, and according to Barrington 'never ceased making dignified obeisances to the multitude', which received him with enthusiasm, crying and cheering 'Long Live the Bishop!' When the equipage reached College Street, Hervey ordered it to halt outside the parliament buildings while the musicians in his procession sounded a fanfare of trumpets which was followed by the rousing beat of the Volunteer March. Lords and Commons retreated nervously indoors, but 'all was peace and harmony', according to Barrington, 'and never did there appear so extraordinary a procession within the realm of Dublin'.

Hervey then drove to Charlemont House, where Lord Charlemont, the commander-in-chief of the Volunteers, a man of tepid views, who had not wished to encourage reform and felt no love for the Colonel of the Londonderry Corps, received him coolly. He stood some way outside his mansion 'so that the subsequent salute might seem more to him as a general than the Bishop . . .' In no way put out, Hervey had his procession reformed and moved off to Merrion Square to stay with his nephew. During the following weeks he continued to roam the city streets showing off his finery, at the same time entertaining lavishly in his nephew's house.

The show was put on partly to gratify his appetite for display; but also to influence the delegates at the Convention to elect him President. Some of his enemies even thought that he was trying to get himself elected Lord Lieutenant by acclaim. But it was the conservative Lord Charlemont who managed to obtain the 'troublesome and dangerous office' of President of the Convention, and who quietly opposed or thwarted any liberal measures put forward by the delegates. Any idea of Catholic franchise was shelved after a bogus letter purporting to come from a Catholic nobleman, Lord Kenmare, stated that Catholics did not wish for any more concessions. Charlemont encouraged the delegates to accept this document as truthful and important.

Hervey did his best to obstruct the President and make his position 'a seat of thorns'. 'Things are going well,' he told him at one point, 'we shall have blood, my lord, we shall have blood.' Richard Lovell Edgeworth, who supported Charlemont, wrote that on one of the last days of the Convention the Bishop invited its most restless members to dinner. 'Before the bottle had made any considerable impression on the company, it was proposed that a motion be made in the Convention for carrying its petition to the door of the House of Commons by the whole Convention

in uniform.' Edgeworth feared that the Commons would interpret this action as a plot to overthrow it or to intimidate it. 'Fortunately for the country, all present became convinced of its
rashness and illegality.' Edgeworth believed that Hervey gave the
dinner solely in order to press for this idea.

In due course a watered-down reform bill was drafted by
Henry Flood; against Charlemont's wishes but with the Bishop's
support it was presented to the House of Commons which felt
strong enough to reject it out of hand. None of Hervey's impetu-
ous and ill-considered efforts was able to forward the Convention's historic aims. 'The volunteer of Derry is of no consequence'
was the general opinion of the lively and truculent little colonel
trying to rouse his comrades to violence in support of its radical
aims. The failure of the Convention halted the whole impetus of
the Volunteer Movement.

Hervey returned to Derry where for a short time he continued
in his forthright political opinions. 'Tyranny is not government
and allegiance is due only to protection,' he told the Bill of Rights
Battalion Volunteers. His advocacy of the unity of Protestant
and Catholic interests so alarmed the government that it seriously
considered arresting him for treason. Northern Liberals and
Catholics sent him scores of grateful addresses. '. . . We trust
that Heaven's Providence *points* you to us as one ennobled instrument to raise our injured kingdom from infamy to glory, from
misery to felicity . . .'

Dublin Castle watched him. 'Lord Bristol has been generally
quiet,' wrote the Lord Lieutenant, the young Duke of Rutland,
'though Lord Hillsborough sends me a Derry Gazette with some
facetious answers to addresses. I shall keep a vigilant eye on his
conduct.'

Lord Rutland need not have worried, for Hervey's political
enthusiasm was waning. He may have become petulant after his
failure at the Convention. His liberal views faded rapidly, so that by
the end of his life he had become utterly reactionary. Meanwhile
Downhill awaited further improvements. 'Downhill is becoming
elegance itself . . . 300,000 trees without doors upon all banks and
upon all the rocks and almost as many pictures and statues within

doors . . .' Not one of the trees has survived the blasts from the sea.

For a brief period before he set out on his travels once more he continued his duties in his usual affable manner. But he was restless, and now lacked the purpose that politics had given. His gout was aggravated by his Epicurean tastes: 'he could drink a bottle of Madeira like a gentleman.' Winters in Downhill were dismal with the wind blowing against all the windows and pervading the great rooms whose dimensions were deliberately large because the Bishop could only breathe properly in a room which was the size of an amphitheatre. Southwards in Europe there was good company and countless antiquities to be collected.

He left Ireland in July 1785, returning for brief periods in 1787 and 1790. After that he abandoned his diocese completely and wandered around a war-torn Europe for the remaining thirteen years of his life. Hotels in half-a-dozen countries changed their name to Bristol after the gracious and lavish-spending prelate, whether he stayed in them or not. Some. like the Bernini-Bristol in Rome, still perpetuate his memory.

In his travels he avoided France. There had been a time when the ideas of liberty and equality, rather too enthusiastically expressed by Frenchmen, would have been regarded by him with the utmost sympathy. But now he considered the French to be 'that nation of baboons' and 'a band of monkies'. He preferred to visit Prussia, where 'I am so occupied and amused, so fêted par tout, that I cannot get on, and my curiosity is as insatiable as if I were five and twenty'. At the court he became the admirer of Countess Lichtenau, the mistress of the king, and took to wearing a portrait of her surrounded with diamonds. Count Dampmartin, the French tutor to the king's children, observed how 'a fatal destiny made the countess meet with Lord Bristol, Bishop of Londonderry, who was remarkable for a revolting combination of witty knowledge, pride, ostentation, *moeurs libres*, causticity, contempt for *les convenances* and irreligion'.

'My common course is a circle,' Hervey wrote to his daughter, Lady Erne, 'and like a planet, a vagabond star, I almost turn round my own axis while I make another revolution around the sun.' He travelled about in a vast carriage, cluttered with baggage so that one observer thought that it looked like the cart of a quack doctor. His cook rode ahead of him to prepare the elaborate meal which awaited him wherever he stopped for the night. He went to Florence where he paid court to the Countess of Albany, the mistress of the poet Alfieri, and widow of Bonny Prince Charlie. She called him 'ce fou Bristol'. He visited Naples often, where he admired 'dearest dear Emma' Hamilton who was under the protection of his old school-mate, Sir William Hamilton. He wrote:

> O Emma, who'd ever be wise
> If madness be loving of thee?

He was quite aware of her frailties. Once he left her salon after a woman with a notorious reputation had been admitted. 'It may be allowed for a bishop to visit one sinner,' he said; 'it is quite unfitting that he shall be seen in a brothel.' Most of his flirtations are assumed to be platonic.

He took to visiting convents where the nuns were deluded into believing he was a Catholic bishop. His ecclesiastical garments included a white hat edged with purple, a coat of crimson silk in summer or of velvet in winter, a black sash spangled with silver, and purple stockings, Often they were set off by Countess Lichtenau's miniature. Vatican authorities constantly objected to his wearing these garments in the heart of Rome.

Rome was his headquarters, and here he kept a lively salon. He was considered a 'volcano' at table for his wit and 'one of the gayest and most fashionable men of the world and a free thinker'. He spent a great deal of his time buying antiques, and he continued his collection with such passion that often he did not have the price of a bottle of Orvieto on him. He tried unsuccessfully to buy the Temple of Vesta at Tivoli, which he thought would adorn one of his building projects—Downhill, the unfinished Ballyscullion or his English inheritance, Ickworth, where his wife lived in impoverishment.

He was cruel to his wife and sons. The elder had no allowance for years and was kept virtually a pauper, while he tried to force the younger into marriage with Countess Lichtenau's daughter by the King of Prussia. He constantly urged his family to economize, even after his income had risen to £60,000 a year. With his two daughters he kept on better terms. A letter survives to the elder, Lady Erne, urging her to come and see him in Rome. She was not to fear sea sickness. 'But to the ship! Lash your carriage to the mast, and in the centre, you know, is little or no motion. Then let down the glass on the windward side for fresh air, but above all else clothe yourself in a pelisse as if it were winter.'

In Ireland he was hardly missed by a population used to absentees. He did not entirely forget his diocese, since the correspondence he conducted with his kinsman, Henry Hervey Bruce, kept him in close touch with its administrative details. Episcopal colleagues were annoyed by his continued sojourn abroad. When two bishops and the Archbishop of Armagh reproached him for neglecting Derry, he sent them three bladders each containing a dried pea and a verse:

> Three large blue bottles sat upon three bladders.
> Blow bottle flies, blow; burst, blow bladder burst;
> A new blown bladder and three blue balls
> Make a great rattle. So rattle, bladder, rattle.
>
>   Bristol.

The Earl of Tyrone, head of the Beresford family, longed for him to die so that he could obtain the see for one of his relations. 'I have an account that the Bishop of Derry is in a wretched and emaciated state', he wrote hopefully to the Duke of Rutland, 'and that we shall hear of his death in a very short time.' Hervey continued to confound his enemies and live on. Former acquaintances might shun him as disreputable, but he was able to give lavish hospitality to scores of visitors in his sumptuous Roman house which was decorated with pictures of his female friends, three of whom posed as Juno, Minerva and Venus in a Judgement of Paris.

In the winter of 1797 he contemplated an expedition to Egypt in search of 'obelisks, columns, sphinks . . . all to be obtained for only the cost of their transport'. He asked Alexander Humbolt, the explorer, whom he had met during one of his rides on horse-back outside Rome, to be his companion and guide, and also ex-tended invitations to two women, Madame Dennis, the wife of an artist and close friend of Lady Hamilton, and the Countess Lich-tenau. They would journey up the Nile in a yacht manned by 'an armoured crew, with artists, scholars etc.' and fitted with an elaborate kitchen and well-provided cellars. He almost persuaded the Countess to come in letters full of double meanings and punning French. 'Quant aux femmes, il faut que vous passiez pour la mienne, et que pour n'être pas violée vous soyez voilée, et alors votre personne est plus sacrée que la mienne . . .' But the death of the Prussian king, Frederick William, put her position in the court at Berlin in jeopardy, and she had to forgo the opportunity he offered her. The expedition never took place. Napoleon also got the idea of visiting Egypt, and his transports filled with troops set sail for Alexandria just as Humboldt reached the French border on his way to meet up with Hervey. When the French army in-vaded Italy, Hervey lost most of his collection of pictures and marbles. For good measure the French locked him up in Milan for nine months as a suspected spy. He was made as comfortable as possible, since he was allowed to order his own food and receive visitors.

Wars and imprisonment could not stop him enjoying himself and spending enough of his fortune to worry his bankers. Miss Catherine Wilmot, an Irish lady resident in Rome, saw him riding and driving past her window a short time before his death:

'His figure is little and his face very sharp and wicked; on his head he wore a purple velvet nightcap with a tassel of gold dangling to his shoulder and a sort of mitre in front, silk stockings and slippers of the same colour, and a short round petticoat such as Bishops wear, fringed with gold around his knees. A loose dressing-gown of silk was thrown over his shoulders. In this Merry Andrew trim he rode on horseback to the never-ending amusement of all Beholders! The last time I saw him he was sitting in his carriage between two Italian women dress'd in white Bed-gown and Night-cap like a witch and giving himself the airs of an Adonis.'

He died suddenly on July 8, 1803 at the age of sixty-three. While riding in blazing heat through the Campagna from Albano to Rome he was seized with an attack of 'gout of the stomach'. He was carried into the outhouse of a cottage whose inhabitants would not admit him because they were unwilling to have a heretic priest die under their roof.

Eight hundred artists of Rome turned up for his obsequies. However, he was not buried in the Eternal City. The Protestant cemetery was not to be laid out for another decade, the result of the Vatican's gratitude to the British government for returning treasures stolen by the French, and meanwhile heretical corpses received undignified treatment. Besides, there was a mausoleum waiting at Ickworth. The great collector was shipped from Naples to London on the man-of-war *Monmouth* wrapped as a piece of antique statuary in deference to the superstitions of the sailors.

The fate of his pictures confiscated by the French is a mystery. In Ireland little remains of all his building and collecting. Downhill and its contents were destroyed by fire in 1851. Most of Ballyscullion was pulled down because the window tax made it too expensive for his heirs to maintain. What was left—some of it still to be seen—was known as the Bishop's Folly. The portico was rescued and taken to Belfast where it decorates the Church of St. George. Another, prettier, folly stands beside the sea; Mrs. Mussenden's temple, dedicated to her beauty, is a fitting symbol of the liberal muddle of his thought with its underground room intended for Catholic priests to say Mass. Irishmen remember him less for his eccentricity than for his rare championship of tolerance and religious liberty—which many of his peers considered to be merely another aspect of his capricious behaviour. A contemporary tribute to him from those who lived in his diocese stands, not in his adopted country, but in the smooth grounds of Ickworth Park, where the citizens of Derry, including the Dissenting minister and the Roman Catholic bishop, subscribed an obelisk to the ecumenical bishop.

Sacred to the Memory of
Frederick, Earl of Bristol, Bishop of Derry,

who during 35 years that he presided
over that see, endeared himself
to all denominations of Christians
resident in his extensive diocese.
He was a friend and protector of them all.
His great patronage was
uniformly administered upon the purest
and most disinterested principles.
Various and important public works
were undertaken at his instigation
and completed by his munificence.
And hostile sects which had long entertained
feelings of deep animosity towards each other
were gradually softened and reconciled
by his influence and example.

Philip Skelton and
other Men of God

PHILIP SKELTON was a friend of the Bishop of Derry, although the two men never actually met. Their backgrounds contrasted sharply; Hervey was almost a caricature of privilege, while Skelton's origins were extremely modest. He was born in 1707 in a village in Co. Antrim named Derrigaghy, the son of a small farmer who also worked as a tanner and a blacksmith. After his mother was widowed while he was still a boy, the family became extremely poor; at one time he had to study at night by the light of a turf fire because he could not afford a candle. He was proud of his background, and in one recorded remark emphasized the most humble of his father's occupations. 'I am no gentleman,' he declared while staying in the house of a prosperous northern landlord. 'My father was only a tanner, yet I would not change him for the best of your fathers, for he was a man of virtue and religion.'

His hard upbringing conditioned his future habits and developed his militant modesty which was in direct contrast to Hervey's love of acquisition and display. While Hervey lived in luxury, Skelton scorned to possess more than the bare essentials of life: a few clothes, and a small library of good books. Plain cooking, a servant and a horse to take him to his widely scattered parishioners were his only other needs. In times of distress most of his possessions were expendable and were sold to help the needy.

Between these outwardly dissimilar characters there existed a a similarity of disposition. Both were gifted and imaginative and pursued their highly original modes of living with parallel

enthusiasm and scorn for conventional attitudes. Their friendship
was conducted by correspondence. As a young curate Skelton
wrote an unorthodox dissertation on doctrine called *Deism
Revealed*. Hervey read it, and he was so impressed by Skelton's
arguments that he wrote to him, beginning a correspondence that
lasted for some years. When Hervey gained his appointment in
1767 as Bishop of Cloyne, he decided to appoint an Irishman as
his chaplain. He asked Skelton to preach his consecration sermon
—a considerable honour for a largely unknown clergyman—at
the same time hinting at future preferment. Skelton hesitated;
first he accepted, and then he sternly refused to be dazzled by
the Bishop's attentions. He wrote that he was quite happy where
he was, his health was not too good, and if he consented to go to
the diocese of Cloyne it would be in order to be nearer to the sun
rather than to his Lordship. Instead of attending the consecration
in Dublin in person, he posted the sermon. Hervey was annoyed.
'The chain of our friendship has been broken in two,' he wrote.
Skelton replied: 'The chain was originally of your Lordship's
forging.'

Hervey forgave Skelton's scorn of patronage, recognizing that
it took courage and strength of will not to accept the temptation
of attending him in promise of reward. After he became Bishop
of Derry he set out to pay Skelton a visit in his remote parish at
Fintona in Co. Tyrone. During a tour of the area which was part
of the diocese, the Bishop made a special journey to see him,
travelling fifteen miles out of his way over hard jogging roads.
Skelton was not at home. This may have been accident or design,
but afterwards Hervey had too many distractions to continue the
friendship.

Skelton's gruff manners may partly have arisen from his poverty-stricken boyhood, but were augmented by his experiences
in one of the most backward livings in Ireland. Before he ended
his clerical career at Fintona, he spent nearly ten years in an even
more remote parish, Pettigo in Co. Donegal. In Skelton's time
this bleak stretch of moorland and bog was well out of reach of
landlords and the changes that their form of civilisation imposed.
He keenly felt his isolation. 'I have often heard him declare,' his

5.　Eleanor Butler and Sarah Ponsonby, the Ladies of Llangollen

6a. Charles Byrne on exhibit with two other giants

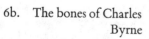

6b. The bones of Charles Byrne

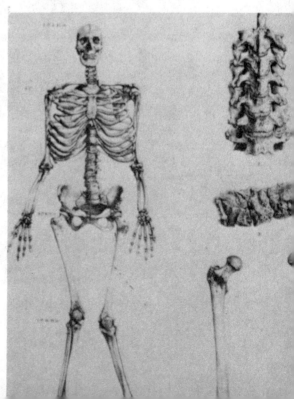

7a.　The Countess of Desmond

7b.　Jonathan Swift. From a
portrait by Isaac Whood

8.   Frederick Hervey, Earl of Bristol and Bishop of Derry. Artist unknown

biographer wrote, 'he was forced to ride seven miles before he could meet with a person of common sense to talk to.' He was surrounded by people who were drunk and quarrelsome, whose 'lingo' he scorned, and who knew less about the gospels than 'North American Indians', and had even less inclination to learn. He considered Pettigo a 'Siberia'.

Although he constantly complained of hardship, the rugged life suited him very well. He took an active interest in all the people who lived in his parish, whether they were Catholic or Protestant. He hired a servant who was a noted boxer, whose horse he fitted with a military saddle provided with pistols; together the two of them would tour the wild countryside, perhaps to tend the sick or comfort the dying or seek out a poteen still or trounce a gang of tinkers for using bad language. He had an odd style of riding, like a tailor, according to witnesses, balanced on the stirrups like a slack wire. 'My education was inverted,' he told a woman who said that he turned out his toes too much, 'I was taught to ride by a dancing master and to dance by a riding master.' In the evenings after his circuits of the wastes of Pettigo, he would return to his lodgings, and if the weather was fine and there was enough light he would tend his garden, which he loved and kept filled with rare and unusual plants. After dark some of his neighbours were so in awe of books that they would gather outside and peer through the window to watch him read by candlelight.

Before coming to Pettigo he had studied medicine for three years because he felt it would be useful. He became an enthusiastic amateur physician. Colds were driven away by a régime of hunger. He was specially interested in psychological difficulties, and the terrors brought about by hallucinations. A woman, who complained of constantly seeing a little old woman dressed in a red cloak and black bonnet sitting in her bedroom, was cured when he whirled a stick and drove the apparition out of the window. A man, haunted by a familiar which persisted in wearing his own large white hat, was advised to sell the hat. A crank who roasted devils over coals was persuaded to drown them instead.

Pettigo was not an area which contained a large number of

Protestants. Sometimes when they were gathered in church, Skelton would lock the door to prevent anyone escaping before he started to deliver one of his alarming admonishing sermons, usually about Hell.

But he was the kindest of men, who gave all the help he could to both Protestants and Catholics. He was unusually sensitive to the misery of the people in his parish. The poverty that he witnessed daily and the effects of disease and hunger were frightening. Particularly hunger. 'If you have not food,' he said, 'beg it; if you can't get for begging, steal, if you can't get for stealing, rob and don't starve.' During the famine of 1757 he not only organized a fairly efficient relief, and sold off all his possessions, including his precious books, but lived on the same raw weeds as the people around him. For relaxation he made snuff from heather. In other famines in 1773 and 1778 at Fintona, he again sold his books and gave the money to people in his parish.

He was subject to bouts of depression which he often cured by inviting guests to partake of wine. He had many admirers who did not hesitate to travel long distances to see him, with more success than the Bishop. Skelton would eagerly invite them into his shabby bookfilled parlour which had an uneven earth floor, and sit them down so that he could discuss his religious doubts with them. He worried about his ultimate salvation and sometimes thought that he was doomed to everlasting fire. More prosaically, he was a demented hypochondriac, and believed that the arthritis that afflicted him—'the Hips' or 'Plaguey Hips'— would kill him at any moment. At regular intervals, when he considered that he was on the point of death, he would gather his friends to witness his demise. His neighbours, Dr. and Mrs. Scott, were often called in so that Dr. Scott could listen to his heartbeats —they were always sound and regular—and prescribe water as a remedy. Once when the usual mournful group of friends was attending Skelton's deathbed, the scene was interrupted by another neighbour, Robert Johns, who burst in crying: 'Make it a day, Sir, and keep it, and don't always be disappointing us thus!'

Skelton was a persuasive preacher; he could, in Gratton's words, 'break the repose of the pulpit'. Most of his sermons had a vivid theme; their object was to persuade his audience of the truth about Hell. To help him he had a 'stock of imagination to set up ten modern poets'. He conveyed the torments of hell fire with a wide range of dramatic gestures, followed by shouts which emphasized the strength of his feelings and the crackle of the flames. His powers of description were considered 'inconceivable'. He had the talent most of his life, and during his short sojourn in London while *Deism Revealed* was being published gave a number of memorable sermons; later he dedicated a collection of them to the citizens of London. In Dublin when he preached about hell in St. Werburgh's Church, one listener at least felt his words 'made him shiver in his place'. In Lisburn on two successive Sundays he spent his time in the pulpit making his congregation laugh and cry alternately, until he himself was so overcome by emotion that the tears streamed down his face.

For all his gifts of oratory and his fame as a writer and religious theorist, his clerical career was undistinguished. This does not seem to be because of his rudeness, since in spite of his ungraceful appearance and opinionated manners he made a deep impression on all who met him. But his refusal to seek advancement from patronage confined him to work in small obscure parishes. He got little promotion, merely a slight rise in his stipend, after he left Pettigo to go first to Devenish near Enniskillen and then to Fintona. In 1780 when he was seventy-two he declared that the northern climate was too harsh, and retired to live in Dublin.

He took lodgings in Dame Street, from where he would walk around the city, a tall stooping figure, dressed in a rusty gown or blue coat covered with snuff worn over a black waistcoat and breeches. His ancient brown wig was one of the sights in Dublin —even at a time when servants tended to make free use of wigs for dusting and polishing Skelton's was unusually tattered. Although he lived at a bookseller's situated next door to the offices of the Dublin *Evening Post*, during the last five years of his life he never read a newspaper. His reason for this was clearly given: 'I have nothing to do with this world, for I am on the point of leaving it.'

He got into debt. As a result he let his beard grow, refusing to

cut it until the debts were paid off. The oddly dressed old man
with his long curling grey beard now looked like 'a Rabbi or a
Turk'. At a meeting of his creditors in 1787 he called for a Bible
and read from the thirtieth chapter of Job.

> But now they that are younger than I have me in derision, whose
> fathers I would have disdained to have set with the dogs of my
> flock.
> Yea, whereto might the strength of their hands profit me, in
> whom old age was perished . . .
> . . . Among the bushes they brayed, under the nettles they were
> gathered together.
> They were children of fools, yea, children of base men: they,
> were viler than the earth.
> And now I am their song, yea, I am their byword.

In the same year he died, having first left instructions that his
throat was to be cut before he was placed in his coffin.

★   ★   ★

By 1787, the year of Skelton's death, the penal laws were beginning to lose their bite. Between the Catholic Relief Act of 1782 and
the Bill of Catholic Emancipation which was passed in 1829, the
last restrictions endured by Roman Catholics in Ireland were
removed. The new freedom was recognized by the founding of
the great College of St. Patrick at Maynooth in 1795, which from
that time educated the majority of Irish priests. Among the endow-
ments that contributed to the College's development was the
Dunboyne Establishment, bequeathed by John Butler, thirteenth
Baron Dunboyne. Lord Dunboyne's relationship with the Catholic
church had been unusual. When, as a young man, he decided to
became a priest, it hesitated to accept him because he had one eye.
Canon law is derived from Hebrew law which forbids anyone to
take up the priesthood if he is blemished: in the words of Levi-
ticus, 'broken footed or broken handed or crookbackt or a dwarf
or that hath a blemish in his eye or be scurvy or scabbed'. Eventually a dispensation was obtained and his ordination was allowed to
take place. He rose to high office, became Bishop of Cork and

occupied the see for twenty-three years. But then, at the age of seventy, he became a Protestant and got married.

Although it was seldom that the Church of Ireland managed such a coup, converts of this quality were not entirely unknown. The celebrated Dean of Killala, the Rev. Walter Blake Kirwan, had been a Jesuit before he joined the Church of Ireland, and in 1777 had been appointed Professor of Natural and Moral Philosophy at Louvain. His namesake, the philosopher and scholar Richard Kirwan, became a Protestant in France and ultimately a Unitarian. During previous periods of religious stress many members of old Gaelic families had supported English rule and turned Protestant. They usually did so in order to keep their lands; they acted for financial and dynastic reasons. These were also the motives that induced the aged Bishop of Cork to resign his bishopric and abjure his faith.

His dilemma began in 1785 when his nephew, Pierce Edmond Butler, the twelfth Lord Dunboyne, died, and he found himself successor to the title. He was distressed to discover that his own heir was only remotely connected to him, being separated in the genealogical line by an interval of a hundred and forty years. Realizing that there was only one way to prevent the extinction of the family's direct line, he decided that he himself must provide another heir. But there were a number of difficulties in his way.

First of all he had to resign his bishopric, before seeking a papal dispensation to give up his priesthood and retract his vows of celibacy. He may have remembered the dispensation he had been given over forty years before and reflected that strictly speaking he was unsuitable material for priesthood. His superiors disagreed, and his request was refused. However he was determined. Seeing there was no way through the Catholic church in which he could seek to preserve his family, he felt that he had no alternative but to abandon the religion that he had served so well. He selected a wife of childbearing age, a lady in her twenties, the daughter of a Protestant cousin, Theobald Butler of Waterford. The ceremony of his recantation and marriage took place on August 19, 1787, in Clonmel Church. Catholic contemporaries were horrified.

Arthur O'Leary considered that, like the Emperor Charles V, he was of an age when men should rather think of their coffins than of their nuptial beds. No other Irish bishop has ever turned apostate. The Pope, who was also in his early seventies, sent him a thunderous letter:

'Pius VI, Sovereign Pontiff to John Butler, Baron Dunboyne and Bishop of Cork, greeting;

'It is not to be believed, venerable brother, with what consternation and anguish of mind we have been seized and overwhelmed, ever since we received authentic information that such was the height of infatuation which your misconduct has reached, that you intended to espouse a certain Protestant female, and dare even now, to live with her in a style of disgraceful concubinage—truly we shuddered with horror at this flagitious proceeding; nor can we now, from the intense agitation of our feelings, find words competent to express our indignation at such an excess of depravity . . .'

Who is to say why the union proved unfruitful? When he came to die in 1800 at the age of eighty-three, Lord Dunboyne was received back into the Catholic faith, and his will with its generous endowment to Maynooth may have emphasized his regret at his behaviour. His reconversion, which happened rather hastily, greatly annoyed his heirs who created another scandal by contesting the legacy under The Penal Laws, which although by this time were seldom enforced, were still in the statute books. They maintained that anyone relapsed from the established religion was incapable of making a will. His confessor, Dr. Gahan, went to prison for a short time rather than testify and violate the secrets of the confessional. A compromise was reached, and Maynooth, instead of receiving the whole of the Dunboyne estate, was given £10,000.

★   ★   ★

Later in the century the Protestant Archbishop of Dublin, Archbishop Whateley was regularly to be seen lounging on the chains outside his palace in Stephen's Green, smoking a long clay pipe. Sometimes he would rush into the Green and climb a tree in which he hid a handkerchief or a pocket knife for his dogs to find. If he felt he needed exercise, he would swing from the branches.

When two old women observed him in the Green exercising his Newfoundland dog and making it go through its repertoire of tricks, their conversation was overheard:

BIDDY: Ah, then Mary, do you know who that is playing with the dog?

MARY: Truth I don't, Biddy; but he's a fine looking man, whoever he is.

BIDDY: That's the Archbishop.

MARY: Do you tell me so? God bless the innocent craythur! Isn't he aisly amused?

BIDDY: He's not our archbishop at all, Mary, he is the Protestant archbishop.

MARY: Oh? The b— ould fool!

At home with Lord Anglesey, the Lord Lieutenant, the Archbishop passed the time before dinner was announced by paring his nails with a pocket scissors and sitting down and stretching his legs on to the mantelpiece, which was covered with Lady Anglesey's precious china. He was extremely fidgety. People who invited him into their homes could expect their chairs to be shattered by his energy in whirling them on their legs. The Lord Lieutenant lost six in this way. Dr. Whateley's attendance at the National Education Board at Antrim House wore a hole in the carpet. Throughout an evening's entertainment his restlessness would be unceasing. 'We were all surprised,' wrote a correspondent, 'at the strange way he had of raising his right leg and foot, doubling it back over the thigh of the left one, and grasping his instep with both hands as though he were strangling some ugly animal. He did this repeatedly during the evening, especially while telling some good stories to which he did ample justice, and during the process the foot thus raised, or rather strangled, was almost on the lap of Provost Lloyd on whose right hand side the Archbishop sat. I can never forget the Chesterfield suavity of the Provost's face, while his fine small black clothing was thus subjected to the treatment of a footmat.'

At a Privy Council meeting Chief Justice Doherty put his hand into his pocket for his handkerchief and found the Archbishop's foot planted there. Often at these meetings Dr. Whateley used to stand before the fire with his coat-tails separated and pulled forward. Once, while he stood like this, an observer, noting that a peer had put on his hat over his bald head for warmth, remarked: 'A bishop keeps uncovered what ought to be covered, and a peer keeps covered what ought to be uncovered.'

He disliked armchairs because they impeded the movements of his arms. His other dislikes included a broken-up countryside, stiff collars, starch, tight garments of all kinds and people with wrongly-shaped heads. For one flat-topped example he proposed 'a new phrenological test . . . take a handful of peas, drop them on the head of a patient; the amount of the man's dishonesty will depend on the number which remain there. If a large number remain, tell the butler to lock up the plate.'

It must be said the he himself was disliked by numerous people, partly because of his odd manners, but largely because he was an Englishman. The government had continued the malpractice of appointing its own nominees to the highest positions in the Church of Ireland. Unlike the Earl of Bristol, Dr. Whateley made little attempt to understand Ireland or enthuse about it. He remained a stranger. On one occasion he directed every parish church and Sunday School in his diocese to sing the hymn that opens:

> I thank the goodness and the grace
> That on my birth hath smiled
> And made me in these Christian days
> A happy English child.

'Dr. Whateley led a life entirely apart—in a measure solitary,' wrote Percy Fitzgerald harshly. 'He conveyed the idea of an uncongenial being, quite disgusted with his banishment. This was conspicuous in his soured face and lean figure, and more especially in his sneering speeches and sarcasms at the natives and their country, which were constantly circulated.' Fitzgerald never came to terms with Whateley's donnish mannerisms and Anglo-Saxon peculiarities, including a fondness for schoolboy conundrums, which may have contributed to his unpopularity.

Q. Why can a man never starve in the desert?

A. Because he can eat all the sand which is there.

Q. But what brought the sandwiches there?

A. Noah sent Ham, and his descendants mustered and bred.

In spite of his uncompromisingly English eccentricities, the tall awkward figure with his dogs (usually of an English breed) is remembered with Stephen's Green as a background for his frolicsome behaviour—not Christ Church Meadows. In Oxford his antics would not have been out of place; in Ireland many found them incomprehensible.

*   *   *

Joshua Jacob, who founded a sect known as the White Quakers, was born about 1805 in Clonmel, a member of a Quaker family. After some years in an uninspiring business career which included commerce in Limerick and running a teashop in Dublin, he set up his own Society of Quakers, which sought to revive the spirit of the very early days of the Movement. The White Quakers assembled at their first yearly meeting in Dublin on May 1, 1843. Their nickname was suggested because they readopted the practice of wearing undyed garments, believing that any clothes but the plainest and most unadorned were emblems of sin. This followed the example of a Quaker named John Woolman, who wore an undyed suit of clothing in 1702 for the same reason.

Even in the seventeenth century Margaret Fox, the widow of George Fox, had condemned those who stressed the importance of rigid conformity in wearing apparel. She protested how 'we must look at no colour, nor make anything that is changeable colours as the hills are . . . but we must be in one dress and one colour. This is a silly poor gospel. It is more fit for us to be covered with God's eternal spirit and clothed with his eternal light . . .' Quakers of that period had exaggerated the strength of their convictions; but two hundred years later Friends who had abandoned their shovel hats and had turned their attention to successful commercial enterprises recalled with embarrassment the behaviour of men like Solomon Eccles (later imprisoned in Ireland). Eccles had destroyed his musical instruments and run naked through the City of London bearing a burning brazier on his long hair and crying, 'Woe unto the bloody city!' It was precisely this sort of passion that had motivated their forebears that the White Quakers tried to revive. Having begun by dressing themselves as plainly as possible, they logically extended the ideas of John Woolman and others by organizing a much-publicized nude procession through the streets of Dublin. They imitated Solomon Eccles, not only by streaking, but in their destruction of anything ornamental or pleasure-giving. Joshua particularly condemned newspapers, bells, clocks and watches. They deplored the cupidity of shopkeepers, comparing them to rotten apples, and demanding, 'Let therefore the trader class be no more!' It was not surprising that they disliked orthodox Quakers, whom they called 'Black Quakers', 'who, professing to be too scrupulous to take an oath, declare that which they know in their hearts in the sight of God to be utterly false, ungrounded and a malicious fabrication of their own'. They attacked individual Friends. 'A Samuel Pim of Mountmellick came into the court of the prison,' wrote Joshua in 1842. (He had been locked up for misappropriating funds derived from the property of orphans.) 'But his guilty conscience kept him at a distance from me . . . as if the people are aware of his wicked spirit, they ran, saying, "He is a Black Quaker!" '

The principal stations of the sect were at Dublin, Clonmel, Waterford and Mountmellick which was the birthplace of Abigail Beal, Joshua's wife. She was also of Quaker stock—Mountmellick had begun as a Quaker settlement—and had been a founder member of the sect. Its beliefs were set forth in 1843 in a series of tracts entitled 'The Progress of Truth'. 'The last trumpet has sounded,' wrote the White Quaker, William Nonner, 'and the last vial of the indignation and the wrath of God is pouring out; the devil is like a roaring lion seeking out whom he may devour, knowing he has but a short time, the last effort of a dying monster is very great.' Joshua himself paid particular attention to the interpretation of dreams. He had his first vision in Waterford on the 24th of the seventh month of 1842. 'This morning I was awoken as I thought with a loud noise saying these words: "It is the truth of God" accompanied by a bright appearance as a vivid flash of light.' From then on the dreams multiplied in intensity and obscurity. They became more general and secular, but Joshua continued to report them and search them for divine significance. One concerned his attendance in the boardroom of the Bank of Ireland, together with all its directors. Another relayed minutely the catching of a wild elephant on the quays of Clonmel. 'I took hold of a rope which was fastened to its legs,' Joshua wrote, 'it was gone so far as to leave but one coil of the rope which was fastened round the post in the ground to which I succeeded in securing the end of the rope; it was in a filthy state with mire and dirt. The post was newly modelled of cut limestone, instead of the simple ones formerly used by the boatmen.'

About 1849 the White Quakers retired to Newlands, a large country house near Dublin, once the home of the murdered Lord Kilwarden. Here they set up a conventional sort of commune which abstained from eating meat and lived largely on bread made from bruised corn. But communes are fragile, and this one did not survive for very long. With the break-up of the community at Newlands, the sect dispersed. When Abigail died, Joshua abandoned all his old principles by going back into business, a betrayal as abrupt as Perrot's had been. He chose a Catholic as his second wife and allowed their children to be brought up as Catholics. But when he died on February 15, 1877, he was buried beside Abigail in a plot they had bought together and fitted with a monument whose bas-relief was emblematic of the purity of their faith.

*   *   *

The hold that religion came to have on George Bernard Shaw's uncle, William Shaw, was vividly described by G.B.S. himself.

'In early manhood he was not only an inveterate smoker, but so insistent a toper that a man who made a bet that he would produce Barney Shaw sober, and knocked him up at six in the morning with the object, lost his bet. But this might have happened to any common drunkard. What gave the peculiar Shaw finish and humour to the case was that my uncle suddenly and instantly gave up smoking and drinking at one blow, and devoted himself to his accomplishment of playing the ophicleide. In this harmless and gentle pursuit he continued, a blameless old bachelor for many years, and then, to the amazement of Dublin, renounced the ophicleide and all its works and married a lady of distinguished social position and great piety. She declined, naturally, to have anything to do with us; and as far as I know, treated the rest of the family in the same way. Anyhow, I never saw her, and only saw my uncle furtively by the roadside after his marriage, where he would make hopeless attempts to save me, in the pious sense of the word, not, perhaps, without some secret Shavian enjoyment of the irreverent pleasantries with which I scattered my path to perdition. He was reputed to sit with a Bible on his knees, and an opera glass to his eyes, watching the ladies' bathing place in Dalkey; and my sister, who was a swimmer, confirmed this gossip as far as the opera glass was concerned.

'But this was only the prelude to a very singular conclusion, or rather catastrophe. The fantastic imagery of the Bible so gained on my uncle that he took off his boots, explaining that he expected to be taken up to heaven at any moment like Elijah, and that he felt that his boots would impede his celestial flight. He then went a step further, and hung his room with all the white fabrics he could lay hands on, alleging he was the Holy Ghost. At last he became silent, and remained so to the end. His wife, warned that his harmless fancies might change to dangerous ones, had him removed to a private asylum in the north of Dublin. My father thought that a musical appeal might prevail with him, and went in search of the ophicleide. But it was nowhere to be found. He took a flute to the asylum instead; for every Shaw of that generation seemed able to play any wind instrument at sight. My uncle, still obstinately mute, contemplated the flute for a while, and then played "Home Sweet Home" on it. My father had to be content with this small success, as nothing more could be got out of his brother. A day or two later, my uncle, impatient for heaven, resolved, to expedite his arrival there. Every possible weapon had been carefully removed from his reach; but his custodians reckoned without the Shavian originality. They had left him somehow within reach of a carpet-bag. He put his head into it and in a strenuous effort to decapitate or strangle himself by closing it on his neck, perished of heart failure. I should be glad to believe that, like Elijah, he got the heavenly reward he sought; for he was a fine upstanding man and a gentle creature, nobody's enemy but his own, as the saying is.'

Spenders and Spongers

ACCORDING to Oliver Goldsmith, the Anglo-Irish acquired a taste for prodigality 'by long conversation with the original natives'. Nearly all eighteenth-century visitors to Ireland commented upon the liberality of Irish squires and townsmen. 'The Irish gentry,' noted John Loveday, the antiquary, who toured the country in 1732, 'are an expensive people, they live in ye most open hospitable manner, continually feasting with one another.' Mrs. Delaney wrote in 1731 how 'the people of this country don't seem solicitous of having good dwellings or more furniture than is absolutely necessary—hardly so much, but they make it up in eating and drinking! I have not seen less than fourteen dishes of meat for dinner and seven for supper during my peregrination'. The English playwright, Richard Cumberland, emphasized the prodigious scenes of hospitality and the mixing of all classes. When he dined out in Dublin, 'I found myself in a company so miscellaneously and whimsically classed that it looked more like a fortuitous concourse of oddities jumbled together from all ranks, orders and descriptions than the effect of invitation and design'. His host, George Faulkner, 'gave good meat and excellent claret in abundance; I sat at his table once from dinner till two in the morning, while George swallowed immense potations with one strawberry at the bottom of the glass, which he said was recommended to him by his doctor for its cooling properties'.

Cumberland spent some time in Galway, where his uncle had been brought over from England in the usual way to become Bishop of Clonfert. One of his neighbours was Lord Eyre, who lived not far from Clonfert in a magnificent house whose ruins are still to be seen. Lord Eyre, 'pretty far advanced in age was so correctly indigenous as never to have been out of Ireland in his life, and not so often from Eyrecourt. Proprietor of a vast extent of soil, not very productive, and inhabiting a spacious mansion not in the best repair, he lived according to the style of the country, with more hospitality than elegance, and whilst his table groaned with abundance, the order and taste of its arrangments was little thought of. The slaughtered ox was hung up whole, and the servitor supplied himself with his dole of flesh sliced off the carcase. His Lordship's day was so appointed as to give the afternoon by much the longest share of it, during which from the early dinner to the hour of rest, he never left the chair, nor did the claret ever quit the table . . . he lived in enviable independence as to reading, and of course he had no books. Not one of the windows of his castle was made to open but luckily he had no liking for fresh air, and the consequence may be better conceived than described.' He still found time, presumably in the morning, for boating on the Shannon and attending to his horses and fighting cocks, which he described as 'the cracks of Ireland'.

Lord Eyre was succeeded by his nephew, Giles Eyre, the original of Lever's Charles O'Malley.

> The King of Oude
> Is mighty proud
> And so were once the ceaysars;
> But ould Giles Eyre
> Would make them stare
> Av he had them with 'the Blazers!'
> He's only a Prince in a small way,
> And knows nothing at all
> Of a six foot wall,
> Oh, he'll never do for Galway!

Perhaps the lack of books at Eyrecourt rendered Giles Eyre illiterate. On one occasion as Colonel of his regiment he received a letter while sitting in the mess. His neighbour, noticing him putting it away in his pocket, told him: 'Stand not upon ceremony, Colonel dear, pray read your letter.' 'Read a letter? Well, you may say read a letter, my dear Captain; but that's not so easy for a man that never learnt to read.' But he could write his name, and he put it, so Lord Gort said, to as many bonds as would thatch Lough Cutra Castle. On £20,000 a year he was able to exceed the imperious discomfort that his uncle had maintained. The stables at Eyrecourt housed between thirty and forty horses, and more than seventy hounds whose howling disturbed the worshippers in the nearby church. (The rector never complained since he had sons for whom he hoped to obtain preferment.) Outside the front door of the house lay a plate of money from which beggars could help themselves, while inside the hospitality was on a princely scale. One of Giles Eyre's extravagances was an election campaign on which he spent £80,000 and then failed to gain the seat. By the time he died he had got through his fortune.

His cousin, Ned Eyre, was equally rich and equally improvident. Another cousin, Dorothea Herbert, had much to say in her Memoirs about Ned and his sister, Mrs. White. (As a girl Mrs. White had been confirmed; 'she was so vexed at being forced to take all her Sins on herself that She stuck her Head full of Iron Pins with the Points up to annoy the Bishop who was terribly Scratched and torn when he laid his hands on his Contumelious Disciple.')

Ned Eyre left Galway as a young man and came to Co. Waterford, where he bought himself a place called Linville near Dorothea's family home at Carrick-on-Suir. At Linville, where he lived with his two constant companions, a pair of spotted labradors whom he called Miss Dapper and Miss Kitsey and treated as his daughters and co-heiresses, he became increasingly absorbed in his peculiar régime of behaviour. Dorothea thought him 'One of the greatest Oddities that Nature or Art ever produced; I say Art, because he studied every possible method to make himself different from Other human Beings'. His clothes were very striking . . . 'of Gayest Colour, Silk or Sattin lined with Persian of a different colour—he wore Sattin shoes and Jet Buckles and had two or three sets of paste Buttons that cost an immensity—His Hair was dressed like a woman's over a Rouleau or Tête, which was then the fashion amongst the Ladies—he sometimes carried a muff, sometimes a fan, and was always painted to the Eyes with the deepest Carmine.' His diet consisted of tea and cold water, sweetmeats and pickles.

He spent most of his time planning 'some ludicrous exploit or excursion and spared no expense in its execution'. Dorothea described in detail a trip taken by herself and her sisters with Ned to Galway and Loughrea Races. They all set off in Ned's specially designed glass coach with the two dogs, various equipages and a cavalcade of servants. Ned was elaborately dressed as a woman.

On arriving in Galway he decided that he must see the remains of his great-aunt. Her vault had to be opened, the coffin lid raised and some of her dust taken away. Such impiety did not pass unnoticed, and a hostile crowd collected, which Ned placated by inviting 'all the Beggars of Galway' to hot toast, tea and chocolate. The invitation had to be repeated and Dorothea complained that 'we had a Publick Breakfast every morning where Myriads attended'.

Ned's other antics in Galway included dressing up one of his hands as a baby to amuse a nurse and child who lived on the opposite side of the street; getting rid of a crowd by sticking out his tongue at it; and loading up the carriage at Loughrea Races with peaches and apricots specially for Miss Dapper now ennobled as Lady Dapper. On the return home to Waterford the carriage was filled with Galway fish—'which soon stank so abominable that there was no bearing it'.

His habits were expensive and money flowed through his hands like water through a net. 'Every year he bought 200 pounds worth of Lottery Tickets though he seldom or ever got a prize of any value.' In spite of his great fortune, he was always in debt, so that by the time he died most of it was gone. This circumstance was suffered by many spenders and generous hosts in particular. Arthur Young was told of a neighbour of Lord Longford whose hospitality 'was unbounded, and it never for a moment came into his head to make any provision for feeding the people he had brought into his house. While credit was to be had, his butler or housekeeper did this for him; his own attention was given solely to the cellar that wine might not be wanting. If claret was secured, with a dead ox or sheep hanging in the slaughterhouse ready for steaks or cutlets, he thought all was well. He was never without company in the house, and with a large party in it would invite another of twice the number. One day the cook came into the breakfast parlour before all the company: "Sir, there's no coals." "Then burn turf." "Sir, there's no turf." "Then cut down a tree." This was a forlorn hope, for in all probability he must have gone three miles to find one, all round the house being long ago safely swept away.'

It was possible, however, to be known for elaborate hospitality and yet not have to get rid of one's whole fortune. A more systematic approach to the problem was worked out by Thomas Mathew of Thomastown Castle, Co. Tipperary, who as a young man decided to devote his life to entertaining his friends. Young Mr. Mathew, the father of the Earl of Landaff, and also the ancestor of Father Mathew, the Apostle of Temperance, was good-looking, widely travelled, an excellent swordsman, and quite wealthy, having inherited an income of around £10,000 a year. But he did not consider this adequate for his princely ideas, so he embarked on a vigorous savings campaign, going abroad for seven years to live in voluntary exile on a meagre income of £600 a year.

When he returned to Ireland, having saved enough money, he set about turning his house into what was virtually a free luxury hotel for his friends. There were forty separate compartments to house them, and every comfort and distraction he could think of in order to make their stay pleasant. A coffee house where they could take breakfast at any hour of the day was furnished in exactly the same manner as a Dublin counterpart, with chessboards and backgammon tables, newspapers and periodicals. Coffee houses were not unknown in large mansions—there was one at Castletown—but few rich hosts went to the trouble of providing a tavern such as Mr. Mathew constructed at one end of Thomastown. Although he seldom drank himself, he had no wish to impose his habits on others. The tavern carefully echoed the preferences of the time with its variety of drink, its billiard room and blue-aproned waiters. Here guests could retire after dinner for an evening's conviviality. If they were sportsmen they might avail themselves of the free fishing and shooting, their guns and rods supplied by Mr. Mathew, or hunt behind one of his two packs. The less energetic could enjoy the gardens around the house and the thousands of acres of deerpark beyond.

With all this opulence Mathew might have been tempted to see himself in the role of grand patron or society host. But this was not the case. His friends were merely those whose company he enjoyed; he chose those 'most comfortable to his taste, inviting them to pass such leisure time as they might have upon their hands at Thomastown'. No efforts were made to encourage them to shine or be brilliant. The only celebrity that he seems to have lured to Thomastown was Swift.

Newly arrived guests were greeted by their host and brought immediately to their apartments. 'This is your castle,' they would be told. 'Here you are to command as absolutely as in your own house; you may breakfast, dine and sup here whenever you please, and invite such of the guests to accompany you as may be most agreeable to you.' He then showed them the common parlour, where, he said, 'a daily ordinary' was kept at which meals were served at any time to those guests who preferred dining in general company. No rules about seating or rank applied. Mathew would give one stipulation: 'From this moment you are never to know me as master of the house, and only to consider me as one of the guests.'

This Haroun al Raschid gesture and a total ban on all forms of gambling were the only strictures he imposed on visitors. The other 'hidden' requirement was that they should enjoy themselves. To help them Mathew got up early every morning so that details of organization would be in order before daybreak. By cockcrow the castle would be gleamingly awake, with the horses groomed and fed, tables laid out for coffee and fires lit. Each guest-room had its appointed servant; these servants would assemble in a special great hall whose walls were lined with numbered bells which jangled when the sleepy visitors upstairs pulled the ropes to summon their breakfast or their shaving water. Mathew absolutely forbade any of his staff to accept tips on the pain of instant dismissal; instead he topped up their wages to the appropriate amounts.

In his *Life of Dean Swift* Thomas Sheridan described Swift's visit to Thomastown. Invited down with Sheridan and a relative of Mathew, the three were met at an inn by their host's private coach filled with wine and provisions. When the coach turned into the gates and the castle appeared to the travellers emerging from the avenue of trees, Swift asked, 'What in the name of God can be the use of such a vast building?' 'Why, Mr. Dean,' said Mr. Mathew's relation, 'there are no less than forty apartments for guests in that house, and all of them probably occupied at this time, except those which are reserved for us.'

Swift promptly told the coachman to turn round and drive back to Dublin, 'for he could not think of mixing with such a crowd'. Within the stalled coach on the avenue his two companions anxiously set about persuading him to change his mind, and after some eloquent pleading he yielded. ' "Well," said he afterwards suddenly, "there is no remedy, I must submit; but I have lost a fortnight in my life." '

The Dean was met at the door by Mathew, who showed him to his apartments where the cook and the butler appeared with the menu and wine list. ' "And is this really so . . . and may I command as in my own house?" Mr. Mathew assured him that he might, and that nothing could be more agreeable to the owner of the mansion than that all under his roof should live conforming only to their own inclinations without the least restraint. "Well then," said Swift, " I invite you and Dr. Sheridan to be my guests while I stay, for I think I shall hardly be tempted to mix with the mob below." '

But again he changed his mind. Intrigued by reports of the entertainment beneath him, the touchy Dean emerged from his chamber after only four days of voluntary exile and joined the main party.

'And now ladies and gentlemen,' he addressed the company before dinner. 'I am come to live among you, and it shall be no fault of mine if we do not pass our time agreeably.' Sheridan's pleasant anecdote concludes with the information that the two weeks' torture originally envisaged lengthened into a four months' stay at Thomastown.

Mathew's contemporaries considered him 'near insane'. But his extravagance was combined with a business sense of getting value for money. It did not matter that his income was spent on so ephemeral a project; he still laboured like a hard-heeled hotelier solely to give pleasure. Unlike other spenders he husbanded his fortune and left it intact to his son.

Few spenders were as thoughtful, and the lamentable list of Irish rakes who dissipated their substance appears to be endless. Most respectable families included a gambler or two. The Edgeworths, for example, had an ancestor, Sir John Edgeworth, nicknamed 'The Prince of Puppies', who would bet on the length of a piece of straw. He was totally improvident, and once sold the ground plot of a house in Dublin to buy a fashionable 'high crowned hat and feathers'. Having lost his estates after James II's accession, he constantly petitioned the king for their return. 'Shall we never have done with the merits of Sir John Edgeworth?' the king complained. Once he absentmindedly presented the king with a letter from his wife, instead of the usual petition. The poor woman, who earlier had all her jewels lost at hazard, was in a state of penury. 'In the name of God, Sir John,' she had written, 'do you think I and my children can live upon the air, or can support such a numerous family?'

Sir John's grandson, Talbot Edgeworth, spent much of his adult life in the Eagle tavern in Exchequer Street pacing up and down a particular board which he had laid claim to. If anyone disputed its ownership with him, he would carefully write his name in a notebook and tell him that he would fight a duel with him —but only when he came of age. He disliked women; 'that they may see and die!' was his general comment on them. He found time away from the Eagle to spend his fortune on furniture for his house and on startling clothes in which he hoped to attract universal attention. For many years he was known for his finery and dashing appearance; but gradually his money ran out and his behaviour grew increasingly peculiar. Eccentricity is a luxury; the impoverished Talbot was certified as a lunatic and ended his days in the Bridewell.

One could become a spender without having the means, and pass a lifetime in financial destitution. The self-induced misery of the poet, Samuel Boyce, which lacked any of the pleasures of dissipation exasperated a wide circle of friends.

Boyce, born in 1708, was the son of a well-known dissenting minister, nicknamed by Dubliners Bishop Boyce. Young Sam went to school in Dublin and then to Glasgow University, where he married imprudently before he was twenty and was obliged to come back to Dublin to live off his father while he worked at being a poet. But Boyce senior died in 1728, and two years later Samuel returned to Edinburgh. A struggling poet usually sought some sort of patronage to help his career, but through a variety of motives—pride, touchiness and laziness—Boyce forfeited every opportunity that came his way of securing help from rich or influential patrons. Once, after writing an elegy entitled *The Tears of the Muses*, regretting the death of Viscountess Stormont, he was offered a sinecure in the Customs by her husband. The day fixed for securing the appointment was showery, and Boyce preferred to lose the job rather than get wet. After some bleak years in Edinburgh his debts forced him to leave Scotland; he went to London where he had been given a number of valuable introductions including a letter to Alexander Pope. When he called round to Pope's lodgings he happened to be out. He never called again.

'Considerations of prudence never entered the head of this unhappy young man,' wrote Theophilus Cibber, from whose *Lives of the Poets* comes most of the information we have about Boyce. Cibber disliked him: 'of all men the furtherest removed from a gentleman; he had no graces of person and fewer still of conversation.' His wife was written off as little more than a strumpet . . . 'and now her circumstances were reduced, her virtue did not improve'. In between indiscretions, Mrs. Boyce was kept constantly busy begging from a wide circle of embarrassed acquaintances whom Boyce considered had a duty to support him.

'You were pleased to give my wife the enclosed shilling,' he wrote to Sir Hans Sloane on February 14, 1738. 'I doubt not but you thought it a good one, but as it happened you will forgive the trouble engendered by the mistake.' Once Samuel Johnson collected on Boyce's behalf. 'The sum', he reported, 'was collected by sixpences at a time when to me sixpences were a serious consideration.' The money was supposed to redeem Boyce's clothes which were in pawn; but within two days they were in the pawnshop again.

His poverty did not prevent him producing quite a considerable body of poetry of which *The Deity*, published in 1749, was the best known. Its opening lines seem to have been heartfelt:

> From earth's low prospect and deceitful aims
> From wealth's allurements and ambition's dreams,
> The lover's raptures, and the hero's views,
> All the false joys mistaken man pursues,
> The schemes of science, the delights of wine,
> Or the more pleasing follies of the nine . . .

Other works included a modern version of Chaucer and *An Historical Review of the Transactions of Europe 1739–47*, published in two volumes. He was paid ten guineas by Robert Walpole for an ode in the manner of Spenser, three pence a line for his work on Chaucer, and for numerous articles he wrote for the *Gentleman's Magazine* received payment by the hundred lines. With proper management and economy this irregular income might have been sufficient to allow him to live comfortably. '[But] can it be believed,' wrote Cibber, 'that often when he received half a guinea in consequence of a supplicating letter, he would go to a tavern, order a supper to be prepared, drink of the richest wines and spend all the money that had just been given him on charity, without having anyone to participate the regale with him, and while his wife and child were starving at home.'

When the begging letters failed he had to resort to subterfuge. He would propose subscriptions to poems in which he had only written the beginning and end. On several occasions he sent out his wife to circulate the news that he was dying in the hope she might squeeze a widow's mite out of his acquaintances.

In 1740 his financial troubles came to a head. The letters were unproductive and clothes that had been pawned could not be redeemed.

The poet lay in bed under a single blanket; even his sheets had been carried off to the pawnbroker. He still had means of earning some sort of living, since he was writing for magazines. He sat up in bed with the blanket wrapped round him, having cut a hole large enough to thrust his arm through to write on the paper he held on his knee. Then he invented a paper collar and shirt. It was a fairly rudimentary garment, consisting of paper slips he had cut out and arranged around his neck and wrists. Wearing a coat over them—he had no breeches—he sometimes visited friends and shocked any ladies who happened to be present.

A friend redeemed his clothes so that he was able to lead a more normal life. The begging letters continued.

'Sir,' went a particular appeal to Mr. Cave, the Editor of the *Gentleman's Magazine*, addressed from the Crown Coffee House on July 21, 1742, 'I wrote to you yesterday about my unhappy case. I am at every moment threatened to be turned out here, because I have not money to pay for my bed two nights past, which is usually paid beforehand, and I am loath to go to the Compter till I can see if my affair can possibly be made up; I hope therefore you will have the humanity to send me half a guinea in support till I finish your papers in my hands . . . I humbly await your answer, having not tasted anything since Tuesday evening I came here, and my coat will be taken off my back for the charge of the bed, so that I may go into prison naked, which is too shocking for me to think of.'

As the years passed his financial position did not improve. 'My salary is wretchedly small (half a guinea a week),' he wrote to another patron, 'both for writing the history and correcting the Press—all I sigh for is a settlement with some degree of independence for my last stage of life.' It was never to happen.

In 1745 his wife died. He had no money to go into mourning for her, but bought a small length of black ribbon for their dog to wear. He soon married again, and four years later, in May 1749, died himself at the age of forty-one. There are different accounts of the event, including one in which he became involved in a brawl with some soldiers, and another, more romantic, having him die a poet, quill in hand, lying in bed composing a poem.

No one would pay for his funeral. Even the warm-hearted Samuel Johnson, who had suggested a final round of the hat to save Sam Boyce from a pauper burial, was unwilling to go to the whole expense himself. A Mr. Stewart from Edinburgh, who canvassed possible contributors, had to report that he 'has quite tired out his friends in his lifetime, and the general answer that I received was that such a contribution was of no service to him, for it was a matter of no importance how or where he was buried'.

His burial had just a little more distinction than that of other paupers, since a separate funeral service was held over him. 'Such was the miserable end of poor Sam,' wrote Cibber, 'who was obliged to be buried in the same charitable manner as his first wife, a burial of which he often mentioned in abhorrence.' Ryan, who in his *Worthies of Ireland* wrote of Boyce's 'unfeeling contempt and ingratitude' and diagnosed his troubles as due to 'general indolence and idleness', concluded that 'men of genius have no right to expect more favourable consequence from impudence and vice than what are common to the mass of mankind'.

Thomas Dermody was another poet who wallowed in poverty and abused his patrons. A natural admirer of Boyce, he wrote sympathetically about his condition:

> In a dark garret where the biting cold
> No cheerful hearth allays, poor Boyce behold!
> A blanket skewere'd his shivering shoulders wears,
> Outrageous hunger at his vitals tears,
> Not one dry crust his tuneful toil requites:
> Yet e'en in famished misery he writes!

Dermody, who was hailed as another Chatterton, wrote passable verse as a small child. Unfortunately his régime of dissipation also started when he was very young, and he is said to have been an alcoholic by the time he was ten. His father, a schoolmaster in Ennis, Co. Clare, was a drunkard, and his son's blatant lifelong lack of sobriety has been blamed on Dermody senior.

We are fortunate enough to have a detailed biography of young Dermody, written by a friend called John Raymond. He was born in Ennis in 1775 and began his classical education at four years of age. By nine he was helping his father teach Latin and Greek, at the same time finding that poetry poured out of him almost as easily as speech. One of his earliest poems survives, expressing his sorrow at the death of his brother from smallpox:

> What dire misfortune hovers o'er my head?
> Why hangs the salt dew on my aching eye?
> Why doth my bosom pant, so sad, so sore,
> That was full blithe before?

Soon after writing this lament he ran away from home, taking with him a couple of shillings, the second volume of *Tom Jones* and a spare shirt. After an adventurous journey on the dusty road from Clare to Dublin, he arrived in the capital, where he promptly sold the shirt. Then for a short time he wandered around the Dublin streets, one of the many homeless waifs with which the city abounded. But there must have been something appealing about this poor ragged young scholar. He was taken in by a locksmith called Lynch and soon afterwards met the first of his much-abused patrons, a Dr. Houlton, who encountered him in a bookshop reading a Greek text. The doctor saw 'a little country lowly boy, meanly habited and evidently not more than ten years old'. He was so impressed with his knowledge of the classics and ability as a poet that he took him home and encouraged him to perform for his friends. Dermody would recite *The Sensitive Linnet*, which he had composed on the road to Dublin, and discuss classical subjects. His favourite authors were Virgil and Horace, 'but he preferred the Georgics of the former to the Aeneid, and the Epistle and the Art of Poetry to any of his works . . .'

Ten weeks after the doctor had discovered the youthful classicist, he was obliged to move out of town, shutting up his house. However, he provided alternative accommodation and some money for the boy. But very soon Dermody was wandering on the streets again. Then he ran into an out-of-work scene painter named Coyle. 'He told me that he had slept four nights in the streets,'

Coyle said later, 'and had left his shirt for the payment of his lodgings. My wife released it and made a pallet bed on the floor; at which he was pleased and grateful.' Lack of clothes and the acquisition of new garments were to be a persistent theme of Dermody's career.

Coyle found a job in a Dublin theatre, and Dermody, although he considered labouring work beneath his dignity, was persuaded to help in various small tasks. Between them he found time to write a lampoon on the rival merits of two theatre managers. This found its way into the Green Room, where it caused a sensation among the actors. One of them, Robert Owenson, made it his business to enquire about the author, whom he found to be 'infantile in appearance and clad in the very garb of wretchedness; with a meagre half-starved but intelligent countenance; a coat much too large for him, and his shoulders and arms seen naked through it; without a waistcoat, shirt or stockings, with a pair of breeches made for a full-grown person, soiled and ragged, reaching to his ankles; his uncovered toes thrust through a pair of old slippers without heels'. Owenson offered him hospitality in his home and gave him some new clothes. Before putting them on Dermody decided to burn the old in a sacrificial rite, but at the last moment he snatched his breeches from the fire and wrote a poem to them.

> This practice all mankind pursue;
> To spurn the old and catch the new.
> Tis thus I cast you far away
> Who warmed me many a chilly day;
> Who kept me from the wind and weather,
> While all your parts were stitched together;
> But now when threadbare, thin and tattered,
> Take strangers who my pride had flattered.
> Yet though I cast you off like lumber,
> Your fame shall chime in jingling number.

Owenson had a relative named Dr. Young who was a senior fellow at Trinity. To him Dermody was sent bearing a poem on the history of the university which he had tossed off as a test of his abilities. Dr. Young, though surprised at his 'shivering, half-starved appearance', offered to supervise his studies and get him through Trinity. He presented him with some classical texts, including a book of Murray's logic. 'Sir,' said Dermody, 'I think I should not like this, for anyone of common sense and little knowledge can quibble without studying to quibble.'

Although his future seemed bright, he was drinking heavily. According to Raymond, 'this ill-fated boy was blind to the happy prospect before him and infatuated with his ruin'. He left the Owenson household, but managed to find another benefactor, the Reverend Gilbert Austin, who took him in and whom the young poet was soon placing among

> . . . proud patrons all so squeamish
> Who damn one for a single blemish.

Mr. Austin was so annoyed at this, that he banished Dermody to his kitchens. But meanwhile he had published his works at his own expense. 'The following collection of poems, it is hoped, will meet with the kind indulgence of the reader. They are all published with a view to obtain support and protection for youthful genius. The author has not yet reached his thirteenth year.' Dermody was, in fact, fourteen.

Ungratefully Dermody left Mr. Austin and returned to Owenson. He began to flit to and fro among different patrons. The Dowager Countess of Moira, to whom Owenson introduced him, ran a fashionable salon in Moira House. Her interest in the young poet resulted in a dramatic pastoral entitled *The Triumph of Gratitude*. Lady Moira went further than merely giving him a subsidy, and removed him from the temptations of the city far into the country at Killeigh, a village in King's County, about fifty miles from Dublin. Here she put him to board with another clergyman, the Reverend Mr. Boyd, while he prepared himself for the university. He stayed in Killeigh for two years, writing poems, stories and essays. At first he was content. 'It is from your bounty I breathe,' he wrote to the Countess, 'and your benevolence supplies the want of a father and mother.'

Soon, he began to find the restrictions imposed on him by

living with a clergyman were irksome. His attitude towards Lady Moira underwent a change. He wrote an essay entitled *The Old Bachelors* in which he aired his opinion of widows. 'A widow, I look upon as the most tremendous wild beast in creation. Her appetite is but whetted by transient enjoyment; her passion is a continual fire; and like the miser's, increases by acquirement.'

His letter of complaint was not very tactful either.

To the Right Honourable Lady Moira.

Your Ladyship generously sent me to school—here I could in the sincerity of my heart say much, but it is all over. Your Ladyship thought it best, I am assured; but in all my misery a year and a half so bitterly I never have passed. For God's sake let the 1st of March be my day of delivery, if ever I am to see the day so welcome.

And again:

The petition of poor Tom to the Right Honourable Lady Moira.
    Sheweth
    That your ladyship's fool
    Is too late at school;
    And needs not a rule
    To keep his head cool;
    For black bogs and mountains and wintry skies
    With some dozen of sighs
    Have made him so sad
    That he is, I'm sure, rather sorry than mad,
    And less witty than wise.

To Mr. Thomas Dermody at the Rev. Mr. Boyd's, Killeigh:

Lady Moira informs Mr. Dermody that Mr. Berwick (who is in the country) has transmitted to her a letter which Dermody had written to him, and she has also received that which Dermody had written to her; both letters indicating his desire and design to withdraw himself from Lady Moira's direction and consequent protection. Lady Moira makes not the least objection to that determination and has inclosed to Mr. Boyd ten guineas that he may enter upon his future schemes and follow his own pursuits not totally in a destitute condition.

Dermody soon spent the ten guineas so that he was again driven to seek out patrons old and new. Henry Grattan and Henry Flood both became interested in his plight, Flood suggesting that he should undertake a long poem in praise of the British constitution, which fortunately was never written. A Mr. White of Grafton Street gave him a guinea after finding him 'lying stretched on a flock pallet without curtains in a dark filthy garret; his shoes besmeared with mud (one of the soles quite gone, the other all broken), lying carelessly by the bedside, his stockings in the same condition and his poor feet all torn and bloody. No wonder . . . he had been at Bellevue, the seat of Mr. La Touche, a rough and stoney road of about sixteen Irish miles, and returned the same day.'

A Mr. Tighe mistook Dermody for a beggar and nearly thrashed him. When he realized his mistake, he gave him five guineas, a snuffbox, a snuff-coloured suit of clothes and a cocked hat, 'the eccentricities of which,' Raymond considered, 'surpassed that of ancient Pistol'. Dermody wore the outfit, although it was much too big for him, 'the breeches being tied below the calf of the leg, the waistcoat lapelled to his knees, the skirts of his coat dangling at his heels, and the hat with a significant and solemn slouch covering both ears'. Then everything was pawned, and again the poet was forced to peddle his rhymes around the countryside dressed in rags. He grew used to travelling barefoot and without stockings to great houses, where he was sometimes turned away at the gate, but often received a tip. Once he visited Grattan at Tinnahinch near Enniskerry, not quite as far as Bellevue from Dublin. The patriot gave him enough money for him to return to the city on a drunken spree. Raymond was woken at his house in Ranelagh to find the window panes being smashed with stones, while the whole neighbourhood, including a nearby nunnery, was woken by Dermody's shouts. He only escaped arrest after Raymond bribed the watch.

He managed to enjoy himself.

In a cold empty garret, contented I sit,
With no sparks to warm me but the sparks of old wit;
On a crazy black stool doleful ditties I sing
And poor as a beggar am blest as a king.

But he had to get money from somewhere.

To the Countess of Moira.
My Lady,
    In the hour of hopeless distress my only last plea must intrude
on you, to whose goodness I entirely owe the former part of
my existence. Spiritless, and overwhelmed by want, I am still
labouring to perfect my studies for the College examination,
assured that my permanent happiness can arise from that
quarter alone.

Lady Moira sent him half a crown.

To the Countess of Moira.
My Lady,
    Thankful for every former instance of your noble and gener-
ous favour, I cannot but wonder at receiving half a crown from
that hand which had bestowed many guineas.

Lord Kilwarden, the Attorney General, did everything in his
power to help him, arranging to pay his tuition and way through
Trinity. Dermody got drunk at his dinner table and then at the
last moment refused to go to College at all. He decided to go and
seek his fortune in England instead. He celebrated his departure in
a poem entitled *Farewell to Ireland*.

Rank nurse of nonsense; on whose thankless coast
The base weed thrives, the nobler bloom is lost;
Parent of pride and poverty, where dwell
Dullness and brogue and calumny,—farewell!

His first attempt to leave his native land proved unsuccessful
because a spate of bad weather prevented his ship from sailing.

It also gave him time to fall into the clutches of the press gang. He sent a desperate appeal to Mr. White, who came and found him in a tender on the Liffey 'with a crew of thoughtless dissolute mortals cooped up in the hold brooding over his misfortunes'. White managed to secure his release, but during the next few weeks Dermody incredibly managed to get himself impressed on two more occasions. Deciding fatalistically that 'as misfortune had hitherto marked him for her own, he was resolved to pursue his fate in other climes', he enlisted in a more orthodox manner and embarked for England on September 17, 1794 as a private in the Wagon Corps.

To the surprise of his old acquaintances he turned out to be an exemplary soldier, serving in a number of campaigns on the Continent and getting wounded twice. With the help of the Moira family he gained rapid promotion, and advanced to corporal, sergeant and finally second lieutenant.

When a truce was called with the French in 1801 he retired on half pay and settled in London, where he very soon reverted to his old habits which reduced him to his customary poverty. Raymond visited him and found that 'a settled melancholy had taken possession of his mind; and his careworn pallid countenance, disfigured by a wound which he had received in action, added to the meanness of his garments, for he was almost naked, exhibited him as in reality a picture of despair'.

New clothes, food, and a job with a London bookseller allowed Dermody to recover his spirits enough to compose a poem entitled *My Own Character*:

When first, I confess, lest you kindly mistake
I'm a compound extreme of the sage and the rake:
Abstracted, licentious, affected, heroic,
A poet, a soldier, a coxcomb, a stoic:
This moment, abstemious as faquir or bramin:
The next, Aristippus-like, swinishly cramming.

He continued to annoy those who offered him support. After he endured a spell in the Fleet Prison for debt Lord Moira refused to give him any more assistance. At the bookshop where he worked, a customer, a peer, asked him his opinion of a certain book.

'My lord, I have already read it; I found too little pleasure in the task to endure the fatigue of again wading through such a mass of dullness.'

'A fatal mistake,' Mr. Wright, the bookseller told him, 'you have forever lost a friend and patron—his lordship is the author!'

'Were the king the author, it is badly written!'

He was taken up by two brand-new patrons. A Mr. Johnson insisted on having him scrubbed clean and presented him with a fashionable suit accompanied by a frilled shirt. Sir James Bland Burges, a poet and baronet, took on the role abandoned by the Moira family. He gave him money and helped him to obtain ten guineas from a literary fund. Again Dermody proved tiresome. There was a cheque which he said he had lost but had in fact cashed, and the perpetual problem of vanishing clothes. He had received yet another suit from Burges, but soon afterwards appeared blind drunk at his house with a black eye, and a wound on his forehead, dressed in rags which were heavy with mud. Sir James refused him further assistance.

Raymond believed that part of Dermody's misfortune was that he was 'in a state of vassalage by unscrupulous friends' to whom he was in perpetual debt. He gives an interesting description of the lodgings where the poet held court. He lived in a garret owned by a cobbler, 'the pallet bed in one corner covered with vegetables, the fireside decorated with numerous pots of foaming porter, and the cobbler's work stool, boat-leg and lapstone used as seats'. Raymond was the most faithful of Dermody's friends and helped him long after most people had given him up. He also tried to reform him.

To John Raymond.
My dear friend,
    I have been most unhappy in incurring your just displeasure —I give you my honour, my oath, I will not taste a glass of intemperate liquor for these ten months to come.

Raymond, too, gave him a suit. Even so Dermody turned up at his house 'without either shoes, stockings, hat, neckcloth or waistcoat; and in a state of intoxication not to be endured'. After throwing down the pawn tickets for his clothes he shouted for something else to wear which Raymond refused to give him. He then 'swore a few oaths, threatened to destroy a sideboard of glass, alarmed the whole family, was turned out of doors, and during the remainder of the night took shelter in a shed fitted up for some cattle in one of the fields leading from Westminster to Chelsea'.

He became consumptive and his last letters were tragic.

'Whatever may have been my past errors and your just indignation,' he wrote to Burges, 'surely this will be softened by the appeal of extreme weakness and extreme sorrow. For two months I have suffered the most wracking torment from an asthmatic complaint without medical (nay, without common) assistance.'

Sometime in June 1802 he escaped his creditors and left London for an abandoned cottage near Sydenham in Kent. 'Pray my dear friend,' he appealed to Raymond, 'write to Lord Moira again: and it will be the last favour conferred on an unfortunate youth. I expect nothing but friendship from you at this fatal period, and therefore will not scruple to ask an extraordinary favour on my death bed. I am in want of everything.'

Raymond, accompanied by a Mr. Allingham, hurried down to Sydenham, where they found Dermody in a derelict house which was more suitable as 'a retreat for a horde of robbers than for a dying man'. There was a stool, some wood scattered on the floor, and a 'crazy bedstead' on which the poet lay beneath a leaking roof through which poured the wind and the rain.

By the time they got him proper rooms on Sydenham Common he was dead. He was buried in Lewisham Church under a tombstone on which Raymond and some of his other past friends inscribed THE FATE OF GENIUS.

Spending could bring the unwary to an even worse conclusion than that of Samuel Boyce and Thomas Dermody. Some years after Dermody's death an Irish traveller was visiting Constantinople. He crossed the Bosphorus to the great cemeteries at Scutari on the Asian shore where among the headstones and cypresses he was surprised to meet a European beggar. Such an encounter was extremely unusual before the days of hippies. Dressed in a tattered white gown and ragged turban the man approached him for alms in the Eastern manner. The traveller stared at the suppliant figure and his astonishment increased; he recognized him.

'Gracious God! Can it be?'

'Alas!' said the unfortunate, covering his face with his hands. 'It is too true. I am Mr. Norcott of the Irish bar.'

Here was the once prosperous Councillor William Norcott trying to live on Turkish charity. But how did he get to Turkey? What had transformed the 'fat, full-faced portly-looking person' that Barrington had known into this 'gaunt and hungry spectre'?

William Norcott, born about 1770, studied law in Trinity and became a barrister. He was an able lawyer, receiving his legal doctorship in 1808. But he had always preferred the gaiety of Dublin social life to anything connected with legal duties. 'The Councillor' was an accomplished guest, an excellent mimic, a free thinker and the writer of some satirical plays. He had learned to lose gracefully at games of piquet with the Duchess of Gordon. As a friend of the Duke of Richmond he was in demand at most of the levees and Castle entertainments. 'He could,' we are told, 'drink as stoutly as the Duke himself, touch the piano as well as a lady or gamble as deeply as any of the gentlemen.'

This last accomplishment was not a useful one. Norcott had the contemptuous attitude towards money shared by richer rakes, and allowed no consideration of prudence to interfere with his pleasures. The descent towards bankruptcy was swift and the day arrived when he found himself destitute.

'Thomas,' he told his servant, 'take one of these pistols and put it to my head; apply the other here, to my heart—fire both together and put me out of my pain—for die I will.' Thomas demurred, and Norcott, recalling the principle of duelling that 'no gentleman shall risk his life without a doctor present', faltered in his resolution.

He was still popular among his friends, a gentle entertaining companion who did not make too much of his misfortune. He preserved his 'full and ruddy cheek, and his glittering cheerful eye'. Among his wide acquaintance was John Wilson Croker, the friend of Wellington, who worked in the Admiralty in London and had co-produced some of Norcott's plays. Croker found him a decent job in Malta, a position which, it was hoped, would provide a short interlude before he was able to return to Ireland and the society that missed him there. But the decision to go so far in an attempt to become solvent proved fatal. Within a short time of taking up the appointment Norcott found himself in disgrace. The actual details are not known, but it seems that he gambled or accumulated private debts that he could not honour. He fled from Malta and went eastwards, disappearing from view.

Conflicting reports of his whereabouts trickled back to Ireland. Barrington heard that 'the last authentic account described him as selling rhubarb in the streets of Smyrna'. Then it was learned that he had arrived in Constantinople. One story had it that he was able to dress in the height of Turkish fashion and had even become a confidant of the Diwan. Barrington thought it unlikely that he was enjoying Turkish delights; selling rhubarb was not a lucrative trade. There was news, too, badly received at home, that he had 'renounced his religion with his hat'.

The truth was more appalling than any surmise. 'His dress was at once the emblem of apostasy and of want,' Sheil wrote in his *Calamities of the Irish Bar*. 'It hung in rags about a person which from a robust magnitude of frame had shrunk to a miserable diminution. He carried starvation in his cheeks, ghastliness and misery overspread his features, and despair was in his glazed and sunken eye.'

Poor Norcott had become not only a beggar, but a criminal; his debts in Turkey had mounted so that the authorities would not allow him to leave the country. His plight was conveyed in numerous letters to his Irish friends, described as 'most heart rending'. Then in 1820 an English traveller in Constantinople took pity on him and gave him funds with which to make his escape. Before his attempt he took 'the desperate step' of renouncing his new faith and reverting to Christianity. Unfortunately the Turks were keeping a close watch on the behaviour of this inconsistent vagabond, and noted the moment when he fled from the city. He had only gone a short distance when he was pursued and captured. He was decapitated on the shores of the Bosphorus and his body was thrown into the sea to join the thousands of others who had incurred the displeasure of the Sublime Porte.

There is always someone to moralize over the fate of the misguided and unfortunate. 'Norcott is dead,' wrote Barrington with asperity. 'He died a disgraced and blasphemous renegado; this confirms an observation of mine throughout life that a free thinker is ever disposed to be also a free actor, and is restrained from the gratification of all the vices only by those laws which provide a punishment for the commission.'

Men of Violence

THE eighteenth century in Ireland was an uneasy period marked by change, migration and speculation. It was overshadowed by the Penal Laws. There was an underlying discontent that would manifest itself in the savagery of 1798. For the Catholics the spirit of anarchy was, as always, linked with the past. The Rapparees were the latest in a line of heroes who were oppressed and betrayed; violence following naturally after the wars was justified in popular tradition. The new settlers had inherited a tradition for criminal violence manifest in the behaviour of the Confederate army and in the career of one of its members, the man from Clare, Captain Blood

> . . . who boldly hath run through
> More villainies than ever England knew,
> And ne'er to any friend he had was true.

The exploits of Blood set an example for years to follow. For economic and social reasons both the landed gentry and the landless Catholics found their lives monotonous, and they filled in time in their own way. The vogue for violence was manifested in the creation of abduction clubs and hellfire clubs, the deeds of bucks and rakes, the assaults of the pinkindindies and the riots in Dublin streets and theatres. It went several stages further than the excesses of Georgian England, and when fighting was refined and canalized in the rules of duelling, Irishmen fought more wildly than other gentlemen of Europe

Duelling was a craze that lasted a long time—from approximately the Battle of the Boyne to the Union. Swift noted it as a national vice and condemned it. It was a sport for the well-to-do as golf is now. Inns kept a special pair of duelling pistols in case forgetful travellers might need them.

Like a medieval knight, a man who aspired to being a duellist had to be a gentleman. 'Does he blaze?' 'Has he smelt powder?' were questions asked of a newcomer to society. An English traveller in 1790 noted that in Dublin duelling was 'much more prevalent than in any other city I ever visited'. Duels were fought to formal rules which varied locally until Galway's 'thirty-six commandments' were adopted throughout Ireland. They were meant to cover every eventuality. Duelling clubs had names like the Knights of Tara, and treasured family pistols might be called something like 'Sweet Lips' or 'The Darling'. One rapier in the Barrington family, which had run through a number of people, was christened 'Skivver the Pullet'.

In Trinity College, the Vice-Provost, Dr. Hodgkinson, advising an undergraduate on the best course of study, recommended: 'My young friend, practise four hours a day at Rigby's pistol gallery, and it will advance you to the woolsack faster than all the Fearnes and Chittys in the library.' 'Scarce a week passes,' wrote Dr. Patrick Duigenan, 'without a duel between some of the students; some of them have been slain, others maimed; the College Park is publicly made the place for learning the exercise of the pistol; shooting at marks by the gownsmen is every day a practice; the very chambers of the College frequently resound with the explosions of pistols.'

At one time the Lord Chancellor, the Chief Justice King's Bench, the Chief Justice Common Pleas, the Master of the Rolls and the Leader of the House of Commons had all fought one or more duels. The Judge of the Prerogative Court fought one barrister and 'frightened another on the ground'. The Right Honourable George Ogle fought Barney Coyle, a distiller, because he was a Papist. Richard Daly, who became manager of the Crow Theatre, fought sixteen times in two years. Duels were undertaken for the flimsiest reasons. Bryan Maguire, who practised his shots at a lighted candle held by his wife, used to throw dirt on the heads of passers-by in order to get a challenge. If they looked up he spat down at them and immediately offered the chance of satisfaction. Crow Ryan of Carrick-on-Suir challenged anyone who said 'boo' to him.

It is difficult to estimate the percentage of duels that ended badly. In Barrington's 'abridgement' of the 'two hundred and twenty-seven memorable and official duels . . . fought during my grand climacteric', he mentions a number of 'hits', but only one fatality, occurring when 'Counsellor O'Connell fought the Orange chieftain; fatal to the champion of Protestant ascendancy'. He adds, however, 'in my time the number of killed and wounded amongst the bar was very considerable. The other learned professions suffered much less'.

The gradual cessation of duelling ran parallel with the decline of abduction. Abduction clubs were a curious Irish phenomenon and a continuing nuisance to rich girls, who were literally pursued by penniless rakes whose motives were more often mercenary than lustful. They were undeterred by the fact that abduction was a capital crime. 'No gentleman or farmer felt himself safe,' wrote Walshe in his *Sketches of Ireland Sixty Years Ago*, 'who had a daughter entitled to a fortune.' Girls were seldom carried off for their beauty. A typical abduction was that of Mary Pike, kidnapped in 1797 by an adventurer named Sir Henry Hayes. She was described as 'homely' but heiress to 'a colossal fortune'. Taken to Sir Henry's house, struggling and kicking up the length of its long avenue, she was set down in his parlour and 'married by a man dressed as a parson'. She tore off the ring that was forced on her finger and hurled it across the room. Eventually Sir Henry gave up, and she returned unharmed to her parents. Barrington described how his aunt, Elizabeth Fitzgerald, a wealthy heiress, fought off twelve suitors who diced for her person. 'She would never grant her favours to man, but preserved her castle and her chastity to the last extreme.'

The unfortunate second Viscount Mountmorres, who was so affected by the troubles in Ireland that he shot himself in 1797, was said to have become deranged from an attempt at abduction that arose from an unhappy love affair twenty years previously. He paid court to a lady who declined him. Learning one morning that she was staying at a certain inn, he surprised her at breakfast and began to bundle her away towards his coach. Her cries brought her friends and servants down on his back, and he got a beating from which he never fully recovered. (Lord Mountmorres had an inflated idea of his powers as an orator. Once he wrote out a speech to be delivered in the Irish House of Lords, and before the debate took place handed a copy of it to the press. He had anticipated its reception by writing in the words, 'cheering', 'clapping' and 'wild applause', at strategic points in the margin. Although the speech was published, it was never delivered, since the debate was postponed.)

The behaviour of Lord Belvedere was contrary to the spirit of the abduction clubs. Robert Rochfort rose through the peerage largely through his own abilities. Born in 1708, he became a Baronet, and then Viscount, Belfield, and in 1757 was created first Earl of Belvedere. Meanwhile, in 1736 he married a sixteen-year-old girl who was cursed with a brutal father as well as a cruel husband. Mary, daughter of Viscount Molesworth, had great beauty and many accomplishments, but no fortune. The marriage was unnerving at the outset; the bridegroom's violent outbursts of rage so alarmed his wife that she escaped to her father's house, to be sent back to her husband the next morning. She settled down with him at Gaulstown, his gloomy residence where his grandfather had entertained Swift. They were reasonably happy, several children were born, and Lord Belfield began to build a beautiful villa six miles away overlooking Lough Ennell. He named it Belvedere. But he spent a good deal of his time in London, where he was ingratiating himself in the court of George II. It was while he was in England that he was sent anonymously a packet of compromising letters written between his wife and his brother, Arthur Rochfort, a married man with a large family. He returned to Gaulstown, where he confronted his wife with this evidence, and was said to have heard her detailed confession which included the admission that his last child was actually his nephew. 'My Lord thereupon locked her up,' wrote Lord Egmont in his gossipy diary. 'My Lord Belfield then went to Lord Molesworth and telling him his unfortunate case, asked his advice what he should do? My Lord replied he might do what he pleased; that having committed such a crime as incest and confest it, he should have no concern about, and the rather because she was only his bastard by his wife before he married her.' Lord Egmont speculated that she might be transported to the West Indies as a vagabond, but Lord Belfield's method of punishment was simpler. He imprisoned her in Gaulstown for thirty years. She had servants whom she could direct, although they were not allowed to speak to her. She could drive around the grounds, but not outside the estate. If she went walking in the garden, she was preceded by a silent footman who rang a bell to keep anyone from coming near. Twelve years after her confinement began, she escaped and made her way to her father's house in Dublin. He refused to admit her, and a day later she was back in her prison.

Her lover, Arthur Rochfort, had escaped to Yorkshire the same night that Lord Belfield had confronted her after hearing that he was threatening to shoot him. He spent some time in France before returning to Ireland fifteen years later, with the hope that his brother, now the Earl of Belvedere, would ignore him. It was a mistake. Lord Belvedere was unrelenting, and immediately had him arrested and charged with £20,000 damages for criminal conversation, a sum he was quite unable to pay. He was imprisoned in the Marshalsea where he died.

Lady Belvedere passed the years at Gaulstown attended by mute servants, never once receiving a visit from her family. Her beauty vanished as her hair became snowy white, while her haggard face wore a wild look and she scarcely spoke above a whisper. She is said to have formed the habit of wandering in the gallery gazing at the pictures as if she was conversing with them. Her husband lived comfortably in his new villa a mere six miles away, maintaining his hothouses at Gaulstown in the grounds where he permitted his wife to wander. From there he was supplied with luxuries for the sumptuous table he maintained at Belvedere. Sir James Caldwell, who visited him shortly before his death, commented on the luxury of Lord Belvedere's hospitality exhibited even to a small number of guests. 'Only think, for us four a complete service of plate, covers and all, two soups, two removes, nine and nine, a dessert in the highest taste, all sorts of wine, burgundy and champagne, a load of meat on the side table, four valets-de-chambre in laced clothes and seven or eight footmen. If the Lord Lieutenant had dined there, there could not have been more elegant entertainment.'

Sir James contrasted Lord Belvedere's 'debauchery and dissipation' with the pious household of his nephew, who lived near-by at a house called Rochfort, and regularly read the Psalms and the Bible after breakfast. Westmeath was dotted with Rochforts; Arthur had been within easy distance of his unhappy mistress, and another brother, George, had been established at Rochfort which was just beside Lough Ennell and within view of Belvedere. Lord Belvedere quarrelled with him to the extent that he could not bear to have his house within sight. Around 1760 he decided to build a sham ruin to block out the particular aspect which he considered belied the name of his residence. At great expense he imported a number of Italian artists to Westmeath to build a remarkable ruined abbey complete with Gothic windows to stand between him and his brother. It is known as the 'jealous wall'.

When he died in 1774 his son came to Gaulstown to release his mother, whom he found dressed in the fashions of thirty years before. 'Is the tyrant dead?' she whispered. She had become pious during her imprisonment; to entertain her, he took her to Rome where she became a Catholic. She had often protested her innocence during her lifetime, and did so for the last time on her death-bed.

Frederic Calvert, sixth Lord Baltimore, became notorious, over in London, when he widened the scope of abduction clubs by recruiting a harem. Baltimore, whose connections with Ireland were sufficiently remote for him to consider himself an English gentleman, had travelled to Turkey and observed the benefits of eastern customs. He wrote a book about the Levant and a collection of maxims entitled *The Wit and Wisdom of the East* which a critic unkindly considered 'no more deserved to be published than his bills on the road for post-horses'. At the same time he gathered ladies for his delight with the aid of two procuresses named Mrs. Harvey and Madame Griffenburg. He took them all with him on his trips abroad. Sometimes there were difficulties. When he arrived in Vienna accompanied by two negro eunuchs and eight women, the chief of police asked him to point out which was his wife. He replied that as an Englishman it was not his practice to discuss his sexual arrangements. If he could not settle the matter with his fists, he would set out instantly on his travels again.

Back in London he cast his bleary eye on Miss Sarah Woodcock during the winter of 1767. She was a young lady of impeccable virtue who worked in a milliner's shop. With the aid of Mrs. Harvey he had her kidnapped and brought to his house. Lord Baltimore's obese and jowly appearance, set off by a nightcap, helped to defend her virtue, and she held out for a week before being brought to his bed, 'her handkerchief wet with tears as if it had been dipped in water'. Later, her outraged family sued him. The word of an aristocrat is a powerful one, and Lord Baltimore, who conducted his own defence, managed to convince the jury that Miss Woodcock had enjoyed sitting on his knee and kissing him, and that she had been 'happy, cheerful and playful' in his house.

*   *   *

'Amongst the gents of the period,' wrote John Walsh, 'was a class called "Bucks" whose whole enjoyment and the business of whose life seemed to consist in eccentricity and violence.' Like the duellists and abductors, bucks faded away after the union when the conforming standards of the nineteenth century took over society. Before that there were scores of them, hovering round the gambling hells. Old taverns like the Eagle on Cork Hill, which were their venues for a long time, eventually became insufficient for their raffish needs, and at the end of the century had been augmented by smart new coffee houses like Lucas's in Exchequer Street and clubs like Daly's and Buck's Lodge.

The Irish branch of the Hell Fire Club was founded in 1735, fourteen years after its counterpart in England. Popular supposition associates it with the gaunt ruin on top of Montpelier Hill, and the odd black mass may have taken place in Mr. Connolly's airy shooting lodge. The club is supposed to have set fire to the place to give to give it a more hellish appearance, while the reputed burning of a lady in a barrel sounds like an outdoor occasion. But most of the antics of its members took place in somewhere like the Eagle; a Dublin tavern would have been more convenient for assemblies to drink Scultheen, the club's special mixture of whiskey and butter.

One member was the gallant Colonel St. Leger, whose admiration for the Duchess of Rutland went to the length of drinking down the water in which she had washed her hands.

'St. Leger,' said the Duke on one occasion, 'you are in luck. Her Grace washes her feet tonight, and you shall have another goblet for dinner.'

The most notorious member of the Club was Richard Parsons, the first Earl of Rosse, sorcerer, dabbler in black magic and, according to the historian, Gilbert, 'a man of humour and frolic'. He admired the rich mad Duchess of Albemarle, who preferred Lord Montagu because he humoured her belief that she was Empress of China by pretending to be the Emperor. Rosse wrote a poem:

> Insulting rival, never boast,
> No wonder if her heart was lost;
> Her senses first were gone . . .

When he was dying in 1741, his neighbour, a censorious cleric named Dean Madden, felt it his duty to write and remind him that he was a blasphemer, profligate, gamester, rioter, and other unpleasant things. Noting that the letter was merely headed 'My Lord', Rosse sent it on to the ultra-pious teetotaller, the Earl of Kildare.

There was a thriving Hell Fire Club in Limerick. A picture exists of its members, who included a woman called Celinda Blennerhassett. Dan Hayes wrote what was probably a deadly accurate description of its activities.

> Eternal scenes of riot, mirth and noise
> With all the thunder of the Nenagh boys

We laugh, we roar, the ceaseless bumpers fly
Till the sun purples o'er the morning sky;
And if unruly passions chance to rise
A willing wench the firgrove still supplies.

Before the advent of the Hellfire Club the Badger's Club had
provided entertainment for the first gentleman of Limerick.
O'Keefe has described the Grand Badger or President, a very old
gentleman who wore a high cap made of badger's skin over a
full powdered wig and sat in a special chair of state.

Limerick produced two famous bucks, the Child and the
Grand Bugle who both displayed contempt for the norms of
behaviour. The Child—otherwise known as the Frolic—was famous for his wild gallop round the walls of Londonderry during
which he jumped the steps at the four gates leading into the town.
On another occasion he turned a theatre performance into an orgy,
reserving two rows of seats for bottles of wine for his friends.
But the theatre was a place where rowdiness could be expected,
and the tendency of the audience to jump on the stage and mingle
with the actors was discouraged by a row of spikes running parallel
with the footlights. In 1787 the Duke of Leinster crippled himself
for life after being impaled on some of them. The more nimble-
footed often managed to pack the stage to the extent that actors
could not play their parts. The Grand Bugle, dressed always at the
height of French fashion, was an inveterate stage hopper; once he
not only joined the actors, but cut a large hole through an elaborate piece of stage scenery through which he regarded the house.
Away from the theatre he was well-known for his disgusting
table manners; from time to time he would prod a piece of beef
on two forks and throw it over his back for good luck. He died,
worn out by every form of dissipation, a debtor in Dublin's
Marshalsea prison.

Beauchamp Bagenal was said to be the handsomest man in
Ireland, who fought all before him and spent all he could muster.
He came from Co. Carlow, where he inherited the family estates
in 1752 at the age of eleven. Later, a high-spirited, good-looking,
wealthy, conceited young man, he made the Grand Tour and

turned it into a rout. The splendour of his travelling establishment eclipsed the households of the petty princes with whom he stayed, while his exploits during his travels became famous back home. Barrington described how he 'fought a prince, jilted a princess, intoxicated the Doge of Venice, carried off a Duchess from Madrid, scaled the walls of a convent in Lisbon, concluded his exploits with a duel at Paris; and returned to Ireland with a sovereign contempt for all continental men and manners, and an inveterate antipathy to all despotic kings and arbitrary governments'. The princess, a plain girl, daughter of the Grand Duke of Mecklenburgh-Strelitz, afterwards married George III of England.

When Bagenal returned to Ireland, he took up his duties as a conventional squire at his house at Dunleckney, Co. Carlow, where he enjoyed having large numbers of people to stay. He was an exacting host. The autocratic manner in which he ran what was virtually a court gave him the nickname of King Bagenal. On his dining table he kept a brace of pistols, one for tapping the barrel of claret, the other for dealing with any of his guests who failed to appreciate it.

Dunleckney provided lavish entertainment for 'all lovers of good wine, good horses, good dogs and good society'. The stud was famous, and the nervous guest might expect to have the best of thoroughbreds at his disposal. But he had to do full justice to the entertainment, and the resulting scenes after all-night dinner parties were lamentable. A clergyman, who spent the night in the park in order to avoid having to take his round, has left a description of the morning after. 'Such of the company who were still able, to walk had procured a flatbacked car on which they heaped the bodies of those who were insensible—then throwing a sheet over them, and illuminating them with candles like an Irish wake, some taking the shafts of the car and others pushing behind, and all setting up the Irish cry, the sensible survivors left their departed insensible friends at their respective homes.'

Later in life Bagenal became interested in the Volunteer movement and raised the first corps in Co. Carlow. Reviewing the Volunteers of Carlow and Kilkenny assembled before Dunleckney, he passed down the lines standing in his carriage with a bottle of claret in one hand and a large glass in the other. Instead of the traditional speech and harangue, he simply invited all the officers to join him in drinking a toast to the Volunteers and three cheers for Ireland. After the review the officers were invited into the house for a private ball while whiskey and claret were distributed to the men. Next morning the park was strewn with bottles, glasses and Volunteers sleeping it off.

Bagenal was not as violent as his reputation suggests. There is no indication that he actually killed any guests who resisted the wavering eye of his pistol and failed to accept another bumper. He fought about a dozen duels, a small number in comparison with such famous duellists as Hairtrigger Dick Martin or Fireball Macnamara. One was against his cousin, Bagenal Hervey, afterwards the tragic Commander-in-Chief of the Leinster rebel army. Bagenal allowed him to shoot first, before crying out: 'You damned young villain, you had liked to have killed your own godfather . . . I only wanted to try if you were brave . . . go to Dunleckney House and order breakfast and I will be there directly!' Another duel was against the Chief Secretary, Colonel Blacquiere, who showed great courage when Bagenal's pistol repeatedly misfired and the proceedings had to begin again each time.

Some duels took place in the churchyard at Killinane. Bagenal was lame—the result of an accident—and he liked to face his opponent leaning against a tombstone. His best-remembered fight took place after he discovered some of his neighbour's pigs rooting in his garden. He sent them back minus their ears and tails with a message to their owner, 'that if only he had a tail, he Bagenal, would sever it from his own dorsal extremity'. He told his friends, 'Now, if he's a gentleman he must burn powder after such a message as that!' His adversary was quite badly wounded. Bagenal faced him sitting in a chair. He was getting old. 'Time was,' he commented, 'that I would have risen before breakfast to fight at sunrise—but we cannot do these things at sixty.' He would not abandon his well-worn weapons completely. 'Rest upon your pistols, my boys,' he advised his guests somewhere around this time, 'occasions will rise in which the use of them is absolutely indispensable.'

His way of life left him the worse for wear. The Quaker, Mary Leadbetter, was at a friend's house, when he arrived declaring that of all things he loved Quakers. 'He entered on crutches having been lately hurt in a duel, and though disfigured by lameness and obscured by intoxication, the grace of his form and the beauty of his countenance were so conspicuous as to excite to no small degree the mingled sensations of admiration, pity and regret. He had entered the world with splendid gifts of nature and possessed a mind not unworthy of them, while drawn into the vortex of dissipation, his mind debased, his constitution shattered, his fortune impaired, he became the wreck which now appeared before us.'

Occasionally he surfaced to a life of responsibility. He was a popular landlord. 'Amongst the people he was beloved,' Barrington considered, 'amongst the gentry popular, and amongst the aristocracy he was dreaded.' He had acquired a seat in the Irish House of Commons early in life, and there he proved to be a liberal member, supporting an independent Parliament and a number of laws designed to bring relief to Catholics. He was also a good family man, although how his wife and children endured the chaos of Dunleckney seems remarkable. A final glimpse of him gives a contrast to the rake and shows that beneath the violent exterior there was a loving heart. He wrote this touching memorial on the tomb of his favourite granddaughter who died in 1800 at the age of thirteen:

'Nevertheless it may not be an unprofitable lesson to say something of her disposition, which was a ready, cheerful, unremitted wish to be of use, and she industriously contrived to be so oftener than anybody could expect, particularly to her grandfather, who through great gratitude and justice here declares that he believes that she was the best child he ever knew except her mother. They united in making life ever desirable to him, though labouring under great infirmity. The loss of such a one will be felt as long as one has feeling, but the recollection is left of every action and every expression of hers from the time she began to have sense to trust and be happy.'

When he died two years later, he was buried beside her.

*   *   *

The violent age culminated in horror in 1798. Of those who per-
petrated the cruelties that took place during the rebellion, some
figures stand out for terror and shame. Hunter Gowan rode into
the town of Gorey at the head of his yeomanry with the finger of
a dead rebel spiked on the tip of his sword, and used it later in
a public house to stir the punch for the officer's mess. The behaviour of the terrible smiling six-footer, Lieutenant Hepenstall, was,
according to Barrington, 'laughed at as the manifestation of
loyalty'. Barrington, who himself enjoyed cruelty with the relish
of an imperial Roman, described with distasteful detail how
Hepenstall would roam about seizing any stray peasant whom he
suspected might be a rebel. He would take off his silk cravat,
and with the aid of a companion use it to string up his victim
behind his back, after which he would 'trot about with his burden
like a jolting carthorse' until the man was dead. When he died
himself, someone wrote,

> Here lie the bones of Hepenstall,
> Judge, jury, gallows, rope and all.

That Hepenstall took the law on his own shoulders was not
altogether surprising. Law in Ireland had a poor reputation.
Judges were considered corrupt and cruel, more interested in
their own advancement than in any transmission of justice.
A number of Hogarthian figures dominated the courts, like
James Egan, a judge of Kilmainham, known as Venison Pasty,
'a huge, coarse-looking red-faced boisterous man'. The Chief
Justice, John Scott, Earl of Clonmell, was known as Copper-
faced Jack from his brazen ways of speaking and the unscrupulous
methods by which he was supposed to have earned his fortune. He
was widely believed to have held lands in trust for Catholics, who
until 1778 were not allowed to own property, and to have dis-
honoured their agreements. Like so many of his contemporaries
he was an experienced duellist, having fought, according to
Barrington, 'Lord Tyrawly (a Privy Councillor), Lord Landaff
and others'.

He wrote a diary which his family were indiscreet enough to
publish after his death. It was full of resolutions which he was

seldom able to keep. In 1774 he meant 'to give up wine and strive to contract my sleep to four hours or at the most six hours in the twenty-four'. A later resolve was to refrain from 'snuff, sleep, swearing, gross eating, sloth, malt liquors, indulgence—and never to take anything after tea but water or wine and water at night'. In vain . . . he grew steadily fatter, until before his death he had become so heavy that he was almost immobile and had to be carried to bed by his servants.

Perhaps his most poignant resolution was made six years after his appointment as Chief Justice of Ireland, when he determined '*seriously* to set about learning my profession'.

More sinister than Clonmell were Lord Clare and Lord Norbury. When Clare died the Dublin populace pelted his coffin with cats, while old Councillor Jeremiah Keeler spoke for many when he said: 'I shall certainly attend his funeral with the greatest pleasure imaginable.'

John Toler, later Lord Norbury, was Ireland's Judge Jeffreys. A contemporary described him as 'fat, podgy, with small grey cunning eyes, which ever sparkled with good humour and irrepressible fun, especially when he was passing sentence of death'. Like Lord Clare he was merciless, but his reputation arose from his particular combination of buffoonery and sadism. His sentences were usually harsh. (When dining with John Philpot Curran, they were served with some tough beef. 'You try it,' said Curran, 'then it will be well and truly hung.')

'What have we here?' he would address a wretch in chains. 'A young man in the flower of life. Yet the flower may never come to fruit.' Once when Curran rose to speak in defence of a client, an ass brayed outside the courthouse window. 'One at a time, please, Mr. Curran,' Norbury told him. 'It was no exaggeration to say,' reported Sheil, 'that the wildest farce upon the stage never raised more laughter than his exhibitions upon the bench, neither could any writer of dramatic drolleries who should undertake to draw him, embody the substantial absurdity of his character in any fictitious representation.'

He lived long (1745–1831) and flourished like the bay tree. Plain Mr. Toler who came from an impoverished family in

Tipperary, boasted that he started his legal career with £50 and a brace of hair-trigger duelling pistols. In 1776 he was elected M.P. for Tralee, and from that time he owed his rapid political advancement to his skill in supporting current government policy and the Protestant interest.

As a prosecuting lawyer he knew little about the law, but 'his whole bearing and aspect breathed a turbulent spirit of domination—a sort of sanguinary "fee, fa, fum" while the dilation of his nostrils and fierceness of his looks expressed . . . the scent of traitor's blood'. He was known as 'Puffendorf' from his habit of inflating his cheeks as he spoke. In 1798, a year after he had got his wife created a Baroness in her own right, he became Attorney General, and in this capacity prosecuted many leading rebels, including the Sheares brothers whom he lumped together as 'ostlers, bakers, carpenters and old clothes men'.

In 1800 in spite of the protestations of Lord Clare, who suggested he was more suited to be an archbishop than a judge, he was made Chief Justice of the Common Pleas and a Baron as a reward for supporting the Union.

'You have sold your country!' a woman heckled him.

'It is very lucky I have a country to sell,' replied his newly-created Lordship.

He tried Robert Emmet, who told him, 'My Lord, were it possible to collect all the blood that you have shed in a common reservoir—for great indeed it must be—your lordship might swim therein.' He was judge for twenty-seven years, presiding over what he himself called 'a racket house' and others described as the Court of Common Plays. His courts were notorious for their rowdiness and he created an environment where people came to watch in the same spirit as they went to the theatre. 'It is a matter of history,' wrote the *Gentleman's Magazine* in its obituary of him, 'that the court of Common Pleas of Dublin was thronged with idlers attracted by the amusement which was to be found— and the humorous conduct of its proceedings. The spirit of the judge naturally entered itself to the council, his principal auxiliaries were Messrs. Grady, Wallace, O'Connell and Gould, who played against each other and occasionally involved the court in a clamour.' In such an atmosphere scores of capital offences were tried. Norbury would enter into court with his grotesque waddle and place a few of his friends beside him on the bench to watch the proceedings. Among the best-known spectators was a mad-man named Toby McCormick, who made a point of attending Norbury's sessions to display his delusion that he and the judge had exchanged identities. He would shout 'Find for the Plaintiff!' after the charges were spoken and before he was hustled outside.

After all the jokes and shouting—Norbury had a stentorian voice—it was time for judgement and sentence. He would address long rambling speeches to the condemned, sprinkled with quota-tions from Milton and Shakespeare, 'flinging his judicial robe half aside, and sometimes casting off his wig'. A typical exhorta-tion was described as 'a wild harangue in which neither law, method or argument could be discovered. It generally consisted of narratives connected with the history of his early life'. He kept hangmen busy; once he sentenced ninety-seven men to death in a day.

Barrington describes an occasion when he was on circuit in Carlow, where he showed up in court 'having a great press of sentences to pass on rebels, etc.', wearing under his robe a costume he had previously put on to attend a masque given by Lady Castlereagh. The day was hot; Lord Norbury prematurely dis-carded his judicial gown and condemned the prisoners before him dressed in 'a green tabinet with mother of pearl buttons, striped yellow and black waistcoat and buff breeches'.

His one well-known act of clemency was towards a murderer whose guilt was indisputable. There was a gasp of astonishment in the court when he recommended the jury to bring in an acquit-tal. The crown prosecutor interrupted the proceedings to remind him that the evidence left no doubt that the man was guilty.

'I know all that, my good fellow,' Norbury replied in a stage whisper, 'but I hanged six men at last Tipperary assizes who were innocent, so I'll let off this poor devil now to square matters.'

Outside the courts he was sought after in company as a wit and a singer, who could deliver 'Black-eyed Susan' and 'Admiral Benbow' charmingly, as well as parts of many glees and catches.

His domestic arrangements were frugal and slovenly. He used to stuff his favourite chair with pieces of paper to augment the horse-hair. His decrepit study with its broken-down pieces of furniture and bookcases containing a few ancient books was described by Sheil. 'In the centre of the room lies a heap of old papers, covered with dust, mingled with political pamphlets written some forty years ago, together with an odd volume of the Irish Parliamentary Debates recording the speeches of Mr. Sergeant Toler . . . a couple of worn out saddles with rusty stirrups hang from the top of one of the bookcases, which are enveloped with cobwebs; and a long line of veteran boots of mouldy leather are arranged on the opposite side of the room. King William's picture stands on the chimney piece with prints of Eclipse and other celebrated racers.'

In court his legal reputation gradually declined further than could be thought possible. He became absent-minded. 'I have repeatedly seen him,' Barrington wrote, 'do things involuntarily which would have been impossible to have done if conscious at the time of his own actions. Though acute in general, he occas-sionally thought of so many things at once, that he lost all recollec-tion whether of place or circumstance.' He also showed a tendency to fall asleep in court. With increasing frequency the gross figure in his red robe trimmed with ermine would be heard snoring loudly through the presentation of a capital charge. Various moves were made to remove him from the bench, including a petition drawn up against him in 1825 by Daniel O'Connell, pointing out how he had slept during an important murder trial. None of the petitions was successful. The old wretch finally re-tired in 1827 at the age of eighty-two and received an Earldom. On his deathbed four years later, he heard that his neighbour, Lord Erne, was also dying. 'James,' he said to his manservant, 'run round to Lord Erne and tell him with my compliments that it will be a dead heat between us.'

George Robert Fitzgerald

GEORGE ROBERT FITZGERALD was a man of his time. 'This reckless duellist, this bold calculating murderer,' wrote a Victorian moralist, 'could not have lived and moved and had his horrid being in any other place or under any other circumstances than in Ireland before the close of the eighteenth century.'

His family was descended from the Desmond branch of the great Geraldine clan, which a century or so before his birth had been transplanted from their lands in Waterford to a forbidding patch of territory in Mayo. Here, west of the Shannon, they turned Protestant and ruled their new lands near Castlebar with the feudal spirit of their ancestors. One of George Robert's minor irritating traits was his tendency to boast about his illustrious pedigree. 'Head as I am of the House of Desmond,' he would repeat frequently, 'and as such most indubitably to be considered as the premier noble in the kingdom . . .'

In fact his father, George Fitzgerald, after serving as an officer in the Austrian army, became an average dissipated Connacht rake. The savagery that George Robert customarily displayed may have been in part inherited from him; but the panache which accompanied his cruelty must have owed something to his Hervey ancestry. His mother was Lady Mary Hervey, the sister of the Earl-Bishop of Derry, and undoubtedly she bequeathed volatile Hervey genes to her son.

She left her husband after five years marriage, quitting Ireland to return to her home in England, with her two infant sons. Before she met George Fitzgerald she had been a maid of honour to Princess Amelia, daughter of George II, and her experience in royal circles had given her a taste for cosmopolitan society.

In Mayo, her husband took a mistress whom his neighbours called a harlot. Much to local indignation she regularly sat beside him as he performed his duties as Judge of Assizes in Castlebar.

His two small boys, George Robert, born in 1748, and Charles Lionel, a year younger, meanwhile enjoyed every golden advantage of association with the English aristocracy. George Robert went to Eton, and when he was old enough, joined the army. He appeared to be a charming and suave young dandy, 'rather small in stature but elegantly made, and of very prepossessing countenance—he was polished to a fault in his address and very agreeable and sparkling in conversation.' But even at this time he had a reputation for bad temper. When someone dared to insult him for a wager and approached him in a coffee house muttering, 'I smell an Irishman!', Fitzgerald, replying, 'You shall never smell another!', took up a knife and cut off his nose.

Then his regiment was posted to Galway where he rediscovered his native land, and found it was the place for him. He could duel to his heart's content. He had already fought his first duel at the age of sixteen against an absent-minded Mr. French who forgot his powder horn and had to borrow his before firing commenced. In Galway an early duel against a sub-lieutenant in his regiment nearly killed him. When a bullet entered his skull, a surgeon had to trepan him; while Fitzgerald, semi-conscious and streaming with blood, implored him to spare his toupee. His father, informed that he was dying, was so upset that he ran through with his rapier a man who offered his condolences. But the son survived, scarred for life. After that he became adept at picking quarrels and provoking likely-looking opponents to issue challenges. In Dublin when the mood took him to fight, he would strike out at people or snatch at their rings and watches. Once he shot off a man's wig. If challenges were unforthcoming in coffee house or theatre, he would resort to standing in the middle of a narrow street crossing, waiting for someone of promising fighting material to jog him so that he could demand immediate satisfaction. He was an expert marksman who boasted that he could hit twenty tins one after the other at a distance of twelve feet apart; alternatively he could hit any part of the human body to a twelfth part of an inch.

In spite of his temperament he had a reputation for charm, and was considered 'gentle and engaging towards the female sex'. One of his Connemara neighbours and duelling opponents commented after his death how the 'elegant and gentlemanly appearance of this man contrasted with the savage treachery of his actions'. He courted and was accepted by a rich and beautiful girl, Jane Conolly, a sister of Thomas Conolly of Castletown. Although Conolly had married a daughter of the Duke of Leinster and had extensive estates in Ireland and England, he was still considered a parvenu, so that socially speaking Fitzgerald was an excellent match for his sister. But Conolly had heard enough about him to be horrified by the prospect of the marriage and tried every means in his power to part the lovers, including barring the door to his future brother-in-law.

Fitzgerald's persistence persuaded Conolly to change his mind and allow the marriage to take place in 1772. The young couple went on an extended honeymoon to France where they were able to make the most of the Hervey connections which gave them the entrée to Versailles and the court of Louis XV. Fitzgerald made his first appearance at court dressed in the height of fashion with his hat and sword knot studded with diamonds, diamonds on his shoe buckles, his coat and vest tailored in the most gleaming and expensive French brocades and velvets, a muff on his left arm, and two emerald watch chains draped across his stomach hung with lines of seals. But he was not a success as a courtier. He started out as favourite of the Comte d'Artois until that nobleman detected him using loaded dice during a game of hazard. When he was invited to join the royal hunt, he confounded the rigid etiquette of the court by riding in front of the royal party and bringing the stag to bay, a privilege exclusively reserved for the king. Worse, during a birthday ball he slapped an importuning creditor in full view of the queen, an action which would have landed him in the Bastille if he had not had the status of a rich influential milord. Outside a Parisian coffee house he drew his rapier and ran a man through who happened to have stepped on his dog. An enraged mob pursued him back to his lodgings, where his carriage was destroyed and a manservant killed.

In 1775, three years after his marriage, he returned to Ireland, where he was to remain until his death. He was twenty-seven years old and had fought just about that number of duels. His debts amounted to £120,000. His wife refused to live with him. 'Fitzgerald is completely broke and gone off to Mayo,' reported his uncle, the Bishop of Derry. 'His wife remains in Dublin.' The unfortunate lady was about to go into a decline which was said to be 'brought on by the levities, quarrels and wild doings of her husband'. But he adored her, and when she died, accompanied her body to Castletown with an ungentlemanly show of grief which people considered immoderate.

He returned to his estate near Castlebar, a little frontier town standing in a poverty-stricken countryside, which had been smartened up to some extent by the Bingham family. Beyond the neat Georgian terraces surrounding the tree-lined mall, the russet bog rolled towards distant mountains. The town, which was the capital of Mayo, had a barracks, and a courthouse with 'a piazza and jail', according to W. H. Maxwell. 'Filled with a cock-fighting dog-spitting gaming gossiping population, it usually wore an air of stagnation—except when there was a petty session or a hanging.' Three miles to the north of Castlebar on the road to Ballina lies Fitzgerald territory. In the eighteenth century it consisted of two estates: Turlough Park, which was in the hands of old George Fitzgerald, and Rockingham, a mile or two away, which his son now strove to improve.

George Robert threw himself into the work of clearing his inheritance. Bogs were drained and land which had never been cultivated was sown with wheat. Soon he was a favourite with his tenantry which prospered under his direction. In a country notorious for absenteeism, where rent rolls went to subsidize extravagance elsewhere, Fitzgerald virtuously emphasized the unusual role he was playing. 'Nor did I take a simple possession of the estate,' he wrote later when he was in prison, 'and afterwards instantly fly away from my demesne to spend the high rents of it in Dublin, London, Paris or Rome . . . On the contrary, I made it my stationary residence—a residence not there to sit and doze away in unnecessary dullness and stupidity a life burthensome to myself and useless to my fellow creatures . . . the gates of hospitality were opened to rich and poor; while morning and evening prayers, administered under my roof, seemed to have drawn down from heaven the invaluable blessings of harmony, content and peace.'

The utter inappropriateness of the last three nouns to describe his mode of life may perhaps emphasize the dream world in which he lived. Not that the turbulence generally associated with Mayo was entirely his fault. The lands which made up most of Galway and Mayo were divided into vast tracts that were more or less empires belonging to a few selected families. The Blakes of Castleblake, the Brownes, the Fitzgeralds and Martins (whose territory consisted of more than a million acres) were dictators in their own properties. There were men like Denis Browne, whom W. H. Maxwell considered 'did much good and some mischief—imprisoned and transported as he pleased; and the peasantry to this day will tell you that he could hang anyone whom he disliked'. These landlords were very powerful; according to Barrington, 'their word was law; their nod would have immediately collected an army of cottagers and colliers or whatever the population was composed of'. Men, women and children were ready to do anything their landlord asked them 'without the slightest consideration as to either its danger or propriety'. Among these rulers, nests of lesser squires, unemployed and restless, vied to be gentlemen. 'If they did not go into the army, they remained at home serving with the militia, but otherwise idle, with little education beyond learning how to ride . . . to play cards . . . to know the catechism. Pistols and cudgels and horsewhips were in every young man's hands at the time.'

Fitzgerald felt himself superficially superior to his boorish neighbours. He was a good conversationalist, an author, who had written an obscure poem entitled *The Riddle*, and a handsome dandy, who, even in Mayo, presented a pleasingly fashionable appearance. He had inherited the love of display that was so evident in his uncle. On any journey he travelled in state, his

servants dressed in blue hussar uniforms faced with yellow and
carrying large sabres, while he himself always wore in his tricorn
a hatband of diamonds or oriental pearls. His most lavish public
show was in 1778 when he decided to enter parliament as member
for Castlebar. He did his best to dazzle citizens of the town, who
considered that the exhibition arranged by the prospective member
for their town would not have disgraced the entry of an Imperial
ambassador into the city of London. He organized festivities
with the aid of seamstresses, tailors, perfumers, musicians and
milliners brought down from Dublin in wagonloads, accompanied
by hordes of beggars. For three days he behaved 'like an Eastern
Nabob', going round in his most lavish clothes, his carriage filled
with guineas sealed up in parcels of fifty each for distribution to
voters; he declared that he would have no dealings with any lesser
sum. It was typical of his spluttering career that after making these
efforts he was not elected.

He was an expert though wild horseman. Maxwell noted that
'his desperate riding was the theme of fox-hunters for many a
year. No park wall or flooded river stopped him—and to this
day' (he wrote in 1830) 'leaps that he surmounted and points
where he crossed the Turlough river are pointed out by the
peasantry'. Once for a bet of two hundred pounds he jumped
his horse over a wall with a fourteen foot drop the other side.
Although he won the bet, the horse died. Later, when he could
bear his neighbours no longer, he avoided them by hunting at
night, his servants lighting his way with torches. At first local
people were terrified by the sound of the hounds baying under
the moon, and a priest tried exorcism to get rid of the devil
in their midst. Soon, however, the midnight call of hounds
aroused no more comment than the hoot of owls; it was merely
'mad Fitzgerald going hunting in the night'.

The threat of invasion by the French gave many isolated landlords the opportunity of raising their own militia. Fitzgerald was
quick to form the Turlough Volunteers, who became the terror
of the neighbourhood, 'a band of desperadoes who knew no will
but his, and had no desire but his pleasure'. As their colonel he
felt justified in fortifying an old rath on the Rockingham property

with six guns taken from a Dutch ship which had been wrecked in Clew Bay. 'Should a Colonel who has command of three companies of Volunteers have a lesser number than six pieces of cannon?'

The duels continued until people lost count. He quarrelled perpetually with neighbours and social equals. Guests at his table often suffered, like the plump man whom he accused of being fat because he was a glutton, adding that the sight of him eating deranged his nerves. Out hunting he regularly lost his temper, and those whom he considered were not the proper 'caste' to take up the sport he simply flogged from the field. Over the years victims of his wrath remembered his insults. 'Go home, Sirrah, you are fitter to follow the plough than the hounds!' 'Quit the field, huntsman, you had better to mind your father's sheep than be here.' 'What, you unwieldy porpoise! Begone to your pigsty, for if you follow the hunt you will certainly break your fat neck!'

He rode over to Westport House, where he took a pot-shot at Denis Browne, and then killed the Brownes' giant wolfhound, an animal called the Prime Sergeant after Lord Altamont's brother, who held that official position. He left a note with the servants that declared: 'Until Lord Altamont showed more charity to the poor, who up until now had only come to his doorway to be barked at and bitten by the overfed monster he had just shot, (which ate all the broken meat due to them), he George Robert Fitzgerald, could not allow any such beast to be kept at Westport.' However, the ladies of the household, Lady Ann, Lady Elizabeth and Lady Charlotte Browne, could each keep a lapdog.

His worst quarrel was with his father. When he married, George Fitzgerald promised to make him an allowance of £1,000 a year to be paid out of the rents from Turlough Park. But the old reprobate squandered the family money so that there was nothing left for his son. George Robert got the Court of the Exchequer to allow him to become the custodian of his father's estate until the debt was paid. In his appeal, George Robert contended that his father was 'sotting and dozing away at Turlough in unmeaning fullness and inactive stupidity, a life burdensome to himself and useless to his creditors'.

The old man was now obliged to live with his undutiful son as a perpetual house guest. The two, shunned by their neighbours, were forced on each other's company and the partnership became loathsome as George Robert did everything possible to annoy and torture his father. There were perpetual arguments about money. Once when old Fitzgerald refused to change his will, his son knocked out three of his teeth. On another celebrated occasion he manacled him all day to a pet bear.

Fitzgerald loved bears, and had brought a number back from France, together with some foxes and particularly ferocious dogs. One of the bears had figured in an incident with the family attorney who happened to be accompanying him down from Dublin to Mayo to deal with some legal matters concerned with the estate. Also sitting in the coach was a 'friend' muffled against the cold in a blue travelling cloak and a scarlet cape with a lot of voluminous white cloth tied round his head. They had started out from Dublin in darkness, and it was not until they reached Kilcock, about thirty miles outside the city, that light streamed into the carriage window from a nearby inn and the attorney realized that he was sitting beside a large Russian bear.

The edition of the Dublin *Penny Journal*, dealing with 'Rogues' and Fitzgerald in particular, made the most of this incident.

' "What's the matter, Harry," said George pretending to awake, "has Bruin been troublesome? He is in general the best of travelling companions; snug and warm, though sometimes cross and apt to snap when you close in on him too much." Fitzgerald handed his friend a stick. "Just, my good Harry, welt him a little, keep him quiet til we reach Kinnegad where we breakfast." ' The attorney declined and burst out of the carriage. 'He stumbled over hillocks, tore through hedges and ditches and never stopped until he came breathless into a little ale house, completely covered with mud and his clothes in rags.'

After his day with the bear, George Fitzgerald was locked up by his son in a cave on the grounds of Rockingham which had been fitted up as a grotto. The remains of the cave can still be seen under a grass-covered mound; it may have suited nymphs, as the inscription over the entrance claimed, but it was an uncomfortable wet hole for an old gentleman. For the first time George Robert had gone too far, and his brother, Charles Lionel, who was also his neighbour, had him seized as he sat on the bench at Ballinrobe assizes. He was brought to Castlebar where he was accused of extreme cruelty. He defended himself by describing his father 'as one of the worst men alive', a defence echoed by his counsel, Remesius Lennon, who intimated that he would be unjust to censure any son for chaining such a public nuisance to a muzzled bear. These pleas went unheeded, and the son was sentenced to two years' imprisonment with a fine of £500. But any attempt to confine him in the Castlebar lock-up was fruitless as long as the Turlough Militia was strong enough to set its colonel free. When its members assembled before the jail and rioted, Fitzgerald was immediately released.

He went home smouldering with fury, found his father and hurried down with him to the shores of Clew Bay, where he bundled him into a fishing smack. Although it was October, and the weather must have been unpredictable, they set off in this small open boat to one of the uninhabited islands that dot the bay. After George Robert had forced his father to land, he set about threatening to murder or abandon him, or to remain with him in this hiding place out of reach of the law until they both starved. Discomfort and cold brought about a brittle agreement. The son agreed to pay the father £3,000 on condition that he dropped all charges of forceful imprisonment. They sailed for home.

Meanwhile Charles Lionel had petitioned the Lord Lieutenant, the Duke of Buckingham, requesting him 'to disarm this formidable and fortified outlaw' in order to release his father from 'thraldom'. His petition was taken very seriously in Dublin, because the Turlough Militia was beginning to be regarded as a particular threat to law and order at a time when the government was passionately concerned about possible rebellion. A company of horse, foot and artillery under the command of Major Longfield set out for the fort which Fitzgerald had surrounded with cannon and protected with his wild yeomanry. He prudently retreated before a shot could be fired, so that in military terms the expedition was a non-starter. 'During the whole march the disposition made by the Major evinced marks of a very superior genius and afforded officers and men the most flattering assurance of success. Fitzgerald, well knowing the skill and bravery of his opponent, spiked his cannon and carried off his store.'

His father, safely on dry land, had gone back on the arrangement he had made in the middle of Clew Bay. George Robert, finding pressures in the west temporarily too much for him, fled to Dublin where he was promptly arrested and put in Newgate. Here he called for pen and paper and began writing appeals to the public. He described himself as 'a staunch Protestant and firmly attached to the Hanoverian succession'. He repeated his condemnation of his father's way of life, 'keeping open house and entertaining at free cost all the unprincipled gambling swindling young fellows of the neighbouring towns he could possibly assemble together, who in their mad frolics had either broken all furniture in his best rooms, or utterly spoiled it with their dressings and powderings, or what was still worse, with the filthy disemboguings from their over-gorged stomachs'. His brother, Charles Lionel, also came in for criticism. 'His conduct in Dublin was, if anything, more scandalous and outré, wantonly and wildly squandering every guinea he could rap or rend upon the lowest and most infamous prostitutes of the town, like another MacHeath, bedizening his Chapelizod Seraglio with silk gowns, stockings, and other glaring, gaudy, silk-suited apparel . . .'

He appeared in court dressed as a beggar except for the diamond band worth fifteen hundred pounds stuck in his ragged hat. The huge crowd of spectators cheered him for the flamboyant gesture, but he was sentenced to imprisonment for a further length of time. Once again he was able to obtain a quick release, possibly because of the influence of his Hervey relations, and retired to his house in Merrion Square to recuperate.

When he returned to the west he found that his banditti had missed him. During his absence a young captain, who went down to try to recruit some of them for service in India, had been badly

9a.   Ruins of Downhill

9b.   The Mussenden Temple

10. Thomas Dermody. From a portrait by Charles Allingham

11a.   George Robert Fitzgerald as a dandy

11b.   George Robert Fitzgerald before
         his execution

12. The Reverend Charles Maturin. From a drawing by W. Brocas

beaten up to cries of 'A George! A George! Long life to our Colonel!' He set about continuing the quarrel he had begun with his neighbour, Dick Martin, nicknamed Hairtrigger Dick from the amount of duels he had won. The two men had hated each other for a long time, and Martin was one of the attorneys who prosecuted Fitzgerald after the complaint by his brother. Fitzgerald had encountered him in Dublin soon after his release from Newgate. They had been at the Crow Theatre, where the famous Mrs. Crawford was playing in *Belvidera*. Fitzgerald said 'Have you anything to say to me?' and Martin replied, 'Only to tell you I have followed you from Castlebar to proclaim you the bully of the Altamonts.' There was an immediate public quarrel in the lobby of the theatre about who had challenged whom. Later Martin sent an emissary to Merrion Square whom Fitzgerald beat up with a cudgel adorned with a green ribbon. Through intermediaries they arranged to duel at Castlebar. Fitzgerald came to the appointment armed with good pistols, while Martin only had old holster pistols. They fired at each other, both receiving trifling wounds which were considered incon- clusive so that another duel was planned the next day in Sligo. But Martin refused to turn up at this second duel, accusing his opponent of appallingly unsportsmanlike behaviour—he had 'plated his body in order to make it bullet proof'.

The next we hear of George Robert is his attendance upon his uncle, when the Earl-Bishop made his stately entrance into Dublin in October 1784, to attend the Volunteer Convention. Fitzgerald commanded the blue and yellow Dragoons surround- ing the Bishop's carriage, and uncle and nephew shared the applause of the Dublin crowds. Hervey's lavish entertainments during the convention took place at George Robert's house in Merrion Square, which he rented for £1,000, money appropriated from the See of Derry. It was rumoured that he had ordained his nephew. 'He has fought one duel even since he has been in orders,' wrote the Reverend Jerome de Salis to Lord Dacre, 'church preferments to the amount of £2,000 a year are given to him or intended for him. I think this to be the most indecent thing, not to say the greatest outrage to society that has happened in

my time.' Much to everyone's relief, the story proved to be un-
true.

There was something rather touching about the friendship of
two men at odds with society. They were always affectionate;
the Bishop chose to disregard Fitzgerald's peccadilloes, while his
nephew admired his uncle who was one of the few people he never
quarrelled with. (Hervey was in Rome at the time of his death,
where he succeeded in keeping the details out of the Italian newspapers.) After the convention Fitzgerald was invited up to Derry,
to be made a freeman. 'Just landed, as it were,' wrote Hervey
breezily to another of his relations, 'to witness the inauguration
of my hospitable nephew as a citizen of this grateful and independent city.' Fitzgerald, for his part, made a graceful speech of
acceptance in which he called the Bishop an 'illuminated and
illuminating constellation' and declared that he himself 'ardently
aspired to emulate the patriotic brilliant example of an uncle, who,
in all his actions, public and private, combined the excellency of
dignity with the dignity of power'. He did not fail to point
out to the city fathers that their new fellow-citizen had an ancestor
who had signed the Magna Carta, and that he was 'the indubitable
immediate heir-male of your Magna Charta Fitzgerald'.

The conferment of the Freedom of Derry directly preceded his
downfall. His life at Castlebar was increasingly friendless. When
he returned he found that his house had been broken into and
ransacked during his absence. His neighbours avoided him and
no respectable servant would remain with him. But his militia
still thrived, and for companions he had two ruffianly employees,
a Scotsman known as Scoth Andrew, coachman, huntsman and
member of the Tulough Corps, and a Welsh attorney named
Timothy Brecknock.

Before long he was quarrelling again. He found a new enemy,
Patrick Randal McDonnell, who had been elected as Colonel of
the Mayo Legion of Volunteers, a position that Fitzgerald coveted
for himself. He felt the insult keenly, especially as he considered
McDonnell, an under-tenant and a Catholic attorney, too much
of a social inferior to challenge to a duel. He took out some of
his bad temper on the citizens of Castlebar who had elected the

colonel over his head, by shooting their dogs and giving a premium to things sold in his own Turlough Market. Then he decided that McDonnell would have to be killed. He concocted a plan with the aid of Timothy Brecknock, who told him it would be perfectly all right legally to arrest McDonnell and have him shot while trying to escape. The plan worked very well; a hundred men of the Turlough Militia were sent to arrest the unfortunate colonel and two friends of his. Only one, a Mr. Gallagher, escaped being murdered by feigning death.

But even in Mayo the law was not entirely flexible. The world was tired of Fighting Fitzgerald, and here at last was an opportunity for getting rid of him. His militia grew frightened and scattered. The very day after McDonnell died, February 21, 1786, a detachment of troops was sent to Turlough House, where they found George Robert hiding in a chest covered over with blankets. He was brought to Castlebar, where an infuriated crowd consisting of supporters of the dead man broke into the jail and almost lynched him. 'They attacked me with sword-canes, they collared me and thrust at me, and several pistol shots were fired.' Six weeks later he was still so shattered by the savagery of the mob that he could not leave his bed and come out of prison. His trial for murder had to be postponed.

It opened on June 11, 1786. The judge was Barry Yelverton, Lord Chief Baron, and the prosecution was conducted by the Attorney General, John Fitzgibbon (later Earl of Clare), with whom Fitzgerald had once fought a duel. Fashionable people flocked to Castlebar to attend and to take bets on whether the accused would be hanged or released. Would his mother's old court connections save him? The general feeling was that he would once again be allowed to flout the law. There was surprise when a verdict of guilty was brought in and he and his companions were condemned.

On the day of his execution George Robert drank a bottle of port and came out completely composed. The crowd saw a small figure, still handsome—he was thirty-eight—'dressed in a ragged coat of the Castletown hunt, a dirty flannel waistcoat and drawers, both of which were without buttons; brown worsted or yarn stockings, a pair of coarse shoes without buckles, and an old round hat, tied round with pack thread'. A print exists, 'an exact portrait' of him at this moment, standing with his hands clenched. When he sprang off the ladder the rope broke in two, hurling him to the ground.

'You see I am once more among you unexpectedly,' he told the crowd. He informed the Sheriff he knew that rope could hang nobody, and desired that he should get another, but not from the same shop. It took some hours before things could be reorganized; they not only got another rope, but another hangman, a convict who agreed to do the job for a free pardon. Fitzgerald sobered up and began to lose his nerve. When they were ready for him again he was shouting for more time, 'even after he had mounted the ladder, thrice downed the cap and thrice raised it again, beseeching each time some minutes for prayer . . .'

Two years later John Wesley, reading one of the many potted biographies that were published after the execution, approved the delay. His journal for July 13, 1789, recorded:

'In the packet going over from Dublin to Parkgate, the sea being smooth, I shut myself up in my chaise and read over the life of the famous Mr. George Fitzgerald . . . I never heard before of so cool, deliberate and relentless a murderer! And yet from the breaking of the rope at his execution which gave him two hours of vehement prayer, there is room to hope he found mercy at last.'

The body was taken down and removed to the windowless shell of Turlough House which rioters had nearly destroyed. It had been so thoroughly looted that not one candlestick could be found. The coffin was set down amid the shambles, lit by candles in bottles, and during the same short summer night George Robert was buried in the family graveyard beneath the round tower that dominates the lonely Fitzgerald estates. The burial was so hurried that afterwards no one could remember where he lay. Much later he was rediscovered; according to a brutal story, a search was made for him in order to recover a ring he was wearing. The flesh had gone from his skull to reveal a great cleft in the bone inflicted during one of his first duels. There was speculation that this wound was the cause of his uncertain temperament.

He left a young daughter who died suddenly in 1794. It was said that her death was brought about by shock after reading an account of her father's execution in the *Gentleman's Magazine* which she found after it had been left carelessly in a bookshelf.

Scholars

THE reputation of scholars for eccentricity has long been recognized. Richard Kirwan's mother became alarmed as she noticed her son's tendency to become a bookworm. From the earliest age he had avoided the pastimes of rural rakes and taken to study. He could conjugate a French verb at five; at seven he wrote an abridgement of ancient history. At seventeen his mother wrote him a distracted letter:

'You see whether I have cause to be uneasy about it when I tell you the misfortune of two that were eminent in that way; one Furlong, who found out the way to make Bath metal grey, by study at last melancholy, let his beard grow and talked to himself; in short, by all I heard, he was lost by it; and the Dominican Friar . . . that was the end of their labours and profound studies, as they fancied. There are several instances of people that were turned or touched, as they call it, by study's which makes me insist so long upon your not falling into the dangerous practice . . .' But her son ignored her directions and persisted in extending the range of his knowledge.

He was born in 1733 at Cregg Castle in Co. Galway, a stronghold built by his great-grandfather in the depths of Connemara. Although his family were of planter stock, they were Catholics, and so cut off by the Penal Laws from higher education in Ireland. It took Kirwan some persistence to persuade his mother to send him to Poitiers where he could complete his education under the Jesuits. In France he was obliged to learn the French language, a task he disliked. However, his tutors, noting his interest in chemistry, restricted his study on that subject to French textbooks, which soon encouraged his fluency in the language. In 1754, after his mother died, he entered St. Omer with the intention of becoming a Jesuit himself. He found that Jesuitical discipline did not suit him, nor in due course did his religion. He picked up an anonymous book on religious controversy in a Paris bookstall and read it regularly during sessions at his hairdresser. As a result he became a Protestant in 1764 and died a Unitarian.

The immediate cause of his abandoning his clerical studies, only a year after he had taken them up, was the death of his elder brother in a duel. Since his parents were also dead, he found himself transformed from an impoverished younger son to a man of property with an income of £4,000 a year. He returned to Galway, 'a tall, elegant, comely young man, given to interceding his discourse with foreign idioms'. He contemplated marriage. 'Miss C— is not taller than Miss F—, very ugly and very fat,' he wrote to his brother. 'Miss H— is very disagreeable to me; and Miss B— does not know how either to read or write . . . if you be not averse to it, I like another of £4,000, who possesses every available qualification.' His brother replied: 'If you are in love with the lady, my being averse to her is of no consequence; but this I know, that before the honeymoon is out you will repent it. £4,000 is nothing to you; it is soon gone.'

His choice was the daughter of a neighbouring landlord, Sir Thomas Blake of Melmo, Co. Galway. Unfortunately instead of her small fortune the lady brought him nothing but debts, so that Kirwan fulfilled his brother's prediction by spending part of his honeymoon in prison. This circumstance, together with his distaste for the life of his fellow squires, induced him to leave the west of Ireland and go to England to continue his education. In England he tried law for a time, and then was absorbed by the new enthusiasm for science. His studies included metaphysics, logic, law, philology, music, mechanical philosophy, chemistry, minera-logy, mining, geology and meteorology. He was awarded the Copley medal for chemistry and made a Fellow of the Royal Society in 1780. His correspondents included leading scientists and the Empress of Russia.

In 1788 he returned to Ireland, having completed twenty years of study abroad. His wife had died after eight years of marriage leaving him with two daughters. He settled down in Dublin, where he was not only recognized as an outstanding savant, but acquired a national reputation as a weather prophet.

He established a meteorological observation centre at his house which was one of the first to be capable of accurate weather readings. Using his information he devised a system of long-range forecasting. He understood the modern theory of rain stresses and recognized the movement of air masses. He analysed the sequence of summaries of the season's weather which had been compiled by Dr. John Rutty, and concluded that the weather during one season depended on the weather of the seasons before. His fame as a forecaster spread to such an extent that many farmers would not grow a crop before they had consulted him by letter. But his methods do not work today, and it seems that basically his forecasts relied on luck.

His reputation as a scholar led him to be elected the second President of the Irish Academy following Lord Charlemont. It also justified many of his mother's fears.

His house at 6 Cavendish Square (now Parnell Square) contained little furniture, and all the chairs and tables there overflowed with books, which also lay in piles on the floor. Here he evolved a daily routine which began when he rose at four o'clock in summer and four-thirty in winter. The drawing-room had a huge fire blazing in it all the year round because he was terrified of catching cold. Before going out into the street he was careful to stand in front of it for some time and then open his coat to catch a little heat. He had, he said, to lay in a sufficient supply of calorific to last for some time. He always wore a slouched hat, both indoors and out, which gave him an excuse for not attending church or castle levees in his capacity of Inspector General of Mines. He wore his hat even in a court of justice. In the street he hurried along, obsessed with retaining the supply of calorific; friends, even the Viceroy, had to run beside him at the same rapid rate if they wanted to keep up. While walking he refused to conduct any conversation.

Because he suffered from dysphagia, and could only swallow with convulsive movements, he always dined alone, attended by his faithful servant, Pope. His diet consisted of milk and ham, and very occasionally a glass of Spanish white wine taken with cake. The wine was dangerous; after drinking it, he said, his temperature would rise from a normal seventy degrees to a hundred and fifty. The ham was cooked on Sunday and reheated every day for the rest of the week.

His servant, Pope, slept in the same room as his master, and one of his special duties was to get up from time to time during the night and refresh him with tea. Sometimes he mistakenly poured the spout in Kirwan's eye, rather than his mouth. Pope mothered the old scholar and took special care to protect him from the public. Once an anxious group of civic dignitaries, including the Lord Mayor, called at Cavendish Square for advice on putting out a fire that was blazing in the city coal yard. Pope opened the door to them and refused to let them in.

'If you were the king himself I dare not admit you.'

'The city coal yard is in flames!'

'If all Ireland were in flames and this house along with it, I dare not; for my master is at dinner.'

After much pleading the delegation was shown into the drawing-room, but just as the Mayor had his hand on the door-handle, he was stopped by Pope's shrill voice: 'Oh, sir, they will get in!'

'What?'

'The flies! The flies!' he shouted, waving a cloth. Kirwan had an obsessive hatred of flies, and paid his servants a small tally on each corpse they produced. In due course, after he had dined, he did see the delegation and gave them sensible advice about putting out the fire with sand.

He was extremely generous, and charitable, although absent-minded about anything to do with money. Correspondence, apart from letters on his chosen subjects, was abhorred. 'Dear Brother,' he once wrote, 'I have read over twice the letter you have pleased to send me, which to me, who hates reading or writing or any business, was a very disgusting task.'

He retained his country estates, which he ran as a model landlord. He strode about his property, wearing his slouched hat and long cloak, accompanied by some enormous dogs—they included

mastiffs, greyhounds and a couple of Irish wolfhounds. He preferred large creatures to small ones since the time his dogs saved
his life when he was attacked while sleeping by six boars. A pet
eagle perched on his shoulder. He had trained it by a Pavlovian
method which he had thought up himself, starving it and employ-
ing a boy to make its life a misery by teasing it. Then he suddenly
appeared with a plate of meat and drove the boy off. Later a
friend shot the bird by mistake, just as it was returning to its
master's shoulder.

One might imagine that such an idiosyncratic personality
would be a recluse, but on the contrary, the house in Cavendish
Square was a centre of fashionable society, where the host entertained brilliantly and amusingly. He could discuss anything from
a theological problem to the chemical properties of the latest
cosmetic. Weekly soirées were held on Thursday ('shaving day')
when ladies were entertained, and Friday, which was devoted
exclusively to visiting gentlemen. Hours were six o'clock to
nine o'clock (eight-thirty in winter). At seven the knocker was
was removed from the hall door; no further guests would be
admitted, and those already within would be undisturbed by
introductions or the noise of the rat-tat-tat outside. Summer and
winter, Kirwan received before the fire, reclining on a couch
rolled in his cloak, with another cloak covering his lower limbs.
Naturally he wore his hat. Time would pass quickly in absorbing
conversation, but when the hour came for guests to leave, they
were expected to go quickly. Kirwan would take out his watch
and his drooping eyes would glance down at it as he wound it.
If this failed as a signal, he took off his shoes and knee-buckles, got
off his sofa and personally escorted them to the door.

The author, Lady Morgan, has left a vivid description of her
first meeting with Kirwan. 'A tall gaunt figure, wrapped from
neck to heel in a dark roquelaure, with a large leaved hat flapped
low over the face, presented the very picture of Guy Fawkes,
with nothing wanted but his dark lantern.' He invited her to
tea in Cavendish Square where she could try his piano and
play his collection of Italian music. She rather hoped to impress
him in her role of Irish harpist instead. But 'Mr. Kirwan called

my taste barbarous and became quite vehement in his expression of abhorrence for Irish music. "Madam," he said, "I left Ireland at your age and full, as you are now, of all the vulgar errors of enthusiastic patriotism;" and again, "I thought there was no poetry like Irish poetry, nor music like Irish music—when I returned I could not endure either."' He then told her that, at Christmas and other festivities, he used to throw open the servant's hall at Cregg Castle to all comers—beggars, bards and story tellers—after the old Connacht fashion. At night he would take his place among them and make each guest tell a story, recite a poem or sing a song in Irish. 'Madam,' he exclaimed, 'it was too much for me, it almost threw me into convulsions.' (In fact, as a young enthusiast for Irish music, he had helped Edward Bunting compile his collections.) Lady Morgan thought that his musical taste had been changed by living in England. To assuage his memories, she took the opportunity of playing various Irish melodies on her harp, including 'Ned of the Hill', which she accompanied by singing. Kirwan was overcome with tears.

'Madam, I won't hear you—'tis terrible—it goes to my soul! It wrings every nerve in my body.'

'Then, Sir, I ask no more, the effects which Irish music produce on you is the proof of its excellence.'

'You may as well say that the howl of a dying dog, which could produce the same effect, is the proof of its excellence. My dear child, give up your Irish howl and study Italian music, you have a true musical organization, but it is all perverted.'

At the time of the Union Kirwan refused a baronetcy, saying that the only distinctions he valued were those to do with the mind. He died in June 1812, in his seventy-ninth year, after catching a cold, in spite of all his precautions, and trying to cure it by the fashionable method of starving. He was buried in Hill Street; later Pope was buried in the same grave.

Kirwan's contemporary, the philosopher and mathemetician, Hamilton Rowan, 'a gigantic old man in old-fashioned dress', shared his passion for large animals, and was always accompanied by two Irish wolfhounds, 'the last of their race'. Lord Cloncurry described a walking tour in England with Rowan. 'I well remember his practice at starting from our inn of a wet morning was to roll himself in the first pool he met, in order that he might be beforehand in the rain . . . He had always some adventure on his hands, two or three of these in which he rescued distressed damsels from the snares and force of ravishers of rank.'

The Reverend John Lanigan, author of a great Ecclesiastical History of Ireland, developed an obsession about stones. Born in Cashel, he was sent to Rome for his education where he became a priest and afterwards Professor of Hebrew at Pavia University. After he returned to Ireland in 1794 almost totally penniless, he found a position in the newly established Royal Dublin Society, as a librarian. In 1799 he began his monumental history, which took him almost thirty years to complete. During his studies he began to show signs of 'erratic temperament'. Once, arguing with a member of the Society, he took a paving stone into the library to squash him flat if he did not yield a point. Fitzpatrick in *Irish Wits and Worthies* quotes the Editor of the Dublin *Evening Post*, a native of Cashel, who remembered the mystification of the townsfolk when Lanigan, on a visit to his native town, spent much time in boiling up some stones in a metal pot belonging to his sisters. No one learned his reason; but it may have been something to do with his impression that stones, or some particular stones, were precious. After he ordered Dean Myler to pray for him they locked him up. The Dean refused, or at least did not pray with the speed Lanigan expected, whereupon the Doctor took some stones out of his pocket and threatened to break the Dean's specially prized engravings of the Seven Sacraments. This had the desired effect of making Myler throw himself on his knees. Poor Lanigan ended his days as a voluntary inmate of Dr. Harty's asylum in Finglas, where he died in 1828.

In Trinity College scholars during the eighteenth century tended to be more rugged and worldly than is usual in academic circles, no doubt because of the circumstances of the time. Richard Baldwin, who was elected Provost in 1717, led his students one Sunday into a battle against the butchers of Ormonde market. 'Follow me, my lads, and I'll head you. I am appointed by your parents and friends to take care of you, and I'll fight for you till I die!' They were brave words, for the butchers of Ormonde Street were formidable, and usually got the best of faction fights with the Protestant Liberty Boys who consisted mainly of tailors and weavers from the Coombe. The butchers armed themselves with their knives and with 'falchions'—sharpened oak staves of casks hardened by being smoked in chimneys. In cases of extreme ill-feeling they were known to hang their opponents by the jaws from meathooks. The Trinity students, armed with massive keys tied to their gowns, helped the Liberty Boys, cheered on by Provost Baldwin, who afterwards attended divine service at St. Patrick's.

Dr. Theaker Wilder, Oliver Goldsmith's tutor, came across a gang of students beside the college pump about to duck a bailiff. 'Gentlemen, gentlemen, for the love of God don't be so cruel as to nail his ears to the pump!' The hint was promptly taken. A more pleasant story concerning Dr. Wilder is his encounter with a girl while crossing a muddy street. He gave her a big kiss. 'Take that for being so pretty!'

Among the accomplishments of the tough self-made Provost, John Hely-Hutchinson, ancestor of Lord Donoughmore, were duelling and dancing. His duels set an example to his students. For one, fought against Mr. Doyle, Master in Chancery, the antagonists went specially to the battlefield of Minden. His dancing earned him the nickname of The Prancer, and a ditty of the period described:

> In minuet step how he advances;
> Strike up the fiddles—see how he dances!
> With his well-turned pumps,
> How he skips and how he jumps!

Another famous dancer, whose zest for the accomplishment bordered on a mania, was Charles Robert Maturin, a clergyman of Huguenot descent, whose ancestor had arrived in Ireland a cripple after spending twenty-six years in the Bastille. Maturin was born in 1782 and took orders after graduating from Trinity. Some time after his ordination he began to write his lurid Gothic novels which became extremely popular. No detail of horror was too much for his refined pen, including this precise description of cannibalism:

'In the agonies of their famished sickness they loathed each other—they could have cursed each other, if they had had breath to curse. It was on the fourth night that I heard the shriek of the wretched female—her lover, in the agony of hunger had fastened his teeth in her shoulder—that bosom on which he had so often luxuriated became a meal to him now . . .'

His most famous novel, *Melmoth the Wanderer*, influenced the work of both Baudelaire and Balzac, and modern vampire tastes have led it to be reprinted in America. Oscar Wilde adopted the name of its hero after his release from prison. A character in *Melmoth* is killed off in an unusually messy manner:

'He fell, trodden in one moment into sanguine and discoloured mud by a thousand feet . . .'

Maturin was not only a novelist, but a dramatist, who took his work to London. His play, *Bertram*, which was praised by Walter Scott and by Byron, earned him £1,000 when it was produced in Drury Lane in 1816. A year later he returned to Dublin, a literary celebrity. He lavishly redecorated his house in York Street, painting the ceilings with clouds and eagles and the wall panels with scenes from his novels. Along with his clerical duties he took up dancing. A contemporary observed: 'His whole port and bearing was that of a man who had burst from a long sleep into a new state of being; always gay, he now became luxurious in his habits and manners. He was the first in the quadrille—the last to depart. The ballroom was his temple of inspiration and worship. So passionately attached was he to dancing, that he originated morning quadrille parties, which met alternately two or three days in the week at the houses of the favourite members of his coterie.' In his own house he arranged that the curtains and shutters in his drawing-room windows were kept closed during the daytime to preserve the illusion of night. Behind them the quadrilles continued.

His early success as a dramatist did not last, and his fortune fluctuated. This affected this clothes which varied from extraordinary opulence to being 'almost ostentatiously shabby'. The poet, James Clarence Mangan, described his walking along York Street in an 'extraordinary double-belted and treble-caped rug of an old garment'. But if he could manage it, he kept his wife sumptuously clothed, even in the extremes of poverty. A payment of a royalty would go to fitting her out with what he considered appropriate dress before any notice was taken of other needs of his household.

He was notoriously absent-minded. Mangan once saw him wearing a boot on one foot and a shoe on the other. He was known to make a social call in his dressing-gown and slippers, and quite often went to parties a day too late. Guests at his table would be kept talking for an hour before they had an opportunity to eat what was before them. After he had written *Melmoth*, he sent it off to his publishers in several different parcels, the pages un-numbered and without connecting words.

While he was writing, as he felt 'the estro of composition coming on him,' he would paste a wafer on his forehead. This was a warning to his family that he was not to be interrupted or disturbed in any way. He died in 1824, aged forty-two, regretted and much loved by his family and parishioners.

One of the most unusual scholars of that highly individualistic age was John ('Jackie') Barrett, the miser and college character who ended his career as Vice-Provost of Trinity, 'a greasy, shabby, croaking, round-faced Provost'. The son of a clergyman, Barrett was born in 1753 in King's County, and very soon proved himself an unusually gifted scholar, endowed with a remarkable memory, especially for languages. Among his achievements were works on astrology and the discovery and editing of a rare copy of St. Matthew's gospel written in Greek which he came across in the college library. He became Professor of Greek and Oriental languages.

His appearance suggested some of his miserly habits. Numerous descriptions emphasized the small bent ungainly figure covered with shabby or ragged garments and a twenty-year-old fellow's gown. In his novel, *Charles O'Malley*, Charles Lever gives a portrait of him in old age. 'Dr. Barrett was, at the time I speak of, close upon seventy years old, scarcely five feet in height, and even that diminutive stature lessened by a stoop. His face was thin, pointed and russet coloured; his nose so aquiline as nearly to meet his projecting chin, and his small grey eyes, red and bleary, peered beneath his well-worn cap with a glance of mingled fear and suspicion. His dress was a suit of the rustiest black, threadbare and patched in several places, while a pair of large brown leather slippers, far too big for his feet, imparted a sliding motion to his walk that added an indescribable meanness to his appearance.' Another observer noted that he always walked with his hands in his pockets, arms held close to his sides.

Among the students his nickname was 'the Sweep'. His rooms in Front Square to the left of the portico of the Examination Hall, dingy and darkened because the windows were never washed, were almost unfurnished apart from books. Dusty volumes were piled high on two dirty old stuffed chairs and a table. As a young recluse reading for his Fellowship, he used to pretend that these sticks of furniture were rival candidates. Chairs, table, basin and bolster off his bed would be ranged before him in a semicircle and given the declared names of candidates, to whom he propounded the sort of questions that might occur in the examination.

The rooms were never warmed, even in the coldest weather, since rather than light a fire he would slip down to the college kitchen to warm himself. Once some students had to resuscitate him with a draught of rum after finding him nearly frozen to death, sitting almost in the dark with one glimmering rushlight stuck to his chair. He always dined on Commons because the food was free. A glutton, he never refused a helping, except on the occasion when, dining with the Provost, he mistook a piece of ice for a plum. 'I'm scalded, by God,' he cried, rushing from the table and demanding an apothecary to examine his mouth.

Normally the only provisions which he was obliged to buy were for his breakfast, which consisted of a pennyworth of bread and a halfpennyworth of milk. On one occasion he sent his servant, an old lady named Catty, for the milk with a penny and instructions to bring back the change. She slipped, broke her leg and was carried off to hospital where she was visited by Barrett.

'D'ye hear, Catty, where's the jug?'

'Oh, Doctor dear, sure the jug was broken, and I couldn't help it!'

'Very good, Catty, that's true, it couldn't be helped; but d'ye see me now, where's my halfpence change?'

In an age of wigs he wore his own hair, which William Blacker, a former student, described as 'black and tinged with grey, and very long, combed back from his forehead and made up behind in three curls or rouleaux which were opened out duly on the Sabbath and being duly primed and loaded with a quantum of powder and pomatum, rolled up again to assume during the week whatever form or appearance he might assume'. He powdered it properly when he had to take examinations. Afterwards he combed out the powder on to a sheet of paper and kept it for the next occasion. It was only at examination time that he took some care with his clothes; the powdered coiffure topped a glossy black dress and new gown, and was surmounted by a lustrous velvet cap. At all other times his garments were ragged and old.

He saved up his guineas—it was said by the sale of accumulated candle ends—and kept them in a sock until he had enough to buy a debenture. The only man he ever lent money to was a Fellow called Magee, afterwards Archbishop of Dublin. Once, while he was lending Magee five pounds, the stocking broke, scattering guineas all over the floor.

'Stop, stop, Magee, do you see me now, get up and stand on the table and I'll pick them up.' Later it was found that one guinea had vanished irrevocably. 'They are all right but one. One is gone, and maybe it rolled into a mousetrap, Magee, and maybe it didn't.' The ensuing quarrel lasted a lifetime, and when Magee was promoted to Bishop, Jacky remarked: 'Do you see me now— I don't care if he was made Bishop of Hell so long as I am not in his lordship's diocese.'

A savant who could only thrive within the shelter of a university, he remained inside for over forty years, venturing out three times a year: twice to go across the street to receive his half-yearly dividend from the bank of Ireland, and once in summer when he would accompany other Fellows on their annual outing to the new observatory at Dunsink. He did make a few other excursions, during which he affected complete ignorance of country matters. In spite of his rural upbringing it was said that he had scarcely observed any aspect of nature beyond the swallows in Front Square. Once he accepted an invitation to Clontarf, a seaside suburb in North Dublin. On his way he saw a sheep and enquired what extraordinary animal it might be. He was delighted to learn that he was seeing 'live mutton' for the first time. At Clontarf he observed the sea was 'a broad flat superficies, like Euclid's definition of a line expanding itself into a surface, and blue, like Xenophon's plain covered with wormwood'.

He went further, to Kerry, to inspect some college estates, which did not impress him. 'I have seen some of them, to be sure, and if bog could be turned into butter, they are very valuable estates indeed.'

Another time he had to give evidence in a law case in Naas, about thirty miles from College Park. In the yard of the inn where he lodged he saw a cock.

'My good man,' he asked an ostler, 'do you see me now, what is this beautiful bird over there?'

'Ah, away with you! You know what it is as well as I do.'

'Indeed I do not; and I'll be greatly obliged if you tell me.'

'Ah, get out; you're humbugging me; you know well it's a cock.'

'Is it indeed? I thank you exceedingly.' When he died they found his copy of Buffon's *Natural History*, where, in the margin of the page on which *gallus domesticus* is described, he had written: 'The ostler was right. It was a cock.'

During the formation of the Volunteers Barrett took great interest in their training. Observing their manoeuvres in College Park, he compared the company to 'one grait lay-goon, just like Julious Say-zairs, do ye see. Sayzair's men had no guns, the like not being invented in those days . . .' An officer drilling in the Park decided to show respect to a Fellow by giving the order 'Present Arms!' Barrett picked up his gown and ran away as fast as he could. On being asked why, he said, 'Well do you see me now, I heard the officer saying Present! and I knew the next word would be Fire!'

At the outbreak of rebellion in 1798 he changed all his securities into hard cash and bought various bogs on which he could run cows.

He was largely inarticulate; it was considered that in spite of his brilliance in languages he could hardly speak English. The hesitancy of his speech was compounded by a habit of nervous swearing and irrelevant interpolations. The Dublin University Magazine gave an example, in which someone had enquired about a Dr. Young.

'Dr. Young was—my, God, my God—born in 1752, he entered —what the deuce is it—College in 1769 and was made a—what the devil's that—Fellow in 1775. He was promoted to the see— what the devil does he want—of Clonfert in 1799 and went to England to consult—the devil—M'Allister I believe . . .'

Because of his tendency to swear, large numbers of students would gather to hear him lecture in Divinity.

His erudition was formidable and he had a reputation for wit. Lever considered that 'a greater or more profound scholar never graced the walls of the college; a distinguished Grecian, learned in all the refinements of a hundred dialects; a deep Orientalist, cunning in all the varieties of Eastern languages and able to reason with a moonshee or chat with a Persian ambassador. With a mind that never ceased enquiring, he possessed a memory ridiculous for its retentiveness even of trifles; no character in history, no event in chronology was unknown to him, and he was referred to by his contemporaries in doubtful and disputed cases, as men consult a lexicon or dictionary.'

Miss Anne Plumptre, who was escorted by Dr. Barrett round the university, noted his phenomenal memory that could rustle up the name of every new book in the library since he became a Fellow; when she asked questions about the history of the College, he was able to discuss the Provosts and Vice-Provosts since the foundation. Her impressions of him were contained in her *Narrative of a Residence in Ireland* published in 1817. Besides acknowledging his erudition, she noted his 'simplicity of manners and utter ignorance of the world'. She went on to narrate a number of well-known stories about his miserliness and to give the information that, although his income as a Fellow was £2,000 a year, he spent scarcely twenty pounds of it except on books.

He evidently read her closely. In the Minutes of the Library dated September 9, 1817, he wrote:

'I put up in the Library and entered in both catalogues the 46 volumes sent in by Mullens last Saturday, with the exception of Miss Anne Plumptre's Narrative which I hope the Board will order to be locked up as too silly and too ill-mannered for a public library . . . Travel in savage countries, Miss Anne, and publish their conversations if you can, but spare the feelings of those who are accustomed to the rules and decencies of civilized life'—a remark that perhaps came oddly from him.

He infuriated visitors by fluttering round them like a bat when he accompanied them on tours of the college. The French naval officer, Charles Dupin, described his treatment 'in the library of the university, which I visited, introduced and conducted by a Doctor belonging to the same university, and which I went over, according to the rules, *not stopping anywhere*. I wished to approach a window from which a tolerably fine prospect was to be enjoyed; but the Doctor who accompanied me, held me back; in his presence and in that of a door-keeper who did not lose sight of us, there was a possibility of my putting a book in my pocket— there are countries where men are first rendered despicable in order that a right may afterwards be assumed to treat them as such'.

Barrett's sayings became known as Barrettiana, and after his death a collection of them was made and circulated round the university. They included examples of his odd speech mannerisms and retorts of students who teased him during his rambling lectures which were also riotous because he could not keep order. A student who flicked a mirror at him to dazzle him was told that he was casting reflections on his superiors. Another called after him 'Sweep! Sweep!' for which he was summoned before the board. 'I will chastize him for scandalum magnatum, for sure amn't I the vice-provost?' The charge was denied. 'How can that be?' demanded the doctor. 'For look you, there was no other sweep in the court, only myself.'

He was too mean to correct examinations with a pencil and used a pin instead. In oral examinations, if he received the correct answer he would say: 'Do you see me now, I'll give you a prod for that,' and thrust the pin through the paper.

In old age he was 'small and obese' and became deaf. A scholar thought he would amuse Commons by intoning, instead of customary Latin formula before a meal, 'Jacky Barrett thinks I'm saying grace Jacky Barrett thinks I'm saying grace Jacky Barrett thinks I'm saying grace . . .' 'May the devil admire me, but Jacky Barrett did *not* think ye were saying grace.'

He died in 1821, a wealthy man, having spent a lifetime accumulating money and neglecting and snubbing his pathetic relatives. A discreditable conversation was overheard between him and a widowed niece who called at his rooms.

THE DOCTOR: What do you want?

SHE: To speak to you, Sir.

HE: Well then? (Interrogatively.)

SHE: Well, Sir, won't you let me in?

HE: I can't go down now, do you see me . . .

SHE: Ah, Sir, only a few words . . .

HE: No, I tell you, go out of that!

When his impoverished nieces visited him he would call out: 'Eh, do you see me now? What, do you come after me till I'm dead?' His will stated: 'I leave everything I am possessed of to feed the hungry and clothe the naked.' His property, given to certain Fellows in trust for charitable purposes, was used sensibly and humanely. An annuity was given to Catty, and after it was decided that members of his family qualified under the will's simple provisions, they were granted a generous portion of the £80,000 he had accumulated.

Richard Pokrich

RICHARD POKRICH was an inventor whose fantastic ideas earned him the nickname of Projecting Pock. The whimsical nature of his schemes led him to be compared with the scientists of Swift's Academy of Ladago on the island of Laputa; it has even been suggested that Swift used the contemporary figure of Pokrich as a model for some of its members. He could easily have worked out a system for distilling sunshine out of cucumbers.

He was born in 1690 in Monaghan, where his father, a soldier who had been dangerously wounded at the siege of Athlone, possessed a large estate. Pokrich senior died in 1715, leaving this estate to his son, together with a comfortable income. Critics of the inventor have suggested that it amounted to £4,000 a year, and that this sudden fortune left in the hands of an unstable young man of twenty-five stimulated him to carry out numerous extravagant ideas. But the £4,000 mentioned may well have been a lump sum. Whatever the truth, Pokrich was to live most of his life in ruinous debt. No one has been able to work out how far this was the result of pouring money into his 'projections', or merely of dissipation.

Although he acquired the reputation for being a mad inventor, not all his ideas were crazy. He thought up an early lifeboat made of 'unsinkable tin' for the use of men-of-war, and a perfectly sensible scheme for linking the Liffey to the Shannon by canals. Perhaps it was these plans which earned him the nickname of 'The Captain.' He was enthusiastic about promoting native industries, and bought a brewery in Dublin. Guinnesses and Leesons established themselves with ale, but Pock's brewery failed. So, too, did his idea of turning the palace of the Archbishop of Tuam at Mount Eccles near Dublin into a cake house, even after he had approached the prelate a number of times with presents of pigeons.

Then his mind turned to bogs. He developed an interest in the most barren, undrained stretches of land which were considered as irreclaimable, and came to the conclusion that they could be planted with vineyards. But soon he considered it simpler to buy or rent thousands of unproductive acres in Co. Wicklow where he planned to rear geese, hoping to supply them to the combined markets of Ireland, England and France. He designed an observatory to be built on a mountain peak, anticipating Ireland's first observatory at Dunsink. There was to be a house for himself located in a nearby snow-filled valley. 'If any person is curious to see the celebrated seat where the Captain did principally reside,' wrote Brockhill Newburgh in his *Essays*, 'he is to descend a craggy mountain, one side almost perpendicular steep, and then to enquire for Pokrich's Paradise, or as some will have it, Pokrich's Purgatory.' But Newburgh was satirizing Pokrich, most of whose plans were confined to paper.

He had an attractive vision of providing every Irishman with a pair of wings, prophesying a day when a man could order up his wings in the same way he could order up his boots. He put forward well-defined ideas about rejuvenating old people and cheating death by means of blood transfusions. Experiments in transfusions had been performed on animals, but the process had not proved reliable. Pokrich was optimistic, and his instructions were precise. 'Take an inflex tube in the nature of a syphon, fix it to the extreme ends in the veins of two different persons to be opened to receive them, the one youthful, adult and sanguine, the other aged, decrepit and withered. The redundant fermenting blood of the one will immediately flow like wine decanted into the shrivelled veins of the other. The effects will be found no less surprising—the wrinkled skin braces, the flesh plumps up and softens, the eyes sparkle. He foresaw inconveniences for doctors and lawyers if everyone lived to the age of Methuselah, so he suggested that an act of Parliament could define a legal death to occur to anyone who lived beyond nine hundred and ninety-nine years. But he did not put all his faith in this scheme for perpetual youth, because he also invented an anti-wrinkle treatment which he practised on himself. 'Take common brown paper, steep it in vinegar, then apply it to the forehead, the skin about the eyes or any other wrinkled part; let it lie on some time, every half hour renewing the application. The wrinkles will not only disappear, but the cheeks flow with a vermeil that excels the power of paint.'

Considering the heights to which his imagination soared, his inventive genius was to be rewarded rather prosaically with the success of his musical glasses.

Musical glasses were not an original idea; Pokrich was not to know that in the Kama Sutra playing on glasses filled with water was one of the sixty-four practices recommended in the sexual education of a young girl. He developed his own glasses after the failure of yet another experiment, when he tried to invent a new instrument consisting of twenty drums. Varying from the smallest treble to the deepest bass, they were arranged in a circle to be played by one musician. 'This gentlemen,' wrote a friend, 'devoted some months wholly to practising upon and improving of this most extraordinary instrument—to the great mortification of all lovers of martial music.'

The glasses evolved from the drums. Pokrich was a frequenter of taverns, and possibly the familiar sight of half-empty tankards suggested the idea. John Carteret Pilkington, the son of Swift's favourite, Mrs. Laetitia Pilkington, met Pokrich late in 1743 in a seaside bar. He later described the engaging down-at-heel character: 'a tall middle-aged gentleman with a bag wig and a sword on . . . who was not amean to being provided with a free drink.' In the course of the evening Pokrich gave him a demonstration of his unusual skills in music.

'He pulled from his sleeve sixteen large pins and from his pocket a small hammer, and with this he drove the pins into a deal table, all ranged one above the other, and some almost in as far as the head; he then took from his side pocket two pieces of brass wire and demanded what tune I would have. I told him "The Black Joke". "Then lay your ears to the table," says he, "hear and admire." I did so, and to my infinite amazement he played it with all its variations, as to sound almost like a dulcimer. Encouraged by the applause I gave to this uncommon instrument, he took a parcel of drinking glasses and tuned them by putting different quantities of water in each; upon these he played a number of the newest tunes in the most elegant taste, giving one delight and satisfaction. He then proceeded to inform me that these were but sleuths of his grand art and discovery, "for," said he, "I have at home glasses as large as bells of my own invention that give you a sound as loud as the organ, but more delicate and pleasing to the ear." '

By the end of the evening, Carteret, who claimed to be a singer, was offered a job to accompany what Pokrich called 'The Angelic Organ' for £100 a year and keep; meanwhile he had to pay for the evening's drinks and also for a coach to bring them back to Pokrich's lodgings. When they arrived he was disappointed to find that Pokrich lived in 'the most littered and dirty hole I have ever seen; the furniture consisted of an old tawdry bed, one rush-bottomed chair, a frame with a number of large glasses on it, and the case of a violincello'.

The Angelic Organ had already been useful to Pokrich when its sweetness lulled two bailiffs who had come to seize him for debt at his brewery at Islandbridge. 'Gentlemen,' he had told them, 'I am your prisoner, but before I do myself the honour to attend you, give me leave as a humble performer in musick to entertain you with a tune.' 'Sir,' one of the bailiffs had answered, 'we came here to execute our warrant, not to hear tunes.' But with the bribe of a bottle of Rosa Salis, he persuaded them to sit and listen to his favourite 'Black Joke' which he played so affectingly that they were moved to forget their duties. 'Sir, upon your parole of honour to keep the secret, we give you your liberty . . .'

Carteret appears not to have been discouraged by the squalor of Pokrich's rooms, or at least he was impressed by his enthusiasm. During the next two months these unlikely partners practised their skills—Pokrich tapping the glasses and rubbing his fingers round them while Carteret accompanied the 'concourse of sweet sounds'. They decided to take the instrument to London and hold its début there. Arrangements were made, but three hours before the concert took place there was a disaster. 'An unmannerly sow' entered the concert room and smashed the glasses in her wanderings. A sow in a concert rooms must be as rare as a bull in a china shop. The money was returned to patrons, the instrument rebuilt and posters reissued:

'For the benefit of Mr. Pokrich, at Mr. Hunt's great Auction Room in Stafford Street on Thursday next will be a Concert of Vocal and Instrumental Music performed by Gentlemen. After the First Overture there will be a Voluntary performance upon the Glasses. Ellin-a-room, the Black Joke, with Additional Variations, the Hurk, the Bonney, Christ Church Bells, to be played in three parts upon the glasses.'

The concert, which took place in February 1744, was a success, and after a lifetime of dismally unsuccessful ventures Pokrich suddenly became famous and moderately wealthy. He was making six pounds a day. The sounds of the Angelic Organ charmed society; Walpole was addicted to them and the poet, Gray, compared them to the singing of nightingales. Goldsmith mentioned them in *The Vicar of Wakefield*.

The Angelic Organ became popular with other musicians and inventors. The composer, Gluck, constructed an improved instrument with a stand of twenty-six glasses tuned with spring water. He played a concert on them. Benjamin Franklin made a more elaborate development with his Armonica, an almost unrecognizable version of the Organ, with a monster series of 120 glasses ranged in rows and played by a keyboard. In an interesting letter to Cesare Beccaria written in 1762, Franklin referred to Pokrich's original idea. 'You have doubtless heard the sweet tone that is drawn from a drinking glass by passing a wet finger round its brim. One Mr. Puckeridge [*sic*], a gentleman from Ireland, was the first who thought of playing tunes formed of such tones. He collected a number of glasses of different sizes, fixed them near each other on a table, and tuned them by putting in the water, more or less as each tone required. The tones were brought out by passing his fingers round the brim.' Beethoven and Mozart wrote music for Franklin's Armonica.

The success of the glasses turned Pokrich's head to other ventures. A little over a year after his first concert, on April 23, 1745, this bachelor of fifty married Mrs. Margaret Winter, a widow who convinced him that she had ample private means. But she brought him nothing but debts, and after eight years of unhappiness she ran off with an actor. The lovers were drowned in a boat accident off the Scottish coast.

Meanwhile her husband unsuccessfully contested a seat in the Irish Parliament and then applied to be chapel master at Armagh Cathedral. The 'poor scarecrow' and 'battered beau' lacked the air of respectability necessary to fill such conventional positions in society. His accompanist, John Carteret, had quarrelled with him during the concert tour, and was soon saying that Pock never gave one genteel entertainment or did one benevolent act. Then Pokrich attracted the ridicule of a distant relative of his, Brockhill Newburgh, who came from Cavan and wrote satirical verse. In private Newburgh was quite kind about his cousin, whom he considered 'a pleasant, jocular and agreeable companion'. He also excluded the Angelic Organ as a subject of his wit, acknowledging that 'it is to this gentleman's original invention that we are indebted for one of the most pleasing instruments within the compass of sound'. But he thought that such a varied personality should be described in detail, and contemplated—or said he contemplated—writing a heroic poem of twenty-four books entitled 'To the Pokrich'. He published some essays which included much material about Pock and an extremely rude and candid dedication to his cousin:

'Unhappy to see a youth who has gone through these seminaries of learning with diligence, credit and reputation, and by his learning and parts encouraged the hopes of proving a useful member of society—at length turn out—what shall I say? a sportsman, jockey, card shuffler, bottle companion;—anything in short, but what parts, learning and a liberal education might have made him.'

Newburgh also wrote a short epistolary poem entitled 'The Projector' which ranged over some of the inventor's more unfortunate ideas.

Thee, the first subject of my muse,
Projecting Pock, to sing I chose:
But schemes unhappily divide
And tear thee from my faithful side . . .

Pokrich, too, wrote poetry among his many preoccupations. His muse had an even more limited talent than Newburgh's but his subject matter was varied and lively. In 1750 he published a *Miscellaneous Works* which he dedicated to that well-known Dublin character, 'His Majesty, Hack-Ball, King of the Beggars, Poets, Projectors, etc., etc.' They were a collection of light-hearted and indecent poems and epigrams ranging from a poem on Chester, to suggestions on running workhouses, a satire on drunkenness and a poem about the new gardens and lying-in-hospital adjoining Great Britain Street which began: 'Rejoice with me, ye wanton ladde's.'

There were also poems about poverty rising from Pokrich's direct experience. Many were written to thank benefactresses who helped him at moments when he was impoverished and harassed by debt. Those who sent him essential provisions inspired such verses as 'A poem upon a lady's desiring the author to send a crock that she might fill it with beef' and 'A poem occasioned by Mistress C—making a present of a pencil'. Another admirer sent him 'Syder and Bacon':

This comes to thank my lovely cousin
For Syder. I received a dozen,
Excepting one, by chance was broken
Just at your door by the same token.

Thanking the lady who sent him two barrels of coals, the poet hinted that he already had enough:

Madam, this comes with humour pleasant
To thank you for your friendly present
Of coals, two barrels I received,
So unexpected and uncrav'd
Such favours are not strange to me,

Where often from ladies, frank and free
Like you, have got without desiring,
A plenteous store of winter's firing.

Pokrich also tried his hand at ribald epigrams like 'On a lady seeing a gentleman making water from her window'. Or:

A lady once her husband found
Kissing her maid upon the ground,
Hussy, said she, this work you'll rue,
Which I still chose myself to do.

He had projected two volumes of verse but only one was printed. Of all his schemes only the musical glasses brought him a small degree of success; otherwise the feverish visionary achieved little. His very last idea misfired. He directed that after his death his body should be preserved in spirits—he would manufacture these himself—and placed in a lead coffin in a public place so that future generations could 'indulge their curiosity in beholding the remains of so illustrious and venerable a personage'. But in 1759 while on a visit to London he was suffocated in a fire at his lodgings at Hamlin's Coffee House near the Royal Exchange, and nothing was left of him to display.

The Stratfords and the Kings

THE Stratfords and the Kings were excessively wealthy families who owned possessions that were large even by eighteenth-century Anglo-Irish standards. Both obtained earldoms, those of Aldborough and Kingston, and for a time produced eccentrics in successive generations.

The Stratfords owned land in south Wicklow, Carlow and Kildare. The first member of the family to live in Ireland had been Robert Stratford, who arrived in 1660; his grandson, John, born in 1689, enlarged the estates over a lifetime of hard work and scheming, married into the ancient Irish family of O'Neill, and commissioned a magnificent house, Belan, near Castledermot in Co. Kildare, the combined work of two of the greatest architects ever to work in Ireland, Francis Bindon and Richard Castle. When he was an old man he obtained an Earldom during one of the pre-Union scrambles for honours. He became 'Earl of Aldborough in the Palatinate of Upper Ormonde', an entirely fictitious location and invented an impressive bogus pedigree for himself. The founder of the family was said to be 'Gualtera de Lupella, vulgarly called Lovel or Tonci' who came 'from Amiens, the capital of Picardy in France to England with William the Conqueror'. It is not uncommon for newly created peers to spruce up their ancestors, but Lord Aldborough went further and announced that his new coat of arms was the same as that of Alexander the Great. Having received his elaborate honours in February 1777, he died four months later.

He was succeeded by his son, Edward Augustus, 'an arrogant and ostentatious man' according to Jonah Barrington, and in the words of an anonymous contemporary 'a petit-maître and a patriot: equally ready to expire at the feet of a fine lady and to die with pleasure for his country's good'. To which Francis Hardy added: 'Neither the one nor the other—a Poor Creature in every way except as to Wealth.' Like many landlords the second earl had a passion for building. Besides improving Belan, he built a charming villa at Seapoint outside Dublin, and in the city Aldborough House on the Royal Canal, now the Stores Department of the General Post Office. He founded a model industrial town called Stratford-on-Slaney, to distinguish it from other Stratfords, which produced lace, plush, ribbons, carpets, linen, stockings and calico printing. In London he constructed Stratford Place with Stratford House at its head—where a century later Mrs. Jerome and her three daughters would settle when they came over from America. One Jerome became the mother of Winston Churchill; another produced Shane Leslie, who wrote of Stratford House:

'This was the unhygienic palace built by Lord Aldborough, commemorated in the epigram:

> Possessed of one fine Stair of State
> It holds no closet nearer than the gate:
> The foods and wine you cannot count
> But there's no Jakes for guests to mount.

'It was a fantastically uncomfortable masterpiece, all staircase and drawing-rooms (What perspective! was Disraeli's comment) The building could be described as Angelica Kauffman above and cesspool below.'

Aldborough House in Dublin (whose offices included a private theatre) also has a pretentious top-lit staircase-hall which Maurice Craig has compared to 'a well shaft or a mine or one of Mr. Howard's penitentiaries'. Lady Hardwicke, wife of the Viceroy, noted in 1801 that '*Otium cum Dignitate* is the motto displayed in the front, and when you enter the porte-cochère, another motto tells you to look around and you will find nothing but beauties' —among them a large heroic panel entitled 'Triumph of Amphitrite' showed Lady Aldborough in a riding habit with Minerva's helmet, sitting on the knee of Lord Aldborough who wore a complete set of regimentals.

Lord Aldborough became a noted collector, and his second wife, who brought him a dowry of £50,000, shared his passion. She was a good sport, making no objection to the Aldborough coach and its pockets being crammed during a journey from London to Dublin with 'living gold and silver fish, pheasants and other livestock'. Her husband's passion for ostentation was revealed during her first visit to Ireland. Determined to give her and the relatives who accompanied her a fitting welcome, he wrote an exacting letter to his agent, Mr. Derenzy at Baltinglass:

> I shall within a month bring over a new Lady Aldborough, and the Duchess of Chandos and Sir John and Lady Henniker. I am desirous of having them received at Ballimore by a small corps of Light Horse, at Stratford by a ditto of Light Foot, at Baltinglass by a ditto of Artillery, and escorted from thence to Belan by a ditto of Grenadiers and Light Horse. I wish also to entertain them while at Belan with two tragedies, two comedies, two musical and other farces, the choice of which I leave to yourselves, but beg be up in your usual parts and no disappointment. I shall have balls as usual, some concerts and a Fête Champêtre . . . The same is to be repeated next year when the Prince of Wales is to honour me with a visit. I hope my towns of Stratford and Baltinglass will make a figure as they pass through, be neat and clean, the . . . church covered in and Baltinglass new bridge completed.

Presumably his in-laws enjoyed the spectacle, although the Prince of Wales never came.

The Earl had a number of brothers with whom he quarrelled incessantly. The borough of Baltinglass was in the patronage of the Stratford family, but there was a constant dispute as to which of the brothers controlled it. Lord Aldborough thought that the best way to solve this difficulty was to have a returning officer on whom he could rely. He chose his sister, Lady Hannah, an appointment which astonished his contemporaries; Barrington described it as 'the most remarkable act of his Lordship's life'. His brothers chose a returning officer of their own, and convention being what it was, were able to defeat his Lordship, Lady Hannah and her lady friends, and keep the borough for themselves. 'The affair made a fine uproar in Dublin.'

In 1792, when Lord Aldborough was building Aldborough House, he disputed over boundaries with a Mr. Beresford. Taking the matter to court, they came before Lord Clare who happened to be Mr. Beresford's uncle and gave judgement in his nephew's favour. Lord Aldborough promptly wrote a satirical book in which he compared the court proceedings with those he had once had with a skipper in Holland. The skipper, who was also a judge, tried the case himself and gave himself a favourable verdict. The book was a huge success since Lord Clare was universally unpopular, and he was so upset that he insisted on bringing the matter before the House of Lords as a breach of privilege. When Lord Aldborough refused to plead unless every word of his book was read out distinctly, Lord Clare, displaying great reluctance, was obliged to read all the offending passages aloud while Lord Aldborough stood beside the woolsack holding a pair of candlesticks to help him see better. Lord Clare had his revenge when his persecutor was sentenced to twelve months' imprisonment and lodged in Newgate in a cell later occupied by Lord Edward Fitzgerald. Lady Aldborough shared her husband's imprisonment, and together they made the little cell as comfortable and luxurious as possible until influence secured Lord Aldborough's release. After a month or so he was freed on paying a fine and two sureties of £50 for good behaviour. He received a magnificent pardon from George III adorned with a painting of the royal coat of arms.

He retired to Belan where he continued to indulge in a passion for extravagant entertainment. He would organize race meetings which lasted a week. During the 1798 rebellion he would drive about the country in his coach attended by outriders, so that his glittering presence would reassure loyalists of his protection. Having added to his fortunes by receiving £15,000 to vote for the Union, Lord Aldborough fell ill. Before he died in 1801 he sought to enliven his deathbed by matchmaking, and invited a large party of young people to Belan, where he planned to marry off those who became attached to each other. His death interrupted the proceedings. He was known as the Earl of a Hundred Wills, although Barrington says that he only made fifty-four.

His brother, the Reverend and Honourable Paul Stratford, nicknamed Holy Paul, lived in a fine old house outside Baltinglass on the banks of the Slaney known as Mount Neill. He insured his residence heavily, and very soon afterwards it caught fire on a windy night. According to Barrington: 'No water was to hand, the flames raged; the tenants bustled, jostled and tumbled over each other in a general uproar and zeal to save his reverence's great house—his reverence alone, meek and resigned, beheld the voracious element devour his hereditary property, piously attributing the evil solely to the just will of providence as a punishment for having vexed his mother some years before her death! Under this impression the Hon. and Rev. Paul adopted the only rational and pious means of extinguishing the conflagration; he fell on his knees before the blazing mansion, and with clasped and uplifted hands, besought the Lord to have mercy and extinguish the flames.

'The people around exerted themselves whilst practicable to bring out the furniture piecemeal and range it on the grass plot. Paul, still on his knees cried out:

' "Stop, stop! Throw all my valuables back into the flames! Never fly, my friends, in the face of heaven. When the Almighty resolved to burn my house, He most certainly intended to destroy the furniture. I feel resigned. The Lord's will be done!"

'The tenants reluctantly obeyed his orders; but unfortunately for "Holy Paul" the insurance company, when applied to for the payment of his losses, differed altogether from his reverence as to the dispensation of providence and absolutely refused to pay any part of the damage incurred.'

The second Earl of Aldborough was succeeded by his brother, John, who lived very quietly at Belan having been deserted by his wife, who preferred to seek a more exciting social environment, first in the villa at Seapoint, then in London and Paris. After her departure the third Earl was looked after by his sister, Lady Deborah, and then by his vivacious daughter, Emily. She sought to enliven Belan by inviting down scores of guests to indulge in racing, cockfighting, gambling and every sort of extravagance she could devise for their entertainment. Lord Aldborough hated them all. Whenever anyone arrived his first question to the newcomer was: 'When do you leave? The coach passes Bolton Hill every morning, and I can send you there to-morrow.' But his efforts to speed guests on their way were quite ineffectual, unlike those of Frederick the Great, who expected compliance with his unmistakable signal for departure: 'I am so sorry to hear you have to leave . . . ah well, pleasant moments cannot last for ever.'

Lord Aldborough was an early riser, and every morning at dawn he would shuffle about the elaborate gardens of Belan long before any gardeners were up. In season he always carried a large basket which he filled up with the best of the newly ripened fruit in order to prevent his guests from eating it. He would creep upstairs again, convinced that no one knew of his depredations, and to make quite sure that his secret was kept, he would carefully clean the mud off his shoes himself so that not even his servants would suspect him.

He died in 1823 and yet another brother became fourth Earl. Benjamin O'Neill Stratford I, was unremarkable. Benjamin's son, Mason Gerard Stratford, followed him as fifth Earl in 1833, and managed to spend a large part of the family fortunes, at the same time acquiring an unpleasant reputation as a seducer, bigamist and rake. He lived in London from where he plundered his Irish properties to pay his debts; Belan was gradually stripped of furniture, mantelpieces, roof slates and stonework, and has been a ruin ever since. When he needed money really badly, he would approach the money-lenders who had previously obliged him with a pistol in his hands, and threaten to blow out their brains there and then. Since he only had a life interest in the property, his creditors usually gave him another loan.

The sixth and last Earl of Aldborough, Benjamin O'Neill Stratford II, succeeded his father in 1849. His life was a complete contrast. Born in 1809, he became a recluse, and retired inside the grounds of Stratford Lodge outside Baltinglass, where for over two decades he brooded about the construction of a giant balloon. In his seclusion he was waited upon by one solitary servant, and since he had no cook, his meals were sent down ready cooked from Dublin every day on the Blessington to Baltinglass Royal Mail Coach. He never journeyed the forty miles up to Dublin to meet people or seek other entertainment. Nothing would distract him from his programme; his sole aim in life, on which he spent most of the remainder of the family fortune, was the triumphant ascent of the biggest balloon ever made.

While it was being prepared and sewn, the balloon was lodged in the grounds of Stratford House in a vast hangar which he had constructed out of chiselled Wicklow granite. Through its great doors, sixty feet high and fifty feet wide, would pass the inflated monster in which he hoped to make a leisurely flight to England, and then another across the channel to France. He had bought a plot of earth on the banks of the Seine on which he hoped to land. The balloon was nearing completion at the time of the Crimean war, and he devised plans for providing it with a floating platform and offering its services to the British army. He visualized sharpshooters being carried over the bloodstained trenches of Sevastopol across the lines to snipe at Russian generals. To his disappointment the war ended too soon.

Then on a Sunday morning in 1856 Stratford House caught fire. The post coach from Athy brought the news to the people of Baltinglass, who gathered round the doomed flame-spitting mansion.

Like his great-uncle Paul, Lord Aldborough was not interested in the fate of his residence. 'Save the balloon house!' he cried, and it was done under his frenzied direction. But the chains of buckets were unable to save its precious contents; a spark caught the silk and the balloon flared and was consumed in a moment. With it went all his purpose in life. Since the big house had burned to the ground, he moved into the blackened balloon house for a time with a few pieces of salvaged furniture. Later he went to Alicante in Spain, where he became more of a recluse than ever. Meals were brought up to his hotel rooms, but the plates and utensils were not removed—when one room became clogged up, he moved to another. He augmented his income by breeding dogs and selling Holloway pills. He died in 1875, the last of the Earls of Aldborough. The Earldom had lasted for almost a century.

The Catholic church in Baltinglass is partly constructed of stone taken from the balloon house. For years many of the fishing-rods in the neighbourhood were made out of the cane salvaged from the burnt balloon.

★   ★   ★

Members of the King family included a murderer, and a scholar who paralleled the sixth Lord Aldborough in powers of concentration directed towards a curious purpose. (I was made physically conscious of the obsessive nature of Lord Kingsborough's scholarship as, sitting in the National Library in Dublin, I watched an attendant staggering towards my desk burdened down with an enormous red-bound volume. 'There's eight more where it came from,' he said indignantly. 'You won't be wanting them now.' I had idly filled in a docket for *Antiquities of Mexico.* Although I knew that Lord Kingborough had spent most of his life writing it, I had been unprepared for this elephantine book and its eight companions in which the peer, who belonged to no university or seat of learning, set out to prove that in ancient times Mexico was colonized by the Jews.)

Lord Kingsborough's grandfather, the second Earl of Kingston, who once employed Arthur Young as a land agent on his estates at Mitchelstown in Co. Cork, is said to have invented pitchcapping, the torture inflicted on rebels during the 1798 rebellion. He was also tried for murder by his peers after shooting a Colonel Fitzgerald who abducted his daughter from a party at Mitchelstown House and was caught and killed after a wild pursuit. The Irish House of Commons was draped in black velvet for the trial and provided with an executioner who carried an axe pointed at Lord Kingston's neck. However, the peers had sympathy for the outraged father, and acquitted him.

His son, the third Earl of Kingston, who had taken part in the chase after his sister, had to wait six years after his father's death before he could take over the estate. His mother, a recluse,

locked him out of the house, and only when she died herself
was he able to enter the family home. He immediately pulled
down this fine Georgian mansion which had been erected only
about thirty years before. He had a castle built in its place. 'I
am no judge of architecture,' he told the architect, George Richard
Pain, 'but it must be larger than any house in Ireland, and have
an entrance tower named the White Knight's Tower. No delay!
It is time for me to enjoy it!'

The castle was finished in 1823 at about the time that a manufacturer thought of starting an industry in Mitchelstown. He
had built a large chimney before Lord Kingston turned his attention to his presence. Horrified at the intrusion, he let it be known
to the townspeople that they had a choice. Unless the stranger left
and his chimney was taken down, he would retire to England. 'I
am come to wish you goodbye, boys,' he told an assembly. 'This
is but a small place and there is not room in it for me and that
man. He says the law is on his side and I dare say it is. Consequently I go to England tomorrow.'

Lord Kingston stayed and it was the manufacturer who packed
his bags. After that, his lordship—whom George IV once described as 'you black whiskered good natured fellow!'—supervised the development of the town. Two churches were built,
one Protestant, one Catholic, a square was laid out and a school
named after his family. But later there was a second challenge to
his authority when his candidate was defeated at an election. He
summoned his tenants from three counties to the castle where he
sat in state waiting to receive them at the end of his hundred-
foot gallery. Suddenly he went mad. 'They are coming to tear
me to pieces! They are coming to tear me to pieces!' he screamed,
leaping from his seat and throwing his arms wide. Later he had
to be confined.

The author of *Antiquities of Mexico* was his eldest son. The
Right Honourable Edward King, Viscount Kingsborough, was
born at Mitchelstown on November 16, 1795. After a boyhood
spent in Ireland he went to Exeter College, where in 1818 he
gained an undistinguished second class degree in classics. Like
many peers he did not bother to take his graduation. He returned

to Ireland where he served as M.P. for Co. Cork, until 1826 when he resigned the seat to his brother Robert, whose loss of it was the onset of their father's madness. Lord Kingsborough gave up politics and every sort of pleasure and pastime, including the idea of marriage, to devote his life to the study of Mexico.

His interest had been aroused in Oxford, where he came across a manuscript called the Mendoza Codex. Not long after the conquest of Mexico, the Spanish Viceroy, Mendoza, Marques de Mondejar, had sent this codex to the Emperor, Charles V. During the long journey to Europe the ship that carried it was captured by the French, and instead of going to the Spanish Emperor, it had found its way to Paris, where it was bought by the Chaplain to the English Embassy. In 1625 it was engraved by the antiquary, Purchs. Then it vanished, to turn up a couple of centuries later in the Bodleian Library, where the sight of it fired Lord Kingsborough with his enthusiasm for Mexico and its past. Although he never found time to visit the country, he was inspired to undertake a colossal task that was to last his lifetime. He decided to trace other Mexican documents that had found their way to Europe over the centuries and compile them for the first time in a series of volumes he would publish himself.

He searched the great collections of Europe, finding his material in the Royal Libraries of Paris, Berlin and Dresden, the imperial Library at Vienna, the Library of the Institute of Bologna and the Borgia Museums. The Vatican possessed a number of important manuscripts. Private individuals like Archbishop Laud and Dr. Seldon had made collections, and so had Lord Kingsborough's contemporary, Sir Thomas Phillips, who vigorously encouraged the project. But, curiously enough, Lord Kingsborough failed to investigate a most important source of Mexican documents—he never went to Spain to inspect the libraries there. Inevitably his detailed compilation was incomplete.

However the presentation of this material was only part of his aim. He did not plan a work of pure scholarship, which was just as well since he had no special knowledge of the languages in which the documents were written or the background they described. But he used them to demonstrate his passionate belief in the early Hebrew colonization of America. He had got the idea from the writings of Montecino. 'We have the authority of a Jew,' he claimed, 'for believing that a colony of Jews had been settled in America long before the age of Columbus, who gives an account of his interview with his Indian brethren who had forgotten Hebrew, were unacquainted with Spanish and spoke to him by means of an interpreter. It is certainly remarkable that they should for so many generations have retained a lively recollection of their Christian persecutions, and should consequently have adopted precautions to prevent the Spaniards discovering their retreat. Their repeated utterance of the syllable Ba! accompanied by furious gesticulations and stamping with their feet, afforded proof also of the fanaticism which still animated them.'

The migrations of the Jews have produced many fanciful theories, and their descendants have been traced all over the Middle East to Afghanistan, India and Africa. Lord Kingsborough reminded his readers that the ancient prophets had foretold that the Jews would be scattered over the face of the earth, and since the earth's surface included all of the New World, it was quite natural to find them in Mexico and Peru. He was undeterred by the commonly held opinion that the New World had only been discovered in 1492. 'Nor will it avail those who wish to insinuate that Moses was perhaps ignorant of the existence of America and therefore did not mean to prophesy that the Jews would be scattered about the continent; since this would be arguing absurdly that human knowledge prescribes limits to Divine inspiration.'

He set about finding similarities between the Mexicans and Jews in their laws, customs and religion. He did this with much ingenuity; he had, his critic, W. H. Prescott, wrote, a good nose for this type of scholarship 'and can scent out a Hebrew root, be it buried never so deep'. Analogies included circumcision, fasting, the use of incense in temples and the cult of sacrifice. He saw a parallel in Christ's crucifixion with that of the Mexican god, Quexalcoatl, whom he also associated with the brazen serpent. 'The Jews considered the brazen serpent which Moses lifted up in the wilderness as a famous figure of the brazen serpent and

Quexalcoatl (which proper name signifies a precious feathered serpent) was so named after the memorable prodigy of the serpent in the wilderness.' He claimed to have traced numerous transcribed accounts taken from the Old Testament in Mexican manuscripts. They included the stories of Noah, Moses and Cain. 'To the fourth chapter of the Book of Genesis which tells the murder of Abel by Cain may perhaps be referred a singular notion of the Mexicans that the sun and the earth drank up the blood of the slain.'

He found prohibitions against the eating of pork in both cultures, and was particularly interested in what he considered similar attitudes to the idea of sacrifice. 'In nothing did the Mexicans more resemble the Jews than in the multitude of their sacrifices. The Jews, it is well known, never tasted blood; and Gemara remarks that though the Mexicans devoured the flesh of human victims, they were never seen to taste the blood.' He eagerly reproduced a traveller's account of circumcision. The fact that Mexican complexions were darker than Semitic he explained with a reference he found in the Old Testament; those 'whose visages were to become blacker than a coal occurs in the fourth chapter of Jeremiah'. It does not precisely, but the confused pronouncements of that gloomy prophet were perfectly suitable to Lord Kingsborough's vague, but sweeping scholarship. The theme of ancient Hebrew migration is scattered through the vast work in hundreds of references and footnotes.

In 1830 the first of the massive volumes entitled *Antiquities of Mexico* was published. Every year for seven years a volume appeared, and two more came out after Lord Kingsborough's death. The source materials included Sahagan's *History of New Mexico*, which he republished after two centuries of neglect, various Aztec drawings and a commentary by the French traveller, Dupai. The thousand fine illustrations were by Augustine Aglio. No pains were spared on the production. 'This work in its magnificence,' wrote Lord Altham, 'recalls to mind patronage of crowned heads and the splendour of the Princely Patrons of Literature.' Others wrote no less eulogistically—'noble . . . colossal . . . magnificent' were adjectives much employed in describing *Antiquities*. 'It was to be wished,' wrote the explorer, Humboldt, 'that some government could publish at its own expense the remains of the ancient American civilizations; for it is only by the comparison of several manuscripts that we can succeed in discovering the meaning of these allegories which are partly astronomical and partly mystic. This enlightened wish has now been realized, not by any government, but by a private individual, Lord Kingsborough.' The *London Monthly Review* confessed that, 'We should have supposed, after we had contemplated the superb materials of which they consist that [these volumes] were the result of some state enterprise undertaken by a spirited and ambitious government, which aimed at exalting the national character and its own by the munificence of its patronage of the fine arts.'

There were critics, however, who, while finding no textual inaccuracies, considered that the presentation was confusing. The plates, for example, were not even numbered. Appleton's *American Biography* commented that 'the work is chiefly valuable for its generally faithful reproductions and facsimiles of Mexican records in Europe' but added that 'their careless arrangement renders them unintelligible except to advanced students of American Archaeology'. The great Mexican historian, W. H. Prescott, while acknowledging the debt that scholarship owed Lord Kingsborough, regretted that 'the purchaser would have been saved some superfluous expense and the reader much inconvenience if the letter press had been in volumes of ordinary size . . . it is not uncommon in works of this magnificent plan, to find utility in some measure sacrificed to show'.

Prescott also made some acid remarks about 'capricious annotations'. He considered the presence of Jews in pre-Columban America as fanciful as the stories of Queen Scheherazade in the *Arabian Nights* and not so entertaining. 'The drift of Lord Kingsborough's speculations is to establish the colonization of Mexico by the Israelites. To this the battery of his logic and learning is directed. For this the hieroglyphics are unriddled, manuscripts compared, monuments delineated. His theory, however, whatever its merits, will scarcely become popular; since instead of being exhibited in a clear and comprehensive form, readily embraced by the mind, it is spread over an infinite number of notes, thickly sprinkled with quotations from languages ancient and modern, till the weary reader, floundering about in the ocean of fragments with no light to guide him, feels like Milton's devil working his way through chaos.'

Undeterred, Lord Kingsborough continued to put forward his highly original ideas in volume after magnificent volume. A complete set cost £120 but later the price was reduced to £36. The publication was not a commercial success, and in fact is believed to have cost him £32,000. He gave away numerous free copies; nine sets of volumes went to the crowned heads of Europe, and two, printed on vellum with coloured plates at a cost of £3,000 each, were presented to the British Museum and to Oxford University, which acknowledged his generosity with a public vote of thanks at Convocation. 'By this munificent undertaking, which no government probably would have, and few individuals could have executed, he had entitled himself to the lasting gratitude of every friend of science.'

His obsession cost him his fortune and, in a roundabout way, his life. After he had spent all his money on the enterprise, debts accrued. He had trouble with his stationer and printer. According to his friend, Sir Thomas Phillips (who had originally been responsible for introducing him to the Codex), he was shamefully cheated by both of them. At the same time, the illustrator Augustine Aglio 'had the ingratitude to claim the copyright of this grand work, altho' Lord Kingsborough was too modest to put his own'.

In 1837 Kingsborough was arrested for debt. The most plausible of several versions of the event is that he refused to pay the stationer a debt which he considered unjust. Possibly things could have been sorted out quickly. But the filthy confines of the Sheriff's Prison in Dublin proved lethal, and very soon after his arrest he died there of typhus on Friday, March 3, 1837. He was forty-two. He died a year before his father, from whom he would have inherited the earldom and an income of £40,000 a year—enough to produce countless vellum sets of *Antiquities of Mexico*.

Buck Whaley and Tiger Roche

BUCK WHALEY became famous, made a lot of money and earned himself the nickname of Jerusalem Whaley by going to Jerusalem for a bet.

Whaley was a typical buck, a spender for whom gambling and other extravagant forms of behaviour were an integral part of the character he created for himself. But he was not violent. He never took to duelling and lacked the cruelty that marked so many of his profligates. His memoirs, motivated by a streak of masochism, are an account of how he got through his fortune by the age of thirty-four. He bewails his degradation with gusto, finding pleasure in the idea of ruination. He wrote them in 1797, intending them to be published after his death as a warning to others, but these instructions were not carried out by his executors who did not want to embarrass his heirs. The manuscript was lost for a century. It eventually turned up in a book sale and the *Memoirs* were published in 1906.

'I was born with strong passions,' they began, 'a lively imagination and a spirit that could brook no restraint. I possessed a restlessness and activity of mind that directed me to the most extravagant pursuits; and the ardour of my disposition never abated till satiety had weakened the power of enjoyment.'

He was the son of Richard 'Burn Chapel' Whaley, nicknamed after an incident in which he demonstrated his dislike of Catholics. The elder Whaley is also remembered for the rhymed cheque which he drew in favour of his wife from La Touche's bank:

> Mr. La Touche
> Open your pouch
> And give unto my darling

Five hundred pounds sterling:
For which this will be your bailey,
Signed Richard Chapell Whaley.

He died in 1769 when his son was only three, leaving a magnificent town house in Stephen's Green, an estate in Wicklow, £60,000 and an income of £7,000 a year which young Thomas began to spend around the age of eighteen. When the Buck was sent abroad to make the Grand Tour, a tutor was engaged and an allowance of £900 a year was set aside for expenses; both proved laughably inadequate. Young Whaley settled in France, where he kept up a country house and a town house in Paris, filled with acquaintances living at his expense. One evening he lost £14,000 at cards and gave the bill for the amount on his banker—La Touche, the same as his father's. When the cheque bounced he had to leave Paris for London in a hurry. Then to Dublin where he went to dine with the Duke of Leinster. One of the company asked what part of the world he planned to visit next, and on the spur of the moment he replied, 'Jerusalem'. The Middle East, scattered with bandits and unscrupulous Ottoman officials, was not a comfortable place to visit at the time, and his fellow bucks were quite happy to bet him £15,000 that he would be unable to get to the Holy City and bring back incontestable proof that he had been there within two years. Before he could set out he had to disentangle himself from another wild scheme. He had just arranged to go round the world in a yacht with a lady whose name he did not disclose in the *Memoirs*. The yacht, a large one of 280 tons, armed with twenty-two cannon, had just been completed by a shipbuilder. But Jerusalem suddenly became more pressing, or perhaps the lengthy cruise was distastful, and Whaley sold off the vessel to the Empress of Russia.

The sudden change from one outrageous scheme to the next was typical of his quixotic behaviour. In a revealing passage he attributed many of his misfortunes to 'the extreme anxiety and impatience I always felt at the approach of any difficulty. To avoid an impending evil I have formed plans so wild and extravagant, and for the most part impractical, that what I had before dreaded appeared light when compared to the distress I incurred by my own precipitate folly'.

He switched his plans so rapidly that it was only a few days after making the wager that he embarked for the Holy Land from the Dublin Quays on October 8, 1788. Thousands of people thronged the pier to get a last glimpse of the daring young man, and a ballad writer composed 'Whaley's Embarkation' to the tune of the 'Rutland Jig'.

> One morning walking George's Quay
> A monstrous crowd stopp'd up the way
> Who came to see a sight so rare,
> A sight that made all Dublin stare,
> Balloons, a Vol review [i.e. Volunteer Review]
> Ne'er gathered such a crew
> As there did take their stand
> This sight for to command
> Tol lol lol tol lol . . .

He sailed to Deal where he was joined for the expedition by a Captain Wilson. From Deal he sailed for Gibraltar with a retinue of servants and 'a large stock of Madeira wine'. Gibraltar was an English military post where the party was entertained by the garrison, and a ball was held by the governor in Whaley's honour, during which the Buck danced the Fandango for three hours. Then the expedition, joined by Captain Hugh Moore, who completed the round trip with Whaley, set out for Smyrna, an important trade centre between east and west. The arrival of the ship was greeted in a gratifying manner by a fifty-gun salute. The party hunted, wore Turkish dress and was lavishly entertained.

Captain Wilson developed rheumatic pains and had to return to England. Whaley took the others, still dressed as Turks, on the overland journey to Constantinople which they reached on his twenty-second birthday. They were given a civic reception and the British Ambassador introduced him to the powerful Abdul Hamid, Admiral of the Turkish Fleet, the real power in Turkey who ruled through the Sultan. Whaley presented him with a pistol that could fire seven balls one after another, and received in return a pélisse and a bottle of Otto de Rose.

On January 21, 1789 he set sail for the Levant in a ship called the *Heureuse Marie* carrying a permit from Abdul Hamid to visit Jerusalem. At St. Jean d'Acre he encountered Al Jazzar, a tough Bosnian, notorious as 'the Butcher', who ruled the whole Levant. Al Jazzar was sitting under a magnolia tree with the British consul in a humiliating position before him, trembling in every limb. He took a fancy to Whaley and told him: 'I am the Lord and Master here, and you are under my protection.' He showed him his harem, where the Buck watched a procession of a hundred women all dressed in white and managed to persuade his host not to smash the back of a gardener with a silver hammer as punishment for breaking the stem of a valuable plant.

Because of fears of bandits the last stage of the journey had to be undertaken by night. At last Whaley found himself in Jerusalem, where he was able to find lodgings in the Convent of Terra Sancta in a room which had been occupied a few years previously by another Irishman, a Mr. Smith-Barry from Cork. Among the legends that rose from his trip was one that he agreed to play ball against the walls of the Holy City. This was not true, but there is no doubt that he went to elaborate pains to acquire proof that he had achieved his purpose. Besides obtaining enough observations to give detailed descriptions of the Holy Places, he asked the superior of the Convent for a signed certificate which he included in his *Memoirs*:

> I, the undersigned, guardian of this convent of St. Mary, certify to all and singular who may read these presents that Messrs. Thomas Whaley and Hugh Moore have on two occasions been present and resided in this convent of Nazareth for a space of three days whereof
>
> given on the 2nd of and signed 5th March, 1789.
> Brother Archangel of Entraigues, Guardian and Superior.

Whaley's return was a leisurely overland progress, and he did not reach Ireland until the summer of 1789. There were bonfires and further celebrations when his fellow bucks handed over their wagers. He estimated he had travelled 7,178 miles in nine months. His expenses were £8,000, so he was £7,000 to the good.

After Jerusalem he had about a decade of dissipation left to him. Most of his money went on gambling in Daly's, the lavish gaming hell where men could throw their money away even in daylight when the rooms were darkened and chandeliers kept glowing to heighten the atmosphere. The rest of his fortune was spent on quixotic enterprises. In London, while losing to another compulsive gambler, Charles James Fox, he devised a scheme for rescuing the King of France from the guillotine. He went to Paris: 'but when I came to the fatal spot, my resolution failed me, and fully convinced that there was not the smallest prospect of rescuing the unfortunate victim from the hands of his murderers, I fled with much precipitancy from this scene of slaughter.'

In his *Memoirs* the famous occasion when he threw himself out of a window into a passing hackney and kissed the fair occupant is placed in Dover. Legend has located the incident outside Daly's or his house in Stephen's Green. Lord Cloncurry said that the jump crippled him for life. He must have mistimed it, because bucks jumped out of windows quite often. In country areas, Barrington wrote, 'very few accidents occurred—usually there was a dunghill of other soft material under the window—the tumble, in truth, was more dirty than dangerous'. Example was set by Dublin street urchins, who commonly dived off the rigging of ships into the Liffey.

Whaley was susceptible to pretty girls. When the sister of a Belfast clergyman was visiting Dublin and standing outside his mansion admiring the façade, he invited her to look inside. After inspecting the various rooms she was asked for her opinion which was so flattering, and she herself so charming, that Whaley made a polite bow and told her: 'This house and all that it contains is mine, and if you wish to make it yours also, you may have the house and the master of it.' The offer was refused, which was as well, because he had a mistress and a number of children. When this lady died he married Lord Cloncurry's sister, who seems to have kept him in better order, since he spent his last months frugally educating his children and writing his memoirs in a contrite spirit. By then his debts had forced him to go into exile.

His inglorious political career kept him solvent for a short time. He represented two constituencies in the Irish House of Commons. The first, Newcastle in Co. Down, had been a safe seat which he acquired at the age of seventeen. After 1797 he changed seats, and it was as member for Enniscorthy that he was bribed £4,000 to vote for the Union. Later he performed another patriotic action by accepting a large sum to vote against it. But no sum was adequate to cover his debts, and he had to sell his estates to pay them. There was a little left over to be used in a final fling.

'With the remainder, amounting to about five thousand pounds, I resolved to try my fortune at play and either retrieve myself or complete my ruin.' After that his financial affairs became so embarrassing that he fled to the Isle of Man. Here he found enough remaining cash to build himself a substantial house which became known as Whaley's Folly, and was subsequently turned into the Fort Ann Hotel. Before starting to build, he imported shiploads of Irish earth to make a foundation in order to win a bet that he could live on Irish soil without living in Ireland. During the autumn of 1800 he paid a visit to England where he died suddenly of a chill at a coaching inn in Knutsford, Cheshire. He was thirty-four years old. His body was placed in a lead coffin and brought to the town's old assembly rooms. Just after the undertakers closed the lid, an Irishman called Mr. Robinson appeared and danced a hornpipe on it.

★   ★   ★

Tiger Roche, was also famous for his nickname gained during a sojourn in foreign parts. But he was named for very different reasons; the range of his unpredictable and often ferocious behaviour offered a contrast with the frivolity of the charming Whaley. Roche was born in 1729, a member of an ancient aristocratic Norman family. His brother was Sir Boyle Roche, the old Parliamentary bore, immortalized for his lateral thinking in a number of sayings which are to be found in dictionaries of quotations. ('Posterity be damned! What has posterity done for us?' 'The best way to avoid danger is to meet in plump.' 'I smell a rat; I see it floating in the sky and darkening the sky; I'll nip it in the bud!' (Attrib.))

Tiger Roche, the younger brother, grew up to be an able and intelligent young man, educated and reasonably wealthy, well-liked by that civilized viceroy, Lord Chesterfield, who offered him a commission in the army when he was sixteen. But he prefered to consort with other bucks and share their senseless pastimes. His career took a sudden turn when after an evening's carousal he and some drunken friends managed to kill a night watchman. He avoided arrest by fleeing to Cork and boarding a ship to America, where he joined the French in their wars against the Indians. When the English and French declared war on one another, he switched to the English side. He became an officer, and might have advanced to high rank if a brother officer had not happened to lose a valuable fowling-piece. Roche was accused of the theft, in spite of his violent protestations of innocence. He was court-martialled and dismissed the service 'with a mark of disgrace and ignominy'. He refused to go away, continuing to claim loudly that he had been wronged and challenging the officer who had accused him to a duel, which was refused. Then he attacked the picket guard with his sword, flew at his persecutor's throat with his teeth bared '. . . and before he could be disengaged, nearly strangled him, dragging away a mouthful of flesh, which in true Indian fashion he afterwards declared "was the sweetest morsel he had ever touched" '. After that he was known as Tiger.

The deficiencies of the British army in America must have been considerable since Tiger was allowed to remain in his regiment as a foot soldier. He was present at the Battle of Ticonderoga. But he found that his reduction to the ranks appeared to be permanent and that he had no opportunity to regain his place as an officer. The situation obsessed him. He had been able to leave a murder behind him by one crossing of the Atlantic, and he must have thought that it would be possible to isolate the next episode of his past safely in America by going back to England where knowledge of the theft was unknown. In London he applied once again for a commission. But details about the fowling-piece leaked out and once again his application was refused. In a personal revival of medieval trial by combat he declared he would fight anyone who doubted his innocence, and set about immediately to prove his point by challenging a Captain Campbell whom he believed had informed on him. The duel resulted in both men being seriously wounded. As soon as he recovered, Tiger challenged and fought his former Colonel, but luckily before there could be further carnage a corporal in the regiment named Bourke gave a death-bed confession that it was he who had stolen the wretched fowling-piece and that Tiger had been wronged all along.

This vindication was enough to restore him to the comfortable status of a buck. A lieutenant at last, he returned to Dublin where the old murder charge had been quietly dropped. Now he was recognized as a respected veteran of the American wars and could marry an heiress and become a man about town, handsome, and skilful at dancing. His fight to prove his innocence and the glamour of his ferocious nickname helped his social popularity. He became a supporter of law and order and an enemy of the pinkindindies. These were expert swordsmen, generally sons of respectable people, who had run wild and formed gangs. Their existence continued until the police force was created. Like all gentlemen, they dressed very formally in full dress with a small sword or, in undress, with a couteau de chasse. They were violent pickpockets who would rob their victims by threatening to nick them with the points of their swords which protruded from their scabbards. They also engaged in the popular Irish pastime of abducting prosperous ladies. One evening while Tiger was strolling along Ormonde Quay, he came across some of them attacking an old gentleman walking with his son and daughter. He was a match for them; Barrington said of him that 'he regarded swords no more than knitting needles, and pinked every man he faced in combat'. Without hesitation he went for them, wounding some

and putting the rest to flight. The incident gave him the idea
of establishing a night patrol to keep the streets safe and provide
'that protection to the citizens which the miserable and decrepit
watch was not able to afford'.

His marriage started to go badly; after he had been through his
wife's fortune, she left him. To avoid his Irish debts he went to
London, but they caught up with him there, and he was arrested
and put in the King's Bench prison. While he was in jail his
personality underwent a metamorphosis. The unbalanced hot
temper, reckless bravery and quickness to avenge any insult
turned overnight into an equally unnatural apathy which made
him submit to insults and blows with a terrible patience or with
tears. People tried to get some of the old aggression out of him,
but they could not stir him. Among his fellow prisoners was
Buck English, one of the most savage of Irish bucks—he is said to
have shot a waiter and had him put on the bill for £50. English,
who had previously quarrelled with Roche, attacked him and beat
him ferociously with a stick. Tiger made no attempt to defend
himself, but merely crouched and cried like a child.

It was only the stone walls around him that brought him to
this condition. When by good fortune he was left a small legacy
which enabled him to pay his debts, he walked through the prison
gates his usual confident self. After this instant rehabilitation he
once again began to cut a dash in society—this time in London.
He became so popular that some of his friends actually nominated
him as propective parliamentary candidate for Middlesex, and
were disappointed when he refused to accept the honour. He
married another heiress and fought with two footpads, one of
whom he put to flight and the other he captured. They were both
brought to trial, where Tiger, recovering his temper, pleaded for
their lives so that they were not hanged but transported. His com-
placency was extreme; once in a billiard room he was observed
playing by himself for a considerable time while others waited
their turn. When someone reminded him about the other gentlemen, he remarked loudly: 'Gentlemen? Why, sir, except you and
me and two or three more, there is not a gentleman in the room!'
Later he added that such a statement could be made without

offence, for 'there was not another in the room that did not con-sider himself one of the two or three gentlemen I excepted'.

After this golden period of popularity and prosperity he ran out of money again and joined the army for a second time. Now he enlisted as Captain of a Company of Foot attached to the East India Company, a position which offered opportunities not only for good fighting, but also for mending his fortune. With luck he might return to his old haunts a wealthy nabob. But no sooner had he boarded the *Vansittart* and set sail in May 1773, for the long wearisome haul around the Cape of Good Hope to India, than Tiger began quarrelling. He had a violent argument with a Captain Ferguson, the sort of affair which could only be sorted out by a duel, When the *Vansittart* arrived at Madeira, her first landfall, Captain Ferguson immediately went ashore to find a firm duelling ground and settle his differences. To his astonishment Roche refused to fight. Once again he behaved as he had in the King's Bench prison, quivering with terror, and making an abject and shameful submission which so disgusted his fellow officers that for the rest of the voyage they banned him from eating at the captain's table and forced him to mix with the common sailors. Perhaps it was claustrophobia that re-duced him to such a wreck; the enclosing timbers of the ship's cabins may have resembled the confined spaces of his cell.

When the *Vansittart* reached Cape Town there was a delay while she waited to be provisioned. Many of the officers went ashore and stayed in the town, among them Captain Ferguson. When, one night, the Captain was found murdered outside his lodgings, suspicion fell on Roche at once; he felt sufficiently uncomfortable to flee into the bush and take refuge with the kaffirs who lived there. The *Vansittart* sailed on without him, but with lurid rumours about his fate; it was said that the Dutch had broken him on the wheel.

The Cape authorities behaved better than that, and gave him a trial in which he was acquitted. Now it was like the fowling-piece all over again, as Roche went through immense efforts to prove himself innocent of murder to his brother officers and to the world in general. First he went to India, sailing on a French ship. When he arrived in Bombay he was arrested and had to go through complicated legal wranglings to get himself shipped back to England to stand trial at the Old Bailey. His trial for the murder of Captain Ferguson took place on December 11, 1775, when he was again acquitted.

He was nearly forty, which was old for a buck. Impecunious, mad, scarred and disgraced—the fiasco of the Madeira duel had become a well-known piece of gossip—he had forfeited the interest of London Society. He returned to India, and there, where it was easy enough to die, he disappeared from public view.

Court Circles

THE young Prince of Wales, later George IV, had a reputation for profligate behaviour which society considered enhanced by the fact that some of his closest friends were Irish rakes. As a young man at the turn of the eighteenth century he chose a number of companions who were thought 'the very *lees* of society', according to one contemporary opinion. Another censorious commentator described them as 'creatures with whom a man of morality of even common decency' could not associate. The most notorious of them were the Barry brothers, rich, elegant spendthrifts who were the first of the Regency bucks. They lived well and died young, so that they just managed to avoid the debtor's prison. In fact their large fortune did not quite hold out, and the last Lord Barrymore had to avoid his creditors by living in France.

The Barrys originally came to Ireland with the Normans and for centuries had taken a prominent part in Irish life. The main branch of the family hesitated to abandon the old faith after the disasters of the Desmond rebellion, but two generations later they turned Protestant and were able to keep hold of a large portion of Co. Cork. Their main seat in that county was at Castle Lyons; with estates in over thirty parishes, they possessed a grand total of over seventy-nine thousand acres. During the eighteenth century they left the rural delights of east Cork and became absentees of the most irresponsible kind, squandering their Irish rents in London.

The Prince of Wales' Barrys were born into a society that was unusually indulged. Peers and their relations were treated with exaggerated deference and expected to behave like oriental despots, lunatics or delayed adolescents. The Barrys did this tradition proud. Orphaned as small boys, they were spoilt by their guardians and grew up with the family contempt for money. Richard, the eldest, born in 1769, who became Lord Barrymore on the death of his father, and inherited the bulk of the fortune, was given a thousand pounds' pocket money while he was still at school.

It was not long before the 'caprices and eccentricities' of these prodigal brothers made them notorious. They were given nicknames, very probably by the Prince himself. Richard was sometimes called Hellmonster, more often Hellgate. His brother, the Honourable Henry Barry, who had the misfortune to be clubfooted, was known as Cripplegate. The third brother, the Honourable Augustus, who had taken holy orders, was a compulsive gambler as his father had been before him, and, because he was so often on the verge of going to prison, his nickname was Newgate. Their sister Caroline, Lady Milfort was christened Billingsgate for her wide use of oaths and generally racy language.

Gillray, the caricaturist, portrayed the brothers as *The Three Scamps*, and in case the point was lost, as *Les Trois Magots*. He drew Lord Barrymore in a boxing attitude and described him in a balloon as A Hellgate Blackguard; Augustus was the Newgate Scrub, and Henry became a Cripplegate Monster cruelly pictured with a cloven hoof. The three set a standard which other Regency bucks tried in vain to emulate, and the Earl in particular was what every aspiring man of fashion tried to be like. A newspaper described how 'this young Lord can drive four or six horses in hand from morn to eve. For contriving, destroying, purchasing, and disposing, none can equal him. He is the coachman, the player, the spendthrift and indeed everything but what his fortune entitles him to be. If none excel him, it is hoped none will equal him. Beware ye youth, how you are entrapped by bad example'.

At his 'cottage' at Walgrave, a few miles from Maidenhead, Barrymore organized a perpetual round of entertainment for his friends which included every type of sport. Besides those that encompassed horsemanship, cricket, cockfighting and boxing were the most popular. A noted boxer called Hooper 'the Tinman' was employed as pugilistic tutor to his Lordship, and accompanied him everywhere as bodyguard. Once he was brought disguised as a clergyman to Vauxhall, where he unfortunately drank too much hot punch. By the end of the evening there was a riot in the gardens as the Tinman went about challenging every man present. In February 1790 he won his employer twenty-five thousand pounds in a bet when he was victorious in a bout against Will Watson, alias Will of the Wisp.

A tall, good-looking young man, Barrymore was strong enough to vault over the back of a horse. He was an exceptionally brilliant horseman, whether he was riding one of the string of race-horses he owned, or at 'the ribbons'—driving teams of four or six horses that pulled his coach. His coachmen, grooms and footmen were dressed in his racing colours, dark-blue livery coats flushed with striking yellow capes, until they resigned in a body, complaining that 'the lower orders took them for infamous characters in penitential garb'. They seemed to have been more willing to dress up in archaic costume used by the huntsmen of Louis XIV in the forests of Fontainebleau, which Barrymore adopted for his own private hunt. While the hunt was in progress, he employed four Negro servants in liveries of silver and scarlet to play 'amusingly' on the horn.

To relax from his sporting activities Barrymore would occasionally go on a 'cooking freak' and cook and serve up dinner to his friends. They could then attend the theatre he had built in 1788, which was modelled after the Opera House in London, and considered the most handsome and luxurious in the kingdom. No expense had been spared on the lavish chandeliers and the gilded armorial bearings of the Barrys set between tiers of decorated boxes, or the sumptuous saloon for the reception of the audience which adjoined the main hall. Between the acts refreshments were served by lines of footmen in liveries of scarlet and gold. The building cost £60,000, and the costumes £2,000.

Barrymore insisted that the sheets on his bed were sewn to the blankets so that no wool could touch his skin. All windows were covered with layers of blankets, and fires had to be extinguished before his Lordship went to bed. By day he and his brothers and friends rode round the countryside uprooting sign-posts and changing pub signs, sending wagons on false missions in search of beer, walking through Walgrave on a hot day wearing nothing but their shirts. Harry Angelo described seeing Lord Barrymore passing through the long straggling street of Colnbrook 'fanning the daylights', breaking every window he could see to the right and left of him with his whip. Once a hansom was observed being driven furiously through London streets with screams coming from its open window: 'Murder, murder, let me go!' It was one of the Barrys doing his imitation of an abducted woman. When rescuers caught up with the cab the brothers thrashed them.

These diversions were very much to the taste of the Prince of Wales, and the brothers were his welcome friends. At the Star and Garter Club they would gather round listening to the Prince warbling 'By the Gently Circling Glass' to great effect; in return Barrymore serenaded Mrs. Fitzherbert in Brighton dressed in the skirts and bodices of his cook. Augustus Barry rode his horse upstairs to Mrs. Fitzherbert's attic and into the garret, where it had to be removed by two blacksmiths. While staying at the Pavilion Barrymore won a bet with the Duke of York as to who could go furthest into the sea fully clothed. Occasionally the Earl went too far with his jests and the Prince was not amused. After one quarrel Barrymore invited His Royal Highness to a sumptuous lunch at Ascot which was to cost £350 a head. The Prince did not turn up, but the Earl did not allow his absence to spoil his appetite and found another friend to do justice to the menu.

By 1792 Barrymore's gambling debts totalled thousands. The £10,000 a year which made up his income could not nearly cover his expenditure, and the bailiffs moved in. Two, disguised as jockeys, arrested him for a trifling debt to a tailor when he was on his way to a Royal Levee. He sold his race-horses and studs to pay creditors, and then the theatre at Walgrave had to go. In October 1792, it was reported that 'Mr Christie sold on the premises, Walgrave, the materials of the Earl of Barrymore's costly temple of Thespius'.

Before he could really suffer from his straitened circumstances, he died. In 1792 he joined the Berkshire Militia, and to the great surprise of his friends and Colonel, became a diligent and painstaking officer. The discipline of military life often suits the dissipated—Dermody had flourished as a soldier. In the summer of 1793 Barrymore was ordered to escort a party of sixteen French prisoners of war to Dover. On the way he stopped at an inn in Folkstone, where he entertained the company to an imitation of a famous theatrical character called 'Hob'. Then, after a last glass of brandy with the landlady, he went outside and jumped into his gig. Beside him was his suzee loaded with swan shot which he had fired on the way down at a number of haphazard sporting targets; now, just as he was showing his driver the direction of the coast of France by pointing his pipe at it, this gun exploded and shot him through the head, pitching him out of the gig away from the bolting horses into the midst of the soldiery.

His death came shortly before his twenty-fourth birthday. In the three years of his majority he had got through about £30,000, and his successor Henry was left financially embarrassed. Henry was a practical man. He set a fashion by letting his groom—or tiger—sit behind him instead of standing, as the previous custom had been. He fought a duel with a Mr. Howarth at Brighton stripped to the waist, because he believed that by undressing he could avoid the danger of clothing—notoriously septic—being driven into his body by a bullet. As his debts mounted he took to wearing the family livery while he gave dinner parties, so that he merely had to stand up when bailiffs arrived in order to disguise himself. But he was forced to go to France, like other bucks, and he died in poverty there. His brother, Augustus—Newgate—had predeceased him. No one had liked him very much; 'he had the curious facility,' a contemporary wrote, 'of exhibiting himself as a perfect gentleman or a perfect blackguard'.

The Prince's other rakish Irish friend was Colonel George Hanger, who wrote his autobiography, *The Life and Adventures and Opinions of Colonel Hanger*, while he languished in a debtor's prison. The book appeared in 1801 with a frontispiece making a pun of the author's name; it shows him swinging from a gibbet, fashionably dressed in frock-coat, high boots, a hat with a cockade and a sword at his side. His long face is dominated by a beaked nose to which he refers complainingly in the text, 'that if I may judge from the length of my nose at my birth, the midwife committed some indignity to my person'.

He describes how he was born in 1751 in Co. Derry, the youngest son of Gabriel Hanger who ten years after his birth was created Baron Coleraine in the peerage of Ireland. 'My father was not in the most distant degree related to Lord Coleraine . . . however, dying without issue or heir to the title, my father, Gabriel Hanger, claimed it with just as much right as the sexton or clerk of the parish.' A closer look at the pedigree reveals that Gabriel Hanger's aunt, Anne, married Henry Hare, Lord Coleraine, whose title her nephew appropriated when it was going begging.

The Hangers, like so many Anglo-Irish, shuffled backwards and forwards between estates in England and Ireland. George went to a school at Reading, and to Eton, where he had a love affair with the daughter of a Windsor greengrocer. In 1771 he joined the army as an ensign in the Foot Guards. After being passed over in promotion he transferred to the German Hessian Corps which saw service in the American wars. In September 1780, he was wounded at the Siege of Charlestown, and two years later retired on half pay. He had followed a prosaic career for a decade. It had not been a period during which he had been able to save any money. Early in his life he formed extremely expensive tastes which the family fortunes were quite insufficient to maintain. After his retirement he had an income of eleven hundred pounds a year, and this was not enough for him to keep up with his friend, the Prince of Wales.

The friendship of the beaky-nosed veteran of the American wars with plump Prinny had already attracted attention, and Hanger, like the Barrys became a favourite subject for caricature. Gilray saw him as Georgey-a-Cock-Horse, a solitary reveller in a frilled shirt riding a nag in front of the Mount Tavern; as Staggering Bobs; or, during the speculative period when the world wondered at the status of Mrs. Fitzherbert, as a revelling companion of the Prince in a rumbustious print entitled 'Wife or no Wife'.

Such notoriety brought expense. Prinny himself was the most colossal spender of the age, forced to make a bigamous marriage to get his debts paid. George Hanger may not have had an unwilling parliament to bail him out, but he endeavoured to live as lavishly as his royal friend. He kept up the pace for a long time, continuing his habit of spending a non-existent fortune on his clothes. 'My morning vestments,' he boasted, 'cost near eighty pounds, and those of the ball above one hundred and eighty . . . It was a satin coat, *brodé en plan et sur les courtères;* and the first satin coat that had made its appearance in this country. All this on a salary as an ensign in the first regiment of footguards, which did not amount to more than four shillings a day; which daily pay,' he added proudly, 'would not have paid my tailor his charges of one single buttonhole to my gala suit.' His garments were not only made in the most lavish materials, but in the most peculiar styles. The silks and satins stiffened by embroidery were of the gaudiest colours, and his rajah's preferences for bright pink and turquoise blue and burning orange were notable even at a time of elaborate men's fashions. His obituary in the *Gentleman's Magazine* allowed that he had been extremely handsome as a young man, 'but his person was disguised by the singularity of his clothes'. Always beautifully powdered, he was instantly recognizable by his brilliant appearance, set off by the flower in his buttonhole, preferably a rose.

He had to budget not only for his gear, but for entertainment and gambling. During the days of his impoverishment he wrote that he disapproved of gambling; but this was years after the occasion that he put three thousand pounds on a horse which fortunately won. There were other races that were lost. Once while he was staying at Carlton House he proposed a race between geese and turkeys. Hanger, backed by the Prince, insisted turkeys would be the fastest runners in a variant of other races where mice, fleas and frogs had taken part. Twenty turkeys and twenty geese, 'the most wholesome and fine-feathered birds,' were selected to run over ten miles for a prize of five hundred pounds to be put up by the backers of the losers. Large side bets were made as the royal party assembled by a dusty summer road and the squawking birds set out. For the first three miles the turkeys held the lead, but as night came on they began to weaken, turning towards the trees at the side of the road. 'In vain the Prince tried to urge them on with his pole, to which a bit of red cloth was attached, in vain Mr. Hanger dislodged one from its roosting place, only to see three or four others comfortably perching a-mongst the branches; in vain was the barley strewn on the road.' The geese won, and both Hanger and the Prince lost a lot of money.

For Prinny it was a little extra indulgence, but Hanger was beginning to be pressed. His debts mounted and he became des-perate, as he sought schemes to raise a little money. He tried to rejoin the army, putting up a plan for recruiting a battalion of ex-convicts to fight the French. But in June 1798 he was arrested and put into the King's Bench Prison for a small debt. 'I gave a bill to a tradesman, not for any debt contracted by me, but for a lady of my acquaintance.'

Many men of society who found themselves in debtor's prisons contrived to keep aside enough money to enjoy a single cell with home comforts. Hanger was forced to rub along on sixpence a day like other common prisoners, who made up the majority of debtors. When he came to write a crusading History of the King's Bench in which he described his own experiences, he pointed out that 'it is the public opinion that no persons surrender to the King's Bench but such who have money in their possession which their creditors cannot lay hold of, so that they are enabled to live there in some degree of comfort; that it is a place of mirth, festivity and joy I have positive proof to the contrary'. He had seen how debtors rotted for years in overcrowded squalor. He himself was fortunate and only had to suffer eighteen months in prison before friends came to his rescue. After he was released in May 1800, 'three noble Earls' wished to set him up in business. One offered him two thousand pounds. 'I took one hundred pounds from him, he pressed the whole upon me almost to an injunction.' Hanger then chose the most inapposite occupation conceivable for an ex-dandy, and announced that he was setting up as a coal merchant. The situation was a gift to Gilray, who caricatured him as George the Coal-Hole, an older, more tattered Colonel carrying a large sack over his back, about to load a cart. If anyone told Hanger that the idea of his being a coal merchant was a fantasy, he would become furiously angry and hit them over the head with a shillelagh. He ended his *Life and Opinions* on a distinctly commercial note, 'By the distinguished favours I have already been honoured with, by a further protection from the public in favouring me with their commands to supply their families with coal, and by their orders which are weekly increasing . . . may the black diamond trade flourish with me.'

He had lost royal favour. The *Gentleman's Magazine* concluded that 'as the Prince advanced in years the eccentric manners of the Colonel became somewhat too free and coarse for the royal taste'. The Prince had objected to Hanger's habit of slamming down odd coins during Royal banquets and shouting out that he was ruined. Hanger simply had not got the money to keep up with his circle. Around this time they met out riding. 'Well, George!' said the Prince. 'How go coals now?' 'Black as ever,' the Colonel told him.

He was not really downcast because his autobiography, published in 1801, had made a sensation. So far, we have only dealt with the Life and Adventures of the Colonel. But it was the Opinions that made the work so popular. One section of the book is full of advice to preachers which includes separate pews and doors for different sexes and trumpet calls and drums for keeping a drowsy congregation awake during a long sermon. He lectured on the advantages of polygamy and the dangers of marriage, concluding, 'Marriage is a good thing, and so is a bone for a dog; but if you tied it to his tail it will drive him mad.' He believed that women should fight duels and mistresses should have a legal right to be maintained by their paramours. His lengthy comments on poverty and his assessment of prostitution (which he favoured) was followed by a dissertation on women's fashion. 'I must confess I am a great admirer of short waists and their clothing; formerly when the women wore strong stiff stays and cork rumps you might as well sit with your arm round an oaken tree with the bark on, as round a lady's waist.'

Much of this was fun, but sometimes Hanger had ideas very much in advance of his time. Suddenly in the midst of some satiric banter, he details a system of sewerage collection from public urinals, more or less describing the sewerage system of a modern city rather than the fearsome cesspits that his contemporaries were used to. The most quoted passage of his book predicted the advent of the American Civil War. 'One of these days the Northern and Southern powers of America will fight as vigorously against each other as they have united to do against the British.'

In 1806, Hanger was given a small army post as a Captain Commissary of the Royal Artillery Drivers. For eleven years he lived quietly within his income. Gone was the fabulous expenditure on clothes, with the extravagance which was a natural consequence of friendship with the prince. Once again he was a sober soldier.

In 1817 his brother died and he found himself in possession of the family's Irish estates and the title of Lord Coleraine. He did not believe in inherited titles. 'This nobleman,' wrote Percy Fitzgerald, 'becoming more eccentric, declined to sign himself by his title and made it an offence to be addressed by it.' He grew 'peevish' at the words 'My Lord'. In the *Life and Adventures* he had written: 'As for the reversionary chance, that, in the wheel of fortune, I may have to the title in our family, I am willing to dispose of it at a very cheap rate to any vain man who seeks for empty honours; for if titles are not bestowed as a reward of merit, they are of no value in my estimation.'

His death at the age of seventy-three on March 31, 1824, from a 'convulsive fit' was widely reported. The obituary writer of the *Gentleman's Magazine* concluded that 'he was so marked a character that he might be considered as one of the most prominent features of his time, and he was courted as well for the peculiarity as for the harmless tendency of his humour'. Since he died without heirs, the unwanted title again fell into abeyance until it was retrieved a century later by Mr. Bonar Law.

*   *   *

13a. Richard Kirwan

13b. Jackie Barrett

14a.   Tiger Roche

14b.   Colonel Hanger's Self Portrait

15. Amanda McKittrick Ros

16a. The Cabinteely Dolmen

16b. Johnny Roche

16c. Adolphus Cooke's Tomb

With the advent of the Victorian age, the elegant dissipations of the Georgians were replaced by a predilection for practical joking. The flamboyance of Henry de la Poer, third Marquis of Waterford, known as Wild Lord Waterford, was however, an echo from the past. According to that great toady, Augustus Hare, Lord Waterford's 'whimsical and extravagant escapades' never fell below the character of a 'chivalrous gentleman'. Born in 1811, he inherited a fortune, much of which he spent on pranks. They were never really cruel; perhaps the worst was painting a policeman bright green and tying him to the railings of a Mayfair house; or painting the hoofs of a parson's horse with aniseed and hunting him with bloodhounds. Once he suggested to a complete stranger that he should knock out his two front teeth in order to hear him whistle. A fellow guest at an inn found that the Marquis had put a donkey in his bed.

Lord Waterford was a keen horseman, and on several occasions rode up the stairs of the Kilkenny Hunt Clubhouse. In London he took it upon himself to become a public benefactor. He descended on an inn in the Haymarket ordering the innkeeper to roll out several casks of gin on to the pavement. He stood in front of them and began to distribute half-pint mugs of gin to passers-by. Soon he was surrounded by London's underworld clamouring for free drinks. A riot ensued, and the police only managed to remove the Marquis from the scene by arresting him for furious driving. Next day he rode into court on his horse right up to the judge's bench, demanding that the horse be cross-examined—only the animal could know how fast he was going. The judge acquitted him.

He bet his friends that he would drive a vehicle down Rotten Row, sacred to horses, and won by dressing up as a workman and driving a water-cart. In a house he had rented, he shot out the eyes of the family portraits and on his own estate at Curraghmore, Co. Waterford, he stuck a cigar through the mouth of one of his ancestors. He asked the Irish railways to make two engines charge each other at full speed, assuring them that he would pay for what happened. In fact he always made good the damage he did. When he sat on all the hats of a London milliner and squashed them flat, he paid her off. A street conjuror said of him:

'. . . His great delight was to make people drunk . . . He was a goodhearted fellow was my Lord; if he played any tricks upon you, he'd always square it up . . . I've seen him jump into an old woman's crockery-ware basket, while she was carrying it along, and smash everything. Sometimes he'd get seven or eight cabs and put a lot of fiddlers and musicians on the roofs, and fill 'em with anybody that liked, and then go off in procession round the streets, he driving the first cab as fast as he could and the bands playing as loud as possible. It's wonderful the games he'd be up to. But he always paid handsomely for whatever damage he did. If he swept all the glasses off a counter, there was the money to make 'em good again . . .'

His death in 1859 was the result of a hunting accident.

Lord Massereene

LIKE Barrymore, Bagenal and Whaley, Clotworthy Skeffington, second Earl Massereene, lost his father when he was young—soon after his fourteenth birthday. Like George Robert Fitzgerald, he suffered an early injury which may have stimulated what contemporaries considered the 'mischief' of his actions. Just after his father's death he fell off a horse and hurt his head so badly that his life was despaired of. When he recovered, it was soon noticed that his way of walking had changed. He would go through the streets with his arms crossed in front of him, clasping his shoulders. When he was asked the reason, he would say that he wished to become stout and broad-shouldered, and if he suppressed the growth of one part of his body, it would break out more strongly in another part.

Early in the seventeenth century the Skeffingtons, who came from Yorkshire, acquired rich farmlands in Co. Antrim, whose acreage increased when they intermarried with another settler family, the Clotworthys. In 1660 a Sir John Clotworthy, who owned sixteen townlands and the town of Antrim, was ennobled by Charles II, becoming Baron Loughneagh and Viscount Massereene. His descendant, Sir Clotworthy Skeffington, gained greater honours when he was created first Earl of Massereene. His eldest son, also called Clotworthy, was born in 1743.

On the death of his father this Clotworthy became second Earl, and seven years later, when he came of age, inherited the family estates. He had been educated at Harrow, where he proved to be a clever boy, winning many prizes. In 1758 he went to Cambridge and did what he pleased. It was observed that his tutor, a fellow of Trinity College, Dublin, 'really taught

him nothing but what he himself delighted in: rowing on the
river down to Ely'.

At eighteen he went abroad, where the formal years of education were followed by a decade of society living. For a short time
he was accompanied by an unfortunate tutor named Mr. Francis
Hutchinson, who had been chosen by his mother to keep him
under observation, and to send her reports on his behaviour.
Two of Mr. Hutchinson's letters have survived in which the
subject of 'carriage' figures largely. 'Madam,' he wrote from
Brussels on October 14, 1760, 'I have deferred writing to your
Ladyship till now in hopes of acquainting you of some change
in Lord Massereene's person. Since our arrival in Brussels, and
not before, his Lordship was resolved not to cross his arms.
Your Ladyship will easily conceive what an advantage this
may prove to his appearance. He says he knows that this change
and the being in good company will alone be sufficient to make
him acquire a proper carriage; I fear he is much mistaken, though
I am confident they will greatly promote it . . .'

On January 23, 1761 the tutor wrote to Ireland that Lord
Massereene was 'very punctual in attendance on his riding, fencing
and dancing masters; but of the three, the last engages the smallest
share of his attention, at least as to minuets and as to what is
much more important, his carriage. I am sorry I have not room
to acquaint your Ladyship of any considerable improvement in
this last particular.'

More ominously, Mr. Hutchinson had reported in the earlier
letter: 'There are such particularities in his Lordship's time and
manner of dressing as will (if not laid aside) occasion his spending
on clothes at least double that sum which would be necessary if
he dressed like other people.'

The Earl was strikingly good-looking, and his manners were
charming, particularly to ladies. He was also a fastidious dandy.
'In his early days he figured very conspicuously in the walks of
fashion,' the *Gentleman's Magazine* noted. A contemporary considered him 'the most superlative coxcomb that Ireland ever
bred'. He would spend hours dressing in his chambers. Horace
Walpole attended a ball given by him in Paris in January 1766

at the Hotel Garni. 'I went at seven, and was told he was not up, at least was at his toilette. Gentlemen arrived, ladies arrived, the Countesses Berkeley and Fife etc.—still no Lord Massereene . . . both ball and cards began, though half the candles were blown out and the fingers of the violinists so frozen that they missed every other note. In short my athletic part of the British constitution bore it for an hour and then I came away before Adonis himself made his appearance.'

These minor peculiarities were a little troubling, but they did not depart outside the behaviour patterns of the aristocracy. It was normal, too, that he should get into debt. When he came of age in 1764, he had already settled in Paris, and he sensibly let the management of his estates continue in the control of his mother. During the next few years his generous allowance of £200 a month could not cover his tailor's bills, gambling losses and the rapacious demands of a series of Parisian ladies. But in spite of the increase in his debts, he might have muddled along indefinitely if he had not got involved in a business venture.

His motives for indulging in wild speculation were edifying, since he wished to recoup some of the family fortune which had been squandered by his father. In order to do so he became the business partner of a devious merchant named Vidari who was an Italian or possibly a Syrian. When Vidari worked out a scheme for supplying salt from the Barbary coast to France or alternatively to the Swiss cantons, Lord Massereene accepted his invitation to subsidize the idea. He passed a number of bills, which in due course when the enterprise collapsed, he was called upon to honour.

The only way to raise the money was on his estates in Ireland. He appointed a Captain John Clarke as his attorney, and sent him over to the family residence of Antrim Castle to take over his mother's duties. Clarke, who had also been deeply involved in the salt speculation, was so eager to obtain the money that it seems certain he was one of Lord Massereene's creditors. Although not a bad man, he was a muddler, and one of his first actions in Antrim was to employ a man named Thomas Thompson, notoriously an enemy of the Massereenes, to deal with the family affairs. The dowager Lady Massereene, with numerous other children to support and to find marriage portions for, played for time and held out against paying her son's debts. After long agitated correspondence she succeeded in obtaining her son's permission to have Thompson dismissed. But she hesitated to send money to Paris; there were a number of practical and legal difficulties, and the situation was complicated by Lord Massereene's capricious behaviour. Together with her advisers she became reluctant to trust him with money while he refused to co-operate with her men of affairs and insisted on ignoring their advice. According to his law agent, William Lyndon, who had the unhappy task of investigating 'this labyrinth—this chaos . . . these unexampled entangled affairs', Lord Massereene's mind was 'filled with vindictive matter'. Lyndon only got abuse for his pains. So did his mother.

Meanwhile the Earl was in a Paris jail. It seemed that he would only be there for a short time before he paid the £30,000 he owed his creditors, who, aware of his large Irish estates, waited for him to tire of imprisonment and pay them off. But there was one difficulty. He insisted that his debts had been fraudulently incurred and refused to acknowledge them. The courts failed to exonerate him, with the result that he developed a violent antipathy towards French justice and the French in general. He was in two minds about what he should do, and continued to write furious letters to his mother demanding sufficient funds to secure his immediate release. After he had been several years in prison, she offered to mortgage a piece of her own property in Derbyshire for £20,000 on condition that she could place a man of business in charge of his affairs. He replied succinctly: 'I will have no man of business. Send me £20,000 by return of post and I will settle my affairs myself.' She refused. The breach between them never healed. He was to spend the next eighteen years incarcerated in Paris, during which time he saw his sister, Lady Leitrim, briefly. Her mission was to stop his marriage to a French woman of whom his mother disapproved. No other member of his family came to visit him and reason with him or commiserate with him.

At the same time that he was abusing his mother and legal

advisers for not giving him money to discharge his debts, his attitude towards his creditors was hardening. He simply would not pay the money. The debts were unjustified and French justice had betrayed him. Very well, he would remain in prison. According to French law a debtor was automatically relieved of his debts if he were imprisoned for twenty-five years; after that they were cancelled and he became a free man. Lord Massereene came to the conclusion that this would be the best solution to his predicament. It would foil his creditors. At the age of twenty-seven he settled down voluntarily to serve time for a quarter of a century.

During most of the early years of his imprisonment, his circumstances were fairly comfortable. He could continue to run up debts—according to one account, they were to total nearly a million livres. He had his own chef and entertained his numerous English friends in style. Stories of his lavishing luxury on his mistresses and paying their dressmaking bills and theatre boxes from his prison cell had some foundation in truth, although they were exaggerated. William Lyndon, who saw him in 1773, found him 'in very good health and spirits, but wavering and unsettled in his schemes as usual . . . At present his Lordship is much influenced by a lady . . . She is decorated with a title and is called *Madame la Marquise de Paysac*, but titles in France are not always like titles in England or Ireland, where they mean something and demand respect . . .' Lyndon suspected Madame of being after Lord Massereene's fortune. However, she faded when his Lordship met and married another woman who could not be accused of self-interest, since she was prepared to die for him.

It is not known how they met or when. Conflicting accounts of the background of Marie-Ann Barcier state that she was the daughter of the governor of the Châtelet prison, where Lord Massereene spent a short time, or that she was the sister of another detainee. The match made the Dowager Lady Massereene fly into hysterics. Lady Leitrim was sent over to Paris to reason with her brother, while from Antrim his mother bombarded the British Ambassador in Paris, the Duke of Dorset, with passionate and unavailing requests to try to forestall the marriage which

upset her as much as her son's long imprisonment. 'I would wish
to prevent such a misfortune as I would dash a cup of poison or
wrench a dagger from a madman.'

Perhaps she did not know the details of her daughter-in-law's
heroism. Among the Massereene papers there is an account,
allegedly dictated by Lady Massereene herself, of her attempts
to secure her husband's release. She first tried some time in 1782,
when he had been in prison for twelve years. He had been transferred to the Hôtel de la Force, where his circumstances had become much more harsh than they had been during the early years
of his confinement. The prison plot in which she became involved,
which was to result in a mass outbreak, not only failed, but had
disastrous consequences when one of the warders was shot dead.
She herself was arrested and put into a dungeon for twenty days.
The strings of her petticoats and her garters were removed to
prevent her from killing herself in her misery. The dungeon
was small and airless and filled with wet straw. At length, aching
with rheumatism and covered in lice, she was removed to the
condemned cell where she spent some time before being reprieved.
Then she was transferred to the notorious Conciergerie for four
months, after which she was allowed to be reunited with her
husband.

Undaunted by her experiences she became more determined
than ever to arrange his escape. Over a long period of time she
smuggled pieces of wood and cord into his cell with which to
construct two ladders. She took impressions of keys, and although
she could not get one for her husband's cell, she managed to
make a hole under the head of his bed with an iron bar. 'This
being a noisy business, was obliged to be done during the day
while my Lord and she made as much noise as possible, he
playing on the fiddle and she singing.'

This attempt, which seems to have taken place in 1787, also
failed. She had given the prison watchdogs some poison, but
one of them failed to die; the turnkeys were woken by its barking
and surprised Lord Massereene in the act of climbing one of his
makeshift ladders. He was dragged off to a dungeon, where he
suffered much the same discomforts as his wife had undergone.

He described them in a pathetic appeal to Lord Carmarthen, the British Foreign Secretary. 'I have been shut up three different times in the *secret* (a place of the greatest horror except the cachot or dungeon), once for fifteen days, once for twenty-four hours and once for six months; the greatest part of this time without *fire, candle, knife, fork, spoon, shoes, stockings* or *shirt*, perfectly *solus* save the quantity of fleas, bugs, lice and some vermin; a mouse became so familiar with my company that it would come and eat crumbs at my feet as I sat; my stockings and shirt when dirty I threw into a corner and remained almost in naturalibus.' He was then sent to the Châtelet for a time 'because the *secrets* and *dungeons there* are more horrible and unwholesome than those here', in La Force. What was worse, he was escorted in irons ('Oh shame to the French nation! And also to the English nation if it goes unpunished!'), and on his return to La Force, with his hands tied with cords.

He was reluctant to make any more attempts to escape. But a year later, when revolutionary fervour was beginning to spill into the Paris streets, his wife finally contrived his release. Several months before the Bastille was stormed there took place the smaller, much less well-known breach of La Force. The mob that assembled outside the prison and smashed open the gates was encouraged with money and entreaties by Lady Massereene. When the final barrier was pulled down, the first prisoner to emerge was her husband. The young dandy whose obstinacy had caused his incarceration eighteen years ago came out bent and grey-headed. 'But no one would pass the gate until Lord M went first, who (having been a-bed when this scene began) appeared without neither hat, coat or waistcoat and only a stick in his hand; which, being seen by one of the populace, he ran up to him with an old sword: "My Lord, this weapon is a poor one of the sort, but it becomes your hand better than that you have." ' Lady Massereene tipped the man two guineas.

After many more adventures they managed to cross the English Channel in May 1798. According to the *Gentleman's Magazine*: 'On landing at Dover he was first to jump out of the boat, and falling on his knees thrice exclaimed, "God bless this land of liberty." ' They lingered in London for some time before crossing over to Ireland in November.

In the halls of Antrim Castle, a frigid reunion took place with his mother. Lord Massereene made no effort to examine the way his estates were run, or to sort out the complications of his neglected affairs. Instead he made himself 'inaccessible' to his family's advisers and left Antrim after a stay of only a few days. He and his wife returned to London where he immediately began to behave as if the long years in prison had never happened. He had learned nothing from his harsh experiences, and soon was persuaded into another bogus business adventure which resulted in debt and imprisonment once again. By the end of 1791 his family estates were in such jeopardy that it was rumoured they would have to be sold up. Shamefully he blamed his wife's extravagance for his debts and deserted her, when, crippled with angina, she was hastening towards an early death as a result of her exertions to free him. Her time in the dungeon had ruined her health. But her story had no happy ending; in 1793 she separated from her husband and was given a pension of £300 a year for what remained of her short life.

Lord Massereene had found another lady. This was Elizabeth Lane, or Blackburn, a girl of nineteen, 'a menial servant in a house immediately opposite his lodgings'. Having a liking for going about naked, he had exposed himself at his window and caught her eye. Soon she was living with him on the promise that when his wife died he would marry her.

Meanwhile he was passing bills to the amount of £9,000 in favour of a swindler named Whaley. Afterwards he claimed to have no recollection of having done so. He gave Whaley the townland of Muckamore in Co. Antrim and even the livestock on the arms out of lease. This adventure landed him twice in prison, where Mrs. Blackburn also came to stay. A loan from his brother-in-law, Lord Leitrim, and a humiliating lawsuit in which he successfully pleaded that he had been a fool eventually freed him, but this time he had to agree to placing his affairs in the control of trustees. At last the old stubbornness was chipped away.

In 1797, a year after his final imprisonment, he returned to Ireland where he set up Mrs. Blackburn as mistress of Antrim Castle. The threatened rebellion was alarming him, since he had a horror of Jacobinism, even though he owed his liberty to the revolutionary spirit inspired by the French Revolution. He considered the United Irishmen 'a plant of Gaelic growth' and set about trying to prune it by forming a yeomanry corps which he trained himself with special manoeuvres of his own devising. He would instruct the entire corps to pile weapons at one end of a field, after which he would march the men down to the opposite end, where he drilled them, making them use their arms and hands as if they were muskets. He would command them to present their left arms and then fire. This meant that each man struck his right hand upon his left hand with a loud clap, 'and he seemed greatly pleased when the clap was well done'. He worked out some special marches. One tortuous movement he called the *Serpentine Walk*, and another, which witnesses considered 'most extraordinary', he named *Eel-in-the-Mud*. Once when his horse grew restless while he was reviewing the corps, he stabbed it in order to make it stand still, breaking his sword in two.

In June 1798, the corps was called upon to help in the defence of Antrim and the castle against Henry Joy McCracken and his rebel corps. After the rebels were raked with canon fire directed at them from the castle's ramparts, they had to retreat. Lord Massereene took little direct part in the action, but nevertheless saw himself as a victorious general, and considered the battle a personal triumph. He began to conduct imaginary conversations about it with Pitt, King George III and the Duke of York. A hostile rendering of one of these monologues was given by Arthur Macartney, one of the counsel at the lawsuit to set aside his will that took place after the Earl's death.

'He would apply to Mr. Pitt to obtain the King's permission to raise a regiment. "And this", said he ,"will be the manner of my application: I will go to London and call upon Mr. Pitt. I will say to him, 'I am the Earl of Massereene, who commanded the corps of yeomanry that gained the great battle of Antrim.' Mr. Pitt will then say to me, 'My Lord Massereene, I am very proud to see you.' I will answer, 'Mr. Pitt, I am now come to request you will obtain his Majesty's permission for me to raise a regiment.' Mr. Pitt will say, 'My Lord Massereene, I am sure his Majesty will have great pleasure in complying with your request; you had better wait upon his majesty yourself, and I will introduce you.' Then, you see, when I am introduced to the King, I will say, 'May it please your Majesty, I am the Earl of Massereene who gained the great battle of Antrim, and I request to have your majesty's permission to raise a regiment for your Majesty's service.' His Majesty will then say to me, 'My Lord Massereene, I am very glad to see your Lordship . . . I will speak to the Duke of York . . .' " '

Admittedly Macartney was not well disposed towards Lord Massereene since the latter had quarrelled with his kinsman, the Rev. George Macartney, vicar of Antrim. The Lord Lieutenant, Lord Hardwicke, had expressly refused to allow Lord Massereene to raise any further troops, let alone the regiment he fondly imagined the King would grant him. On the other hand, the Rev. Macartney was allowed to raise a corps in Antrim independent of his own. In an intemperate letter to Lord Hardwicke Lord Massereene described the vicar as 'foaming at the mouth like a man in a canine madness . . . a man than whom a more mad exists not out of Bedlam . . . a coward . . . a friend to numbers of United villains, a fellow void of honour, probity and every virtue . . . infernal monster . . . the vicar, not of Jesus Christ but of Satan.'

In Antrim Castle Mrs. Blackburn had made friends with a disreputable father and son named O'Doran or Doran. Doran senior had been a Catholic priest, but later joined the Church of Ireland, and received from Lord Massereene the living of Killead which was worth £500 a year. His son became Lady Massereene's lover, probably during her husband's lifetime, and married her after his death. Other members of the family, Doran's wife and daughters, cheerfully endured Lord Massereene's unreliable behaviour towards ladies and listened to his repertoire of obscene songs.

With the aid of Doran father and son, Lady Massereene assumed complete control over the estates and over her husband's progressively enfeebled mind. The three of them managed to ensure that he quarrelled with all his neighbours; the row with Macartney which ended with Lord Massereene challenging the clergyman's son to a duel, was only one of their successes. Soon the Earl had no outside friends. Mrs. Blackburn also completed his estrangement with his mother and brothers. His feelings towards his mother were increasingly hostile. He had seen her once since his return from France, and now he saw her no more. He refused to pay the old lady's annuity, so that she had to sue him. According to Macartney, Mrs. Blackburn 'made him believe that his mother was an old witch and a whore; and so atrocious was her conduct that upon one occasion when sailing in a boat with him, she said: "I wish we had your mother tied by the legs dragging after us." His answer was so indecent that I will not repeat it.' A lieutenant McCullough who gave evidence at the trial said that 'she often spoke of his brother William as a rebel and a robber, and said that his old mother was a witch withered away with her crimes, and that hell would never be full till she was there'. Her son came to believe it, and when she was dying, he was heard to say that the devils were in waiting to take her soul to hell.

Lord Massereene liked shadow-boxing in his shirt before a mirror, and when he had put in a good blow, he would flex his arm muscles and cry out: 'Sweet little Massa!' Lieutenant McCullough, who remembered him as a 'wild man', described how 'sometimes he would take it into his head to dine on the platform on the roof of the house, and upon these occasions it was necessary to hoist up chairs, tables and provisions by a pulley. The company ascended by a small ladder in the inside of the house, and often when they had scarcely begun dinner, he would rise up and say he would sit no longer there, and in a moment order chairs, table and dinner to be lowered into one of the rooms'. A rich man's whim.

Lieutenant McCullough also recalled how after playing cricket the Earl would lay the bats on a sofa in the drawing-room and send Lady Massereene from the dining-room to see if they were sweating. 'He said he never knew any man that had lived from the

Creation, but believed that by a proper exercise a man might be made to live for ever.'

On the death of his first wife in 1803, Lord Massereene married Mrs. Blackburn and regularized a relationship that had caused scandal far beyond the bounds of Co. Antrim. He called her 'Lord Chancellor of the Woolsack' and other pet names. In 1804 Lord and Lady Massereene, together with various members of the Doran family, paid a visit to Dublin where they lodged with an apothecary named Sowen. Here a pet dog became ill. Her Ladyship took it out in a carriage in order to seek medical advice. When she brought it home, she laid it down on the drawing-room carpet, weeping over it while Lord Massereene tried to console her. 'His Lordship took the dog in his arms,' Mrs. Sowen recollected some years later, 'and carried it to an open window to give it a little air; after some time he brought it in and laid it again on the carpet. Lady M. exclaimed the dog was dying fast —it was certainly gone. His Lordship assured her that it was not and told her that he had seen many people die, but that was not the way they died; and in order to convince her that the dog was not so near death as she supposed, he would show her the manner in which people commonly died; he then stretched himself on the carpet, continued quiet for a little time, then turned himself from side to side, began to distort his features, stare with his eyes, throw about his arms, work himself into the appearance of convulsions and then expire . . .' Next morning it became apparent that in spite of his protestations the dog was well and truly dead. 'The carcase was suffered to remain some time in the drawing-room and towards the evening was carried into the bedroom of Miss Doran to be waked. Next day a number of people came to [the] house, among whom was a plumber with a lead coffin for the dog, and a carpenter with an outer shell. The plumber's account was £4.11. When the carcase was put into the coffin, a car was procured to carry it to Antrim Castle, and positive orders were given that fifty dogs should attend the funeral in white scarfs and all the dogs of the parish should be present.'

A year before his death Lord Massereene was persuaded to leave his wife the whole Massereene estate except for 'a guinea each to his brothers and one to Lady Leitrim and £200 to Mr. Smyth the Collector of Larne'. He died in March 1805, his lady having successfully struggled to the last moment to prevent his relations from seeing him.

His brothers brought a lawsuit against his widow to combat the terms of the will. The case for the family rested on the fact that Lord Massereene was insane, and many witnesses were summoned to relate his peculiarities. After four year's litigation the brothers gained a verdict, not on the grounds of insanity, but on his wife's undue influence over him. Lady Massereene was paid off very comfortably with a lump sum of £15,000 and an annuity of £800 for life. The verdict may have been a gentlemanly one; it was not customary to declare peers mad unless there was no other alternative. Perhaps a kind and accurate opinion was that of Mrs. Sowen, the apothecary's wife, who 'had previously heard a report that he was a lunatic, but she then thought that if he was a lunatic he was the pleasantest one she had ever met.'

Amanda Ros

ANNA MARGARET MCKITTRICK was born in 1860, the fourth child of the headmaster of Drumnass High School near Ballynahinch, Co. Down. Later she wrote that she had been called after the heroine of a novel called *The Children of the Abbey* which she had the temerity to claim she had never read, although she assumed it 'no doubt a nice book'. She adopted the heroine's full name, and after her marriage to Andy Ros called herself Amanda Malvina Fitzalan Anna Margaret McLelland McKitterick Ros.

Her parents came from solid Ulster farming stock, and all her life she was torn between the respectability of her background and the pressures of her voluptuous imagination. She was still a girl when she became convinced of her aristocratic connections. Later she would claim, 'by birth I am an Irishwoman—though a dash of German blood piebalds my veins . . . My father traced descent from Sitric, son of Almanc, King of the Danes . . . The McKittrick family was originally written as "Kittrick" and they were directly descended from Danish royalty'. Royalty and the aristocracy were her delight. 'Lords, ladies, countesses and ambassadors are my chief patrons,' she told another correspondent proudly; 'in fact I hold letters concerning my works from all crowned heads except the Czar of Russia and the Emperor of Austria. I don't say this in a spirit of boasting, for I detest bombast.'

She began to write—she said—at the age of six.

> When baby's yours I tried to write
> Upon a slate from morn to night.

After she left school she was sent to Dublin to Marlborough College to train as a teacher. While she was there she fell in love with a kindly red-bearded railway official fifteen years her senior. She married him when she was twenty and went to live with him hin Larne, a seaside town in Co. Antrim where he had been rewarded with the position of station master, having worked his way up from a porter. Larne was not altogether the quiet limit of the world, since it was, and still is, linked to Scotland by the Stranraer ferry. Amanda made the most of this, and also of Andy Ros's prosaic origins. After he died she remembered how 'he was a perfect gentleman in every way. He dined with every gentleman of note who crossed in vessels to Larne harbour, viz. Lord Londonderry, Lord Roberts . . . he was a fine English scholar, could speak Russian, French and Norwegian fluently. One day Lord Randolph Churchill caught his arm and they walked arm in arm to the Oldfleet Hotel and dined together'.

Meanwhile her first and best-known book, *Irene Iddesleigh*, which she had begun in her teens was published privately in 1897. It had an unremarkable romantic plot; young Irene marries an older man, later elopes with her first love and is punished by becoming an outcast of society. But the alliterative names of the protagonists—Osbert Otwell, Irene Iddesleigh—the metaphors, which a critic has described as Molotov cocktails, and the passionate rambling prose with its own rules of grammar formed a style unique in English literature.

'Sympathize with me indeed!' ran the opening passage. 'Ah no! Cast your sympathy on the chill waves of troubled waters; fling it on the oases of futurity; dash it against the rock of gossip; or, better still, allow it to remain within the false and faithless bosom of buried scorn.' The hero, Sir John Dunfern of Dunfern, 'though a man of 40 summers . . . never yet had entertained the thought of yielding up his bacheloric ideas to supplace them with others which eventually should coincide with those of a different sex'. His meeting with the fair Irene in strained formal circumstances—'How the titter of tainted mockery ran through the whole apartment!'—changed everything.

One of the author's habitual grammatical blunders was to begin a sentence with a phrase that belongs to the previous sentence and is unrelated to the subject it governs. 'On entering the chamber of sickness with a new bottle of medicine sent from London, Sir John raised himself slightly on his left elbow.' She broadened the meaning of words: 'north' and 'south', for example, could be interpreted in new ways. The 'bald north' of Lord Gifford's statue referred to the top of the head; 'south' could mean a man's trousers or Hell.

In a later novel, *Helen Huddleston*, her common use of alliterative names went a step further when she called a number of characters charmingly after fruit. Sir Christopher Currant, the Duke of Greengage and Sir Peter Plum were set against Madam Pear, Mrs. Strawberry, and a maid called Lily Lentil. Her biographer, Jack Loudan, claims that she genuinely found nothing incongruous about this. He interviewed her while she was actually working on the novel. 'Why did you choose these names!' 'Because they are the right names for such people,' he was told. 'What else would I call them?'

This is the book where Susan Sylvester appears, her face 'charged with misty patches of pure distress'. Elsewhere she is to be found 'a mass of moist anxiety, stooping over Lord Raspberry where he lay motionless (as if he had bidden farewell to the world and its teeming varieties of humanity) on a gorgeously appointed bed that held within its exquisitely carved creations years before three crowned heads, two of whom abused its virtuous embellishments, thereby robbing them of further encroachments within either its coaxing elegance, inculcating a desire to follow the dictates of a cleanly conscience'. Parts of *Helen Huddleston* are written in dialect which even the natives of her own Co. Down could not understand. 'How soniver, it seems Beer nex no name til keep dye thing goin' ir to keep dthe grandfther ive it birrelin ahes capital's lack mae own.'

Amanda also wrote poetry.

> She rises mostly every day
> At sunrise, noon or night.
> Her one and only thought is where's
> The drink to make her tight
> For it very often happens

That bipeds so inclined
Would practise tricks more filthy
Than drinking too much wine.

Lines on Westminster Abbey

Holy Moses! Have a look!
Flesh decayed in every nook.
Some rare bits of brain lie here,
Mortal loads of beef and beer . . .

She had an obsession with the state of the body after death. At its most exalted she visualized Queen Victoria in her tomb at Frogmore 'where this Queenly Death-Diamond of the first and purest water reposeth in her Royal Cradle of Calm'. Others fared less comfortably, like this critic:

My! What a bubbly vapoury box of vanity!
A litter of worms, a relic of humanity.

Critics were generally hard on her. One described her as the 'World's worst author'. An American thought her 'a poor tame woman, wife of a workman, escaping on paper from the knowledge that things have always been dour and plain around her and that they would never be anything else'. She was touchy about bad reviews. 'I see a criticism in the Irish News of the 8th inst. by some donkeyosity who calls himself Billy Moore and I style Hogwash.' Another critic was called 'Poor Ape'; indeed, before her literary career was finished she had composed scores of highly ingenious epithets for her enemies. Mr. Loudan has listed them; they include apprentices to the scatheing trade, brain washers (possibly the earliest, certainly an original use of this term), clay crabs of corruption, drunken ignorant dross, evil-minded snapshots of spleen, hogwashing hooligans, maggoty throng, scandalizers of books, scorchers of rare talent, street arabs, talent wipers of wormy orders and worms.

Her most famous reply to a critic was a ten-thousand-word piece of invective headed 'St. Scandalbags', directed against

D. B. Wyndham Lewis who reviewed *Irene Iddesleigh* unkindly in the *Daily Mail* in 1926. It began:

'Under the long and honoured and peaceful reign of our Good and Gracious and Peace-Loving Queen Victoria, stirring and many and multitudinous were the events, fashions and effronteries that happened, were formed and committed throughout the realms of her August Control. But all these events, fashions and effronteries were as midge on a camel's back to the stale spuings, the ungrammatical effortless efforts of a "criticising crowdrop" to be found bespattering a column—a *whole* column! (with not even a *bite* out of it) of the celestial-like-celebrated-talent-tarnisher and by name, "*The Daily Mail*".'

Irene Iddesleigh was, after all, her masterpiece, and she considered it worthy of nomination for the Nobel Prize. She called her house after her heroine, and it appeared on her famous visiting card: Mrs. Amanda Ros—AUTHORESS—'AT HOME' ALWAYS TO THE HONOURABLE—Iddesleigh, Ireland—Telegrams, 'Iddesleigh, Ireland'.

'I am pleased to say,' she could write to a correspondent in 1927 a year after her attack on Lewis, 'this work now rests upon the shelf of "classic" for which reason I presume the critics, lately have done their utmost to murder both the book and its author; nevertheless—*I Still Live* and the book shall never die.

'Their bayonets of bastard sheen with their scurrilous punctures of jealousy jadery affect neither the book nor its author financially, but on the contrary, will not be overlooked by me in the near future.'

Besides critics she had her fans. Perhaps they did not include all the members of the Amanda Ros society formed at St. John's College, Cambridge, by undergraduates who used to send her flattering letters in order to encourage her extraordinary replies. Nevertheless she claimed that she received tributes from admirers throughout the world. 'I expect I will be talked about at the end of 1000 years.'

In 1923 Aldous Huxley wrote a sympathetic article about her, which mildly pointed out that her ambitions were more than her abilities. She was extremely pleased and regarded it as the highest praise she had ever received. When 'St. Scandalbags' was reprinted in 1954, Anthony Powell thought there were affinities between Amanda and Shakespeare in her handling of language. He also found a resemblance between a passage from 'St. Scandalbags' and an extract from James Joyce's *Ulysses* which he used to emphasize that Amanda Ros was a 'genuine native Irish writer'.

But she could also sound like John Perrot the Quaker, who wrote how he 'did make sobs as an ease to my soul and sustained myself with the grievousness of groanes; there were sighings as a spouse in my bed and tears as my solace to her . . .' Amanda's ecstasies may perhaps be traced to her non-comformist upbringing; the Bible, absorbed as a girl at Ballynahinch, played a part in forming her style which appears to be a bizarre combination of the Old Testament and the Victorian novel, set off by her own uniquely immoderate handling of language.

She did not read widely outside her formative influences, remaining largely ignorant of the mass of English literature and the works of her contemporaries. She was convinced of the worthlessness of many fashionably acclaimed writers. Revolted by *Alice in Wonderland*, she severely condemned Lewis Carroll. 'I hold any man wearing a clerical coat, especially, for a hundred and one reasons, should receive 100 strokes of the birch to celebrate into that region he best deserves for writing such idiotic nonsensical whimsical disjointed piece of abject happenings, bursting with Stygian Style Expressions lined throughout with a prickly patterned policy the Gods would grant and decentminded abhor . . .'

Lawyers as well as critics excited Amanda's scorn. Her excursions in litigation were numerous and inspired many an earthy note of abuse. 'Sir,' she wrote to a lawyer in 1905, 'it has just come to my notice that you had the tinker-like impertinence to send me the enclosed. Would you be surprised to learn that I don't owe Porter one cent? If not, I'm here to inform you. What importation are you, by the by? I thought Belfast already stuffed with priggish prey. And you demand my damned 2/6 for writing "this" piece of toilet paper. Well, I wouldn't give

you 2/6 for all the W.C. requisites in Belfast and solicitors,
included, mark you . . .'

In 1908 she was left a limekiln with some land, a legacy which
was to involve her with six different solicitors in various lawsuits.
She took a leading part in her own defence. One barrister was
threatened with her stick. 'Have some manners, Sir—don't inter-
rupt a lady when she's speaking to a gentleman.' On another
occasion she displayed a banner in the streets of Larne on which
was inscribed some of her grievances against two leading lawyers.
Crowds would gather round her trap as she argued her case in
the open air; before leaving for home her habit was to take out a
toy trumpet and blow two raspberries in the direction of her
enemies' office. The case dragged on for five years before judgement was given against her.

Law and Church played a prominent and unflattering role in
her writing. Characters in her novels included Bishop Barelegs
and the lawyer, Goliath Ginbottle. In *Helen Huddleston* she described Barney Blocter, K.C., with Joycean zest: 'his jaw beggar-
plated and boraxed with flaxen fluffy hairy fringe crimped towards
the south, his mouth an olio of odour and Portland Pegs ditched
round with a wall of bright red brick; his tongue a live tooth-
brush; and his chin a baggy sauceboat.'

Among her books of poetry, *Poems of Puncture*, described as a
'filthy debt to dishonest lawyers', contained twenty-seven poems
of which eleven abused the legal profession.

> Readers, did you ever hear
> Of Mickey Monkey-face McBlair?
> His snout is long with a flattish top,
> Lined inside with a slimy crop.
> His mouth like a slit in a money box
> portrays his kindred to a fox . . .

Lawyer Jock is described as 'the Ugliest Brute in England',

His face so shaped like a butter spade, was of colour a
  corpsey-pale
With a treacherous look in every nook from the top of it
  down to his —.

The death of an old antagonist, Jamie Jarr, brought no hint of regret or forgiveness.

> His mouth now shut for ever,
> His lying tongue still and nevermore
> Can stab you in the dark
> Earth is by far the richer,
> Hell—one boarder more—
> Heaven rejoices to be free
> From such a legal bore.

Corruption and the law are combined in her nasty *Epitaph on Largebones*.

> Beneath me here in stinking clumps
> Lies Lawyer Largebones all in lumps;
> A rotten mass of clockholed clay,
> Which grows more honeycombed each day.
> See how the rats have scratched his face?
> Now so unlike the human race;
> I very much regret I can't
> Assist them in their eager 'bent'.

In 1917 Andy Ros died. He was a popular citizen of Larne and a large crowd of civic dignitaries assembled for the funeral. Amanda carefully vetted the wreaths; those which came from people she disapproved of were put in a barrow and returned the day before Andy was buried. She instructed her messenger to wheel them from door to door. One rejected wreath from the new station master of Larne was returned with the cryptic note: *Keep it for the funeral of X.* During the funeral procession Amanda, having spied several people she disliked, ordered the hearse to trot away from the mourners following on foot.

After the death of her husband she was obliged to convert the ground floor of her house into two shops and let them out. One was taken by a man who sold sweets and toffee apples, doing much business on Sunday. This was not a routine any strict Presbyterian could approve of; she tried to discourage customers by ringing a large brass bell as they came to the door and hanging

out a banner on which was written: ALL DESECRATORS
OF THE SABBATH SHALL BE PUNISHED.

In 1926 she got married for the second time to a prosperous
Co. Down farmer called Mr. Rogers. Eight years later her last
book of poems *Fumes of Formation*, appeared, 'hatched with a mind
fringed with fumes of formation, the ingenious innings of inspiration and thorny tincture of thought.' Jack Loudan describes
her in old age as 'a tall stately woman with bright black twinkling
eyes behind a pair of shining pince-nez, a black lace cap arranged
neatly on her head, a white cameo brooch on the high neck
of her black dress. There was something superbly Victorian about
her.'

She outlived her second husband and 'joined the boundless
battalion of the breathless' in February 1939, at the age of seventy-
eight.

Folly and Death and
Adolphus Cooke

When man grows staid and wise
Getting a house and home where he may move
Within the circle of his breath,
        Schooling his eyes;
That dumb inclosure maketh love
Unto the coffin that attends his death.

In this final chapter I have linked some builders and occupiers
of follies and tombs with others who, like George Herbert, sought
for reminders of death in the routine of their everyday lives.
Death becomes a preoccupation for many eccentrics, even if
they do not often 'step into their voluntarie graves' with the
alacrity of the hermit, observed by de Latocnaye, who lived in
a hut made of coffin boards. This recluse arrived one day at the
ruins of Muckross Abbey outside Killarney and set up his residence
in a window. He did not like to be regarded by the curious; one
early tourist who paid him too much attention—for he was good-
looking—was told: 'Take care of these eyes, they have done a
great deal of harm!' He spent two years in the abbey window
expiating some crimes and depending on charity for his livelihood
before vanishing as mysteriously as he first appeared.

Wandering near Dublin, de Lactonaye found a family living
under a dolmen. The cumbersome pile, with its vast slanting
cap of rain-washed granite supported on six boulders, still stands
near the village of Cabinteely at the bottom of a suburban garden.
The inside chamber, which measures approximately ten feet by

six, was probably more comfortable and weather-proof than many homes of the poor. It was cheerfully occupied by a father, mother, ten children, dog, cat, goat and pig, until the owner of the land on which it stood persuaded them all to move into a cabin, so that he could more easily show off his interesting prehistoric possession to his friends. The Cabinteely dolmen was not unique in its adaptation as a dwelling place; another at Haroldstown near Rathvilly in Co. Carlow is said to have been inhabited right up to modern times, and probably there were other large prehistoric tombs where the destitute and homeless chose to live.

A dolmen would have been more comfortable than 'the Rat Hole' at Bray which, before the coming of the railway turned Bray into the Brighton of Ireland, was almost the only building on the sea front. Here, if death were not a perpetual reminder, decay was. The little hovel was owned by a fisherman whom Joyce in his *Neighbourhood of Dublin* described as 'eccentric, solitary, tar-begrimed . . . who took a delight in surrounding his unattractive abode with ill-smelling heaps of manure, offal, seaweed and every other abomination that came within his reach, until at last it became difficult to distinguish between the dwelling and these strange accessories. To what end he accumulated these malodorous tumuli none who knew him could surmise; but that he enjoyed the possession of them could be open to no doubt, as he was to be seen there daily during his leisure hours, regaling his nose and eyes on their perfume and proportions.'

Around 1860 in the woods of Co. Cork Johnny Roche settled down to make tombstones and build a castle for himself. He was born sometime before the famine at Walltown near Mallow, where he picked up his skills as a carpenter and blacksmith from his father, although he never received any formal training as a craftsman. He emigrated to America for three years, until, on the break-up of his marriage, he returned to Cork. Beside the Awbeg river a few miles below Doneraile he built a mill for preparing wool and homespuns and also for the manufacture of tombstones. He had already become well-known for unusual enterprises and local people recited:

This is another of Roche's toys
That does little work but makes great noise.

Soon the mill was adapted to the more traditional job of grinding corn while Johnny Roche turned to a more ambitious undertaking. In an area which is thickly covered with the stumps and ruins of old castles, he decided to build his own, similar in spirit to those round about. He was a poor man and set out to do every spadeful of the work himself. For three years he toiled, drawing lime from nearby Mallow in his donkey and cart, collecting stones to his site by the river, and as the strange building became higher, devising a winch to pull the materials up to where he sat. When it was completed it was nicknamed Castle Curious.

Although a little worn, the framework of Johnny's castle still stands. It consists of an oval tower twenty-seven feet in length and forty-five feet high, topped by two oval turrets that run at right angles to the main building. At the base of the tower a slab of granite is engraved with fine lettering: John Roche, 1870. It is not quite what he set out to achieve since it is no more like the frowning Nagle fortress nearby than a pepperpot resembles a grandfather clock. Situated on a beautiful curve of the river, it has an air of fragility imposed by the limitations of one man's strength, that turns it into a fairy castle. In his time one of the turrets carried a flag showing a flying angel and the outside was ornamented with grotesque heads.

Here Johnny lived for the rest of his life in a labyrinth of rooms, now all in ruin, making use of his private well, so that there was no need to use St. Bernard's holy well, situated within a few feet of him. He would lean out of a window in his tower and abuse the pilgrims who came to leave their votive offerings, calling them public nuisances and gatherings of thieves. Using the castle as a base, or moving about the countryside on the special bicycle he constructed himself, or in his travelling coach drawn by two mules complete with such amenities as stove and bed, he indulged in his skills and interests. He could draw teeth, mend clocks, produce sculpture, construct a large water-clock, play on the bagpipes or violin, dance, whistle or sing.

He had himself photographed in loose clothes he made himself, a wide-brimmed Rabbinical hat topping his bearded face with sharp quizzical eyes, a violin in one hand, a mortar in the other. His best friend was a retired dragoon named Nixon, who was clerk to the clergyman at Wallstown. Nixon asked Roche to design his tombstone if he should predecease him. In due course Johnny came to erect a pole and flag over the grave of his friend whose headstone was inscribed simply: HERE LIES NIXON. He planned something more elaborate for himself and collected stones for his tomb and composed his epitaph.

> Here lies the body of poor John Roche
> He had his faults, but don't reproach;
> For while alive his heart was mellow;
> An artist, genius and comic fellow.

But he died before his plans were complete and was buried without elaboration in nearby Templeroan.

Some people like to be buried where there is a view which they assume they will be able to enjoy. There are two graves with good vantage points in the Knockmealdown mountains. Grubb's Grave, belonging to Mr. Samuel Grubb, a Quaker who died in the 1920s, is situated on the north slope of the Sugar Loaf Hill, 2,144 feet high. Mr. Grubb directed that he should be buried standing bolt upright in a tomb that imitates the hill, a cairn of whitened masonry which overlooks his estate, Castlegrace House, lying in the valley below. On the highest point of all, the actual summit of Knockmealdown Mountain, 2,609 feet above sea level, lies Henry Eeles, a gentleman of Youghal, who published some tracts upon electricity. In their book on Ireland published in 1841, Col. and Mrs. Hall summarized the speculation that arose about his burial.

'The . . . *History of Waterford* states that Mr. Eeles had his horse and dog interred with him on the summit of the mountain. We have, however, the testimony of his relatives and representative that the statement is incorrect . . . Rumour has, of course, added largely to the fact that the eccentric gentleman selected his last home apart from crowds. We have not only heard the addition of the steed and hound, but were told by many that by his directions an iron rod was driven through his body, in order that it might attract the lightning to descend to consume him utterly.'

In 1956 General Sir Denis Kirwan Bernard left instructions that he was to be buried at the summit of Knockmaa in Co. Galway. His horse, which had predeceased him, had been buried in a field halfway up and another lay some distance away. Knockmaa, a fairy hill called after Maeve, is traditionally regarded as the Otherworld seat of Finvarra, the King of the Connacht Fairies. On the summit there is a prehistoric cairn (the Carn Ceasarach of medieval legend) and a cross over the general's grave engraved with his name and dates facing the Galway plain which stretches to Lough Corrib and the mountains beyond. The panorama is magnificent, and like Mr. Grubb, the general thought he could enjoy it better if he were buried upright. Unfortunately since Knockmaa is made up of limestone slabs, the site was found to be too stony to carry out his wish, and he has had to lie in the conventional manner. His burial met with another hitch when it was found that his chosen resting place was a few feet outside his estate in the possession of another farmer. Matters were sorted out and no one could have a finer view.

The death of a loved one can obsess people. Dorothea Herbert tells of a good-looking young widow who became unhinged by the death of her husband. She painted every inch of her house in Clontarf black. Even the flower-pots were blackened, and so were the stalls and mangers in her stables. A white horse, lodged in them while they were wet, 'having well rubbed its snowy hide, it was led out to its master an elegant Pye bald'. The widow then invited in an upholsterer to do some alterations. 'He was shown at Midday into a large dark Room where the fair widow sat (with a Taper burning) in the deepest Woe and dressed in her Sables received him—she then showed him every hole and corner of the house—bespoke hangings of black Paper for every room—Black Beds, black chair covers, black Window curtains . . .' She commanded her maid—also dressed in black—to lock him in a room until he agreed to do the work. He escaped after giving 'one Spring from the Top of the stairs to the Bottom'.

A concern for the death of his wife was surprisingly and touchingly revealed in the will of the great Dublin philanthropist, Thomas Pleasants. He wrote it when he was over ninety on fifteen separate pieces of paper. The beneficiaries included Joshua Pasley who received six guineas a year for life 'so that he might continue to put 2/6 into the poor box of any church he might choose to go on Sunday'. A servant was left a special legacy in recompense for her wonderful exertions on the night when the rain deluged the bedroom. He left his cook the copper utensils which she was so fond of keeping bright, and two other servants received sums of money because they were always attentive to him 'and kept themselves clear of the shameful fashions that females in general and of all descriptions are now, unfortunately for their minds, as well as their bodies under the influence of . . .' Lastly he reiterated his constant memory of his wife by desiring that her slippers, which since her death he had placed under his pillow every night before he went to sleep, should now be put in his coffin.

But pure eccentricity is an egotistical exercise, and the concern of William Thompson and Adolphus Cooke about their ultimate future was selfish.

Outside Ireland William Thompson has a universal claim to fame. Born in 1775 the son of one of the richest merchants in Cork, he visited France as a young man and became a disciple of the Comte de Saint-Simon, the philosopher and early expounder of Socialist theory. He met Bentham and Owen and became a member of a group of thinkers who had an important bearing on the development of modern Socialist thinking. Karl Marx is said to have been impressed by Thompson's pioneer work, and Sidney and Beatrice Webb have described Marx as 'the illustrious disciple of Thompson and Hodgkin'. There is a bust of Thompson in the International Communist Museum in Prague, although it is doubtful if many people who make a reverential tour of that establishment realize that it represents an autocratic old bachelor who ruled over several thousand tenants in the wilds of south-west Ireland, and at the same time showed a range of eccentricities that are still remembered in the area where he was a landlord.

Before considering his peculiarities, it would be as well to remember his achievements. Among his most important publications were *An Inquiry into the Principles of the Distribution of Wealth* and *Labour Rewarded* in both of which he put forward his influential ideas about Socialism. Many of his other beliefs were strikingly advanced for his time. He was an early advocate of a free state school system, and, as a good follower of Saint-Simon, who adopted a reverential attitude to *Woman*, a passionate believer in female emancipation.

His family did not like his new ideas at all, and were horrified to learn of the conversion of the 'Red Republican', especially when he said that he also supported Catholic Emancipation. The estrangement that began when he was a young man continued after his father's death in 1814; although he inherited the bulk of his property, three years later he was declared a bankrupt after a dispute with his relations concerning a charge put upon the estate. Years of litigation followed, which concluded with his having to sell a portion of his land to appease his sisters. But he remained fairly wealthy, and, determined to break with the custom of absentee landlordism, he settled down at Carhoogarriff, his estate near Glandore, a wild remote fishing village in West Cork. Here, on seventeen hundred acres of bog and rock, he carried out a number of philanthropic projects to help the local people. He also set about forming an experiment in co-operative living.

He had written a pamphlet entitled *Practical Directions for the Speedy and Economic Establishments of Communities on the Principle of Mutual Cooperation, United Possessions, Equality of Exertions and of the Means of Enjoyment*. He was influenced by Robert Owen, who first thought up a master plan for communal living on the assumption that man's character was the product of his environment. Owen came to Ireland to lecture on the idea of the co-operative, and impressed two forward-looking landlords, John Scott Vandeleur of Co. Clare and Thompson. Thompson took up the idea at once, proposing an immediate foundation fifteen miles from Cork. Although this did not come to anything, two years later in 1829 he began a co-operative experiment at Carhoogarriff. John Finch, who visited it in 1834, a year after his death, reported some of his developments to a select committee of the House of Commons. Peasants had been granted allotments of three to twenty acres and provided with specially built cottages. Because of the lack of dram shops 'the whole place had become sober and industrious . . . the village magistrate had reported that scarcely a case of crime came before him in a year'.

In the midst of this exemplary atmosphere Thompson had walked about Glandore with a tricolour tied to the end of his walking stick. An acquaintance, Mrs. Wheeler, described him as wearing 'the old plain flannel petticoat about his neck in guise of a cloak, and that seduisant hat, put on in the true Thompson cock'. He was a teetotaller and non-smoker, and for the last seventeen years of his life a vegetarian, declaring that he could read and write better without meat. For breakfast he ate bread and jam, while lunch consisted of turnips and potatoes. Although he would not take eggs or butter, his diet contained two luxuries, tea and honey, which he produced from his own hives. Once a mouse got stuck in his honey and he licked it clean before releasing it.

He gave chemical experiments in public, so that his tenants, already awed by his atheism, considered him a wizard. He pulled their teeth and treated their illnesses, while carrying out experiments in practical farming. For some time after he heard that the flesh and bones of all living animals contain the same ingredients as wood, he fed his pigs on a diet of sawdust, peat and straw.

His famous tower, a hundred feet high, built like a round tower with a little conical roof, was a landmark until quite recently. He used it like Montaigne as a retreat, and also as a look-out from where he could watch the activities of the co-operative.

The co-operative had only just got under way when he died at his house at Clonkeen on March 28, 1833. The cause of his death was probably pneumonia. He said during a particularly violent paroxysm of coughing: 'Ah! if only I could live for ever, be for ever young, active joyous and useful; but as it is, I must make the best of a short life.'

As a militant rationalist and free thinker who believed that reason must ultimately triumph over dogma, he had particularly disliked all varieties of clergymen and priests. One clergyman who recovered from an illness under his ministration was told to give thanks to his pills and the devil rather than God. He considered priests 'rapacious parasites, ghost dealers in creed and spiritual brimstone', and declared that 'if a Turkish and Irish child were exchanged in infancy, the Irish Mohammedan would grow up to look at Christians as monsters who worshipped three gods, and whose priests ordained and compounded the divine nature of the communion service'.

Local people, Catholics and Protestants alike, disapproved when they observed that he got a Christian burial. This had been insisted upon by his nephew, Mr. White, a connection of the Earls of Bantry, who hoped to inherit the property. After the funeral was over Thompson's will was read out, and it was discovered that he had given explicit instructions forbidding 'any priest, Christian, Mohammedan or Hindu' to meddle with his remains. His body had to be dug up from Drombeg cemetery to comply with his wish that it should be put on display 'to aid in conquering the foolish and frequently most mischievous prejudice against the public examination of corpses'. There is confusion about the fate of his skeleton whose ribs he instructed were to be 'tipped with silver so that it might present a fashionable appearance'. The will directed that it should be left to the first co-operative successfully established in either Great Britain or Ireland. But a Dr. Donovan later claimed that he had been given the job of preparing the corpse on condition of 'stringing up the bones and sending them as a memento of love to Mrs. Wheeler'. Mrs. Anna Wheeler was an early believer in the emancipation of women and the mother-in-law of Edward Bulwer-Lytton. Whether she received her gift is not known. She did not get the skull which was left to a French phrenologist named Monsieur Baume. 'Came across from London to claim the cranium to lecture on its physical development', the Frenchman wrote.

Thompson left his estate to the Co-operative Movement. The will was contested by his relations, and the case dragged on for a miserable twenty-five years before judgement was given in their favour. By that time most of the money had vanished into the pockets of lawyers, justifying Thompson's opinions about the legal profession which were as forceful as his estimate of priests. The co-operative soon languished; nothing remains at Glandore except for a few almost indistinguishable stumps of buildings rising from the side of a hill. The tower went to make a road. As the Salford Co-operative Institution fearfully predicted in a hymn that closed a memorial oration on the occasion of his death:

> Pity dropping hangs her head
> Sorrowing o'er our Thompson dead;
> Death—stern death has from her won.
> Tell, O Guardian Angel, tell,
> Was lost our cause when Thompson fell?

★   ★   ★

Adolphus Cooke shared with William Thompson an interest in what happened to his body after his death, although he was less practical. He believed in reincarnation. This made him unfailingly courteous to his father, whom he believed had returned to earth in the guise of a turkey cock. He instructed his men servants to take off their hats to this bird every time they passed it, while women had to genuflect and bend one knee.

He represented the extreme in country house eccentrics whose wealth encouraged oddness and yet helped him to skirt the boundary of true madness. An account of his life and death, highlighting the original features of his circumstances and behaviour, makes an interesting conclusion to this catalogue of Irish eccentricity.

He owned a big estate in Westmeath where his ancestors had settled late in the seventeenth century. In 1742 a Cooke remodelled the family mansion, Cookesborough, making the doors, windows and wall recesses arched. This was to bring them in line with his chairs which all had balloon backs. Even the stables, coach-houses and other offices in the yard had curved orifices. The windows were very expensive, and most of them refused to open.

Other members of the family kept racehorses, greyhounds and gamecocks with which they gambled away bits of their land. One Cooke, attending a race meeting in England, was heard to call out as he watched his horse go down to the start: 'He is off now with the Wood of Ra'honnell on his back!' The wood was lost.

Adolphus Cooke came to possess the substantial remainder of the property in a roundabout way. He was illegitimate; Robert Cooke followed the family's wild traditions when he fathered him in 1792. At his birth, Robert's wife, who had given him two legitimate sons, left him at once, The servant who was the baby's mother was sent away, and the infant farmed out to be nursed by a woman named Mary Kelly. He was never allowed near the Big House, but was confined with his foster mother in a two-roomed thatch cottage beside what is still known as the Nurse's Pond. From Cookesborough his father took a distant but efficient interest in his welfare, seeing that the cottage was kept in good condition and arranging for a basket of provisions to be sent down every day for the needs of nurse and growing boy. They never got more than one day's supply at a time. Each item had to be accounted for, the potatoes weighed and the salt measured; even the sods of turf for the fire had to be counted. On one day in the year Mrs. Kelly was allowed to go to Mullingar to buy the child clothes and shoes, charging the bills to Mr. Cooke.

When the time came, Adolphus was sent to school in England, and afterwards served in the army. He was in Spain and Portugal under Wellington, and visited Africa and India. Perhaps it was while he was abroad that he became interested in reincarnation. But he may have been converted to the idea from his reading. Over his lifetime he collected nine thousand books, although he failed to own a copy of the Bible.

Meanwhile both his half-brothers had predeceased their father. One was drowned in Lough Swilly in 1811, and the other died without issue in 1823. When Robert Cooke died in 1835 without a legitimate heir, he bequeathed his property to Adolphus, who, at

the age of forty-three, left the army and came home to take possession of Cookesborough. The demesne and farm around the house
contained about seven hundred acres, while the rest of the property, which totalled over four thousand acres, was let out to
tenants.

It soon became clear that the ex-soldier had inclinations to
vary the conventional role of an Irish landlord. The taint of
illegitimacy may have affected his behaviour. First of all he gave
two curious employees whom he called 'gentlemen of nature's
stamp' positions of trust on his farm. His steward, Tom Cruise,
whom he had selected from the local workhouse was a big heavy
man, much addicted to sport. His passion for attending sporting
fixtures made him travel long distances. He would collect subscriptions for these events and at the same time ask the local parish
priest to announce them at Sunday Mass. Once, he interrupted a
sermon by calling out: 'Father, you are forgetting to tell them
about the sports at Longfield today.' Aldophus's second most
trusted servant was Billy Dunne, a tall raw-boned man of
about fifty, renowned for his flat feet. The children of Mullingar
taunted him by shouting that they would spit on his toe. He
had a passion for drilling imaginary troops, and an admiration
for the newly created police force which inspired him, during
fair or race days, to parade around in cast off policeman's clothes
with a straw rope round his waist from which hung a stick he
would call his bayonet.

With the help of these aides Adolphus organized his work-
force on a system that was a cross between army discipline and
a landlord's paternalism. The people on his estate were well looked
after, receiving two blankets at Christmas, a pension and funeral
expenses. But they had to conform to rigid rules of conduct under
pain of instant dismissal. Every morning Adolphus would lead
his men off to work, wheeling a wheelbarrow. He would give
the commands, 'Fall in! March in Step!' and behind him in a line
came each workman with his own barrow filled with tools.
When anyone entered his employment he was given the barrow,
together with spade, fork, shovel, pickaxe, scythe, river knife and
drag, each marked with his initials. If he lost any of these tools

he would be dismissed. At the end of a working day Adolphus would be there with his barrow to lead his people home; they would line up behind him again and walk back in step. On one occasion when they were working late digging drains, some of the men in their hurry put extra tools into the master's own barrow. As a punishment he kept them out far into the evening by stopping the column every hundred yards to rest for long periods.

Like Dean Swift he hated children. One family living on the estate spent years concealing their children, fearful of being evicted. A vagrant, asking Adolphus for a little help, received five pounds when he informed him that he was childless. Another, hoping to appeal to his generosity by announcing that he had a wife and twelve little ones, was to told go away because he was a naughty man.

A gatekeeper who had let in unwanted visitors to the estate was told that as a punishment he must get rid of his wife and replace her with another. 'The bigamy law is against you, and it is a law that ought to be repealed,' the man was told.

The animals at Cookesborough were treated unusually. Although Cooke bred beautiful horses, having imported some of the best blood of the day, many of the colts remained unbroken, and were allowed to enjoy themselves until they were ten or twelve years old. Once he was told that a bullock had stumbled into a river and was drowning. After consultation with Dunne and Cruise he gave instructions that all his other cattle should be driven to the bank of the river. 'There they will have an opportunity of seeing their companion drowning, and it will be a warning and a caution to each and everyone during their mortal tenure to shun water.'

A bull who threatened his master in the Bull Paddock was challenged to a fight. Adolphus, declaring that he had no notion of being turned out of his own field by his own bull, dressed himself in a red coat and went out to meet it with a sword. During the battle that followed the bull gained the upper hand until a maidservant came running to help. She set the dogs at the animal and opened the heavy iron gate into the paddock wide enough to allow the matador to escape. He sacked her on the spot, telling her that only the best should be allowed to survive.

His special preoccupation was the crows of the estate. He hated the noise they made, during February and March when they were nesting. He would be out much of the day gazing up at the tall Scotch firs, and if he heard the birds squabble he would become very excited, showing corresponding relief when the row was over. Trees and shrubs were never allowed to be cut because crows used them as resting places or made their homes in them. One year he went further and directed a detail of his men to gather twigs and brushwood and make the nests themselves. Some of them got tired of this work, and settled down to rest in a sandpit, leaving one man to watch. Adolphus surprised them, but only sacked the careless watchman, saying: 'You have let in the enemy!' But neither the crows nor the jackdaws would use his nests.

He believed that he was surrounded by the strongest and best fed crows in Ireland, well able to withstand any invaders. Their worst enemies were the crows from nearby Killucan. If his men wished to ingratiate themselves with him, they would tell him that his honour's crows had fought a terrific battle with the Killucan crows, which they had won, leaving thousands dead and wounded. He would stand up and clap his hands. Anyone who shot, trapped or ill-treated a Cookesborough crow was dismissed or evicted.

The belief in reincarnation led to confusion about the identity of certain creatures. The turkey cock received due reverence because he was considered to be the late Robert Cooke. But there were doubts, which led to the reprieve of the dog Gusty.

Gusty, a large red setter, was one of Adolphus's favourite dogs, an affectionate animal, well liked by the staff and friendly with strangers. But he was apt to stray. On each occasion Adolphus would send a dozen men from Cookesborough out to scour the the countryside to find him. When he was brought home his master would severely reprimand him for his wandering habits and love of low company, and command that he should be kept in solitary confinement for three days and placed on short rations.

After several such imprisonments Adolphus decided to give Gusty one last chance. In the presence of most of his workmen, who were summoned as witnesses, Gusty was warned that if he strayed once again he would be hanged like any common criminal, and to impress the point on him he was shown the rope and the tree.

Gusty took no notice, and soon afterwards was found near Mullingar late in the evening with some common dogs. Adolphus ordered his trial to take place the following morning in the great hall at ten o'clock with all his staff present. Billy Dunne and Tom Cruise acted as special advisers and a jury was chosen. Two labourers gave evidence of how Gusty had been found and how he had resisted arrest. The jury went into another room, and after an absence of two hours they returned with a verdict of 'Guilty of Misbehaviour', which they thought would best please the judge. On passing sentence Adolphus emphasized the heinousness of the crime for which Gusty was convicted—ingratitude to a good master who had fed and nurtured him with tender care since he was a puppy. Gusty was told that after he was dead a tombstone would be erected over his grave with the following inscription:

Executed for high crimes and misdemeanours
GUSTY
Once the favourite setter dog of
Adolphus Cooke, Esq.,
Cookesborough,
And it is earnestly hoped that his sad fate will be a
warning to other dogs against so offending.
Tuesday, 8th May, 1860.

But who was to hang him? None of the staff was eager to do the job, since they were fairly sure that the hangman would be dismissed after the execution. In due course a man called 'The Bug Mee' consented to dispose of him. 'To plaze your honour I'll hang him; and I'd hang the missus and childer too, if it came to that.' He was instructed to carry out the execution next morning at one of the seven lime trees a quarter of a mile from the house. He disappeared towards them with Gusty and the rope, but returned a little while later with Gusty alive. Adolphus met him and thundered: 'How was it you did not carry out my instructions?' The Bug Mee replied: 'Your honour, I was knotting the rope on his neck when he put the heart across me. He began speaking to me in some kind of foreign language. So, I said to myself, I'd bring him back to you because there is something in him.' 'So, Mee,' Adolphus replied, 'you do believe as I do.' 'Your honour, wouldn't anyone believe if he saw what I saw? Who knows, but it's the ould gentleman himself that is living with?' 'You can be right, Mee.' So Gusty was brought back into the house, and like the turkey cock he lived to a ripe old age.

As he grew older, Adolphus became concerned about his own future. At first his ideas about burial were comparatively simple. He wrote:

> When the day arrives that I must die
> In some lonely spot let my body lie
> Where no mortal was laid before
> There let me rest for evermore
> Let there be no stone to mark my bed
> Nor o'er me let a prayer be said,
> O let me not implore in vain
> Let this spot be in my demesne.

Then his funeral arrangements became more elaborate. He built himself a massive marble vault on the Cookesborough estate, forty feet square and forty feet deep so that he would not be disturbed by the screams of jackdaws. He personally supervised the construction of marble steps leading down into a room with an arched roof lined with marble slabs. Inside was a great fireplace, in front of which he put a marble chair and table and a lectern. The surrounding shelves were filled with books and on the table he planned a regular supply of pens, ink and paper. He directed that he should be embalmed and placed in a sitting position before the fire, which, together with the hanging brass lamp overhead, should be kept perpetually alight.

When he died in 1876 his wishes were not carried out. The rector of Killucan with whom he had a number of disagreements ('Leave bye that Bible—I would sooner hear the Koran . . .')

would not comply with his arrangements and had him buried instead under the stone beehive where he had already interred his father and his nurse. The vault with its marble chair has been demolished, but the beehive tomb, which looks as if a giant bird had laid an egg end up, survives in Reynella churchyard near his home. It is twelve feet high and forty-two feet in circumference.

Adolphus made three wills. The first was in favour of a Scottish nephew who came to visit him bringing his fiancée. The couple were welcomed, and preparations were made for a banquet and ball to be held in their honour. They were taken for a tour around the estate which included an inspection of the marble vault whose refinements were explained. The girl sat down on the big chair and asked: 'Is this how you will look in it?' Her host flew into a rage, telling the couple to leave the house on the spot. The same day he changed his will, after sending the horseload of drink and provisions meant for the banquet down to his men working on his bogs.

His second will left the property to a cousin, Dr. Wellington Purdon, who lived nearby. Dr. Purdon was a follower of hounds, and one day the Westmeath pack came into Cookesborough, the Doctor behind them, and killed a fox in front of Adolphus. He was most upset. He did not always see himself spending the after-life sitting and reading improving books. Sometimes he imagined that he would return to earth as a bird, but increasingly he felt that he might become a fox. He hated hunting, and changed his will again to exclude Dr. Purdon, at the same time ordering his men to dig a number of exceptionally deep foxholes and trenches lined with stone which he could use in case of need. He was worried about being hunted in the next life, but consoled himself with the reflection that he had a good knowledge of the topography of the district. It may have been to no avail. A fox was killed by the Westmeaths in the kitchen of Cookesborough very soon after he died. Dease's *History of the Westmeath Hunt* remarks that 'the kitchen was a fit and proper place to find a Cooke'. (Adolphus may have known that thirty miles away at Larch Hill, Kilcock, a Mr. Watson had also built himself an earth for use after his death. This earth is highly ornamental; the great mound which covers the dome-shaped chamber is decorated with a pepperpot tower, probably erected by Mr. Watson's widow, who had an obsession for building follies. After his death food was regularly laid out for Mr. Watson beside his earth, and hounds were directed never to draw his coverts.)

The third will left the Cookesborough estate to a younger son of the Earl of Longford. The Honourable Mr. Edward Pakenham had very few prospects and was perfectly willing to hyphenate his name and become Pakenham-Cooke in order to obtain the inheritance. Dr. Purdon contested this will on the grounds that Adolphus had been of unsound mind. The case was first heard at the Common Pleas Summer Assizes at Mullingar. Among the witnesses called was a Dr. William Williams, who disliked Dr. Purdon and was prepared to swear that Adolphus was sane. He had known him for thirty-six years, and although he admitted that he was a difficult patient—after he cured him of a serious illness, he was never invited to the house again—he contended that the old gentleman enjoyed making himself out queerer than he was. Dr. Williams was cross-examined about the occasion when Cooke informed him that he was becoming a screech owl.

DOCTOR: I told him that I admired screech owls very much.

COUNSEL: Do you admire screech owls?

DOCTOR: Well, I said I liked places that had birds and crows and rooks . . . that they generally accompanied old demesnes and old families.

COUNSEL: Can you give me the exact words he used when he said his voice was becoming like that of a screech owl?

DOCTOR: He said, 'This is the first day I perceived my voice becoming like that of a screech owl.' He was very hoarse at the time.

HIS LORDSHIP (intervening): Did you ever hear a man saying he was as hoarse as a raven?'

DOCTOR: I did.

HIS LORDSHIP: Now, when Mr. Cooke said his voice was becoming like that of a screech owl, do you think he supposed he was a screech owl?

DOCTOR: I do not.

The verdict was in favour of Pakenham-Cooke, concluding that Adolphus was not mad. The judge summed up: 'I believe that his belief as to what might happen to him after his death is no proof of want of capacity if there is any other proof of capacity. If a man believes he will turn into a successful screech owl after his death, that is no proof that he is incapable.'

Dr. Purdon took the case to the High Court in Dublin. The Bug Mee gave evidence. Again the verdict was in favour of Pakenham-Cooke. But by this time legal proceedings had lasted so long that the lawyers were the only gainers. The Pakenhams and the Purdons were not on speaking terms for a generation or so. The Cookesborough estate was declared bankrupt, and its owner, considering that it was not worth while carrying out the wishes of his benefactor, dropped the Cooke from his name and became plain Mr. Pakenham once more.

Selected Books

Ackworth, Bernard. *Jonathan Swift*. London, 1947

Anon. *Some Account of the Progress of the Truth as it is in Jesus*. Mountmellick, 1842

Anon. *The Life and Times of G. R. Fitzgerald*. Dublin, 1787

Anon. *Memoirs of the late G. R. Fitzgerald Gentleman of Mayo*. Dublin, 1787

Anon. *Perrot against the Pope*. London, 1662

Austin, Dobson. *The Paladin of Philanthropy*. London, 1947

Bagenal, P. H. *Vicissitudes of an Anglo-Irish Family*. London, 1925

Barrington, Sir Jonah. *Historic Memoirs of Ireland*. 2 Vols. London, 1835

Barrington, Sir Jonah. *Personal Sketches of his Own Times*. 3 Vols. London, 1830–2

Bergin, O. J. *Irish Bardic Poets*. Dublin, 1970

Besse, J. *Sufferings of the Quakers*. 3 Vols. London, 1733–8

Bieler, L. *The Irish Penitentials*. Dublin, 1963

Boles, W. *Remarks from Cork City*. Cork, 1737

Bowen, Elizabeth. *Bowenscourt*. London, 1942

Brennan's Ecclesiastical History. Dublin, 1840

Brook, R. *The Brimming River*. Dublin, 1961

Burdy. Rev. S. *Life of Phillip Skelton*. Edited Norman Moor. Oxford, 1914

Burke, Thomas. *Vagabond Minstrel*. London, 1936

Butler, Hubert. *Ten Thousand Saints*. Kilkenny, 1973

Cambrensis, Giraldus. *Topography of Ireland*. London, 1968

Cameron, C. H. *History of the Royal College of Surgeons*. Dublin, 1910

Carroll, K. L. *John Perrot*. Supplement No. 33, Friends Historical Society. London, 1971

Caulfield, James. *Portraits of Remarkable People*. 4 Vols. London, 1820

Chadwicke, N. K. *The Age of the Saints of the Catholic Church*. Oxford, 1967

Chavasse, Claude. *The Story of Baltinglass*. Kilkenny, 1970

Childe-Pemberton, W. S. *The Earl Bishop*. 2 Vols. London, 1924

Cibber, Theophilus. *Lives of the Poets*. London, 1753

Clarke, Desmond. *Richard Lovell Edgeworth*. Dublin, 1969

Cloncurry, V. B. Lawless, Second Baron. *Personal Recollections*. London, 1849

Colles, Ramsay. *In Castle and Court*. London, 1909

Craig, Maurice. *Dublin 1660–1860*. Dublin, 1969

Creevy, P. J. *Adolphus Cooke of Cookesborough*. Longford, 1970

Croker, T. C. *Researches in the South of Ireland*. London, 1924

Cuiv, B. O. *Irish Men of Learning*. Dublin, 1961

Cullen, L. M. *Life in Ireland*. London, 1968

Cumberland, Richard. *Memoirs*. London, 1806

Dixon, F. E. *Richard Poekrich*. Dublin Historical Record, 1946–9

Donovan, M. *Royal Irish Academy 1847–50 Vol. IV*. Dublin, 1899

Eddy, William Alfred (ed.). *Satires and Personal Writings by Jonathan Swift*. Oxford, 1932

Fitzgerald, Percy. *Recollections of Dublin Castle*. Dublin, 1902

Fitzpatrick, W. J. *Memoirs of Richard Whately* (2 Vols). London, 1864

Fleetwood, J. *History of Medicine in Ireland*. Dublin, 1951

Flower, Robin. *The Irish Tradition*. Oxford, 1947

Fothergill, Brian. *The Mitred Earl*. London, 1974

Gerard, Francis. *Picturesque Dublin Old and New*. London, 1898

Gilbert, J. T. *A History of Dublin*. 3 Vols. Dublin, 1854–9

Gillespie Elgy. *The Liberties of Dublin*. Dublin, 1973

Gogarty, Oliver St. John. *As I was walking down Sackville Street*. London, 1937

Greatrakes, Valentine. *A Brief Account of his Life*. London, 1660

Guinness, Desmond and William Ryan. *Irish houses and castles*. London, 1971

Hanger, Col. Robert. *The Life and Times of Colonel Hanger*. London, 1801

Harrison, W. *Memorable Dublin Houses*. Dublin, 1890

Hartigan, A. B. S. *The Family of Eyre*. Reading, 1899

Herbert, J. D. *Irish Varieties*. Dublin, 1836

Howe, G. *Dorothea Herbert*. London, 1929

Hutchinson, R. *Biographia Medica*. London, 1799

Idman, Nilo. *C. R. Maturin*. Helsingfors, 1923

Joyce, P. W. *Social History of Ancient Ireland*. London, 1903

Joyce, Weston St. John. *The Neighbourhood of Dublin*. Dublin, 1921

Killanin, Lord and M. V. Duignan. *Shell Guide to Ireland*. London, 1962

King, Edward, Viscount Kingsborough. *Antiquities of Mexico*. London, 1830–1839

Knapp and Baldwin. *Newgate Calendar*. 3 Vols. London, 1824

Kobler, John. *The Reluctant Surgeon*. London, 1960

Lanigan, J. *Ecclesiastical History of Ireland*. Dublin, 1822

Leadbeater Papers. Dublin, 1862

Lever, Charles. *Charles O' Malley*. London, 1842

Longford, C. *A biography of Dublin*. London, 1936

Loudan, Jack. *O Rare Amanda*. London, 1954

MacAlister, Alexander. *Memoirs of James MacCartney*. London, 1900

MacManus, M. J. *Irish Cavalcade 1550–1850*. London and Dublin, 1939

MacThomas, Eamonn. *Me Jewel and Darlin' Dublin*. Dublin, 1974

Madden, O. *Revelations of Ireland*. Dublin, 1848

Malcomson, A. P. W. *The extraordinary career of the 2nd Earl of Massereene*. Belfast, 1972

Mason, T. W. *The Islands of Ireland*. Reprinted Cork, 1967

Mavor, Elizabeth. *The Ladies of Llangollen*. London, 1971

Maxwell, Constantia. *Country and town life under the Georges*. London, 1940

Maxwell, Constantia. *Dublin under the Georges*. Revised London, 1956

Maxwell, Constantia. *A History of T.C.D.* London, 1946

McCall, P. J. *In the shadow of St. Patrick*. Dublin, 1894

McCarthy, M. *Fighting Fitzgerald*. London, 1930

McLysaght, E. *Irish Life in the seventeenth century*. Cork, 1950

Middleton-Murray, J. *Swift*. London, 1954

Moran, M. *Memoirs of Zozimus*. Dublin, 1971

Newburgh, B. *Essays, Political, moral, critical*. Dublin, 1769

O'Brien, *Liberties of Dublin*. Dublin, 1973

O'Donoghue, D. J. *Pokrich, Irish Musical Genius*. Dublin, 1899

O'Keefe, J. *Recollections*. London, 1826

O'Keefe, J. S. *The Frenzy of Suibhne*. Irish Texts Society. 1913

Old Kerry Records

Orrery Papers. Dublin, 1941

Pankhurst, R. K. P. *William Thompson*. London, 1954

Pearson, Hesketh. *A Life of Bernard Shaw*. London, 1942

Penn, William. *My Irish Journal*. (1669–70). London, 1942

Perrot, J. *A narrative of some of the sufferings of J.P. in the city of Rome*. London, 1661

    A sea of the seeds sufferings. London, 1661, etc.

Peter, A. *Sketches of Old Dublin*. Dublin, 1907

Peter, A. *Sketches of Ireland*. Dublin, 1925

Phillips, Charles. *Curran and his contemporaries*. London, 1818

Plumtre, Ann. *Narrative of a Residence in Ireland*. London, 1817

Porter, Classon. *Frederick Augustus Hervey*. Belfast, 1884

Raymond, John. *Dermody*. 2 Vols. London, 1806

Robinson, J. R. *The last Earls of Barrymore*. London, 1893

Ros, Amanda. *Irene Iddesleigh*. London, 1898. *Helen Huddleston, Fumes of Formation*, etc.

Ryan, J. *Irish Monasticism*. Dublin, 1931

Ryan, R. *Worthies of Ireland*. London, 1821

Sewel, William. *The history of the rise and progress of the Christian People called Quakers*. London, 1772

Seymour, St. John D. *Irish witchcraft and demonology*. Dublin, 1913

Shaw, G. B. *John Bull's other island*. Introduction. London, 1930

Sheil, R. L. *Sketches of the Irish Bar*. London, 1855

Smith, C. *History of Waterford*. Dublin, 1746

Smith, C. *The Antient and Present State of the County and City of Cork*. Dublin, 1751

Swift, Jonathan. *Gulliver's Travels*. Introduction by Michael Foot. London, 1967

Tuckey's Cork Remembrancer. Cork, 1837

Walsh, J. E. *Sketches of Ireland sixty years ago*. London. 1847

Walshe, J. R. *Frederick Augustus Hervey*. London, 1972

Whaley, Buck. *Memoirs*. Edited Sir E. Sullivan. London, 1906

White, Terence de Vere. *The Story of the Royal Dublin Society*. Tralee, 1955

Widdess, J. D. H. *History of the Royal College of Physicians of Ireland*. Dublin, 1965

Wilde, Jane Francesca (Lady). *Ancient Legends of Ireland*. London, 1888

Wood, J. *Annals of Westmeath*. Dublin, 1907

Woodmartin, W. G. *Elder Faiths in Ireland*. 2 Vols. London, 1902

Magazines, Journals, Newspapers etc.:

Allibone. *Dictionary of American Biography*

Annual Register. 1937

Appleton's Dictionary of British and American Authors.

Brinton, A. P. 'The Million Dollar Bet.' (Extracted from *Aramco World*, Nov.–Dec. 1967)

Crone, J. S. *A Concise Dictionary of Irish Biography*. Dublin, 1928

Dictionary of National Biography.

Dublin Historical Record

Dublin Penny Journal. 1840

Dublin University Magazine. January, 1840

Fraser's Magazine, 1838

Gentleman's Magazine, passim

Grace's Annals

Guinness Book of Records

Hermathena. E. J. Gwynn No. 44, Supp. 1–2. *Rule of Tallaght*

Irish Independent

Irish Press

Irish Texts Society. *The Frenzy of Sweeny*, Vol. XII, 1910

Irish Times

Journal of the Cork Historical and Archaelogical Society, passim

Journal of the Kildare Archaeological Society

Journal of the Royal Society of Antiquaries

The Listener

New Statesman

The Observer

Old Kerry Records The Times.

Walker's Hibernian Magazine

Index